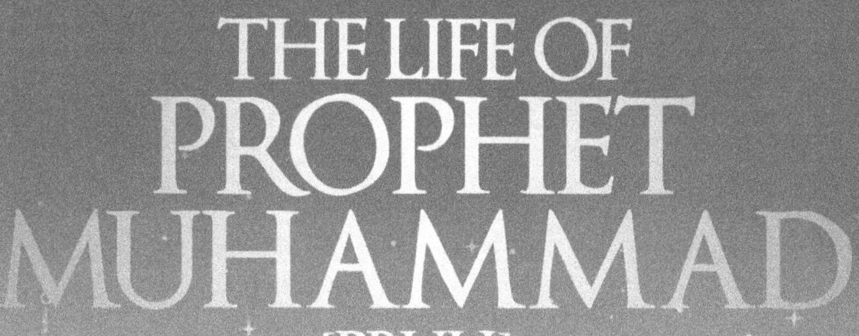

THE LIFE OF PROPHET MUHAMMAD [PBUH]

THE GIFT OF DUROOD AND SALAAM

Virtues of Durood, 40 Durood and Incidents regarding Love for Rasulullah [PBUH]

Written by: Mufti Zakariyya Makada

PUBLISHED BY
ISLAMIC BOOK STORE

The Life of Prophet Muhammad [PBUH]

THE GIFT OF DUROOD AND SALAAM

Virtues of Durood and Incidents regarding Love for Rasulullah ﷺ

PUBLISHED BY

Islamic Book Store, Gujarat, India. 394601

Written by: Mufti Zakariyya Makada

Madrasah Ta'leemuddeen
4 Third Avenue
P.O. Box 26393
Isipingo Beach
4115
South Africa

Tel: (+27) 31 902 9818
Fax: (+27) 31 902 5681
E-mail: info@ihyaauddeen.co.za
Websites: http://ihyaauddeen.co.za
                              http://ihyaaussunnah.com
                              http://muftionline.co.za
                              http://whatisislam.co.za
                              http://al-islaam.co.za

First Edition: Zul Qa'dah 1441 / July 2020

CONTENTS

The Love and Obedience Displayed by the Pious for Rasulullah صَلَّى اللّٰهُ عَلَيْهِ وَسَلَّمَ

INTRODUCTION

بسم الله الرحمن الرحيم الحمد لله رب العالمين والصلاة والسلام على أشرف الأنبياء والمرسلين

سيدنا ومولانا محمد وآله وصحبه أجمعين وبعد

All praise is due to Allah تَبَارَكَوَتَعَالَى and may His choicest Durood (salutations) and Salaam (peace) descend upon the noblest of Ambiyaa and Rasuls, our master and leader, Hazrat Muhammad صَلَّىٱللَّهُعَلَيْهِوَسَلَّمَ, as well as upon his blessed household and all his illustrious companions رَضِيَٱللَّهُعَنْهُمْ.

It is the belief of every believer that after Allah تَبَارَكَوَتَعَالَى, those who enjoy the highest rank are the Ambiyaa (may Allah's تَبَارَكَوَتَعَالَى choicest blessings rain upon them), and from the galaxy of Ambiyaa عَلَيْهِمُٱلسَّلَامُ, the highest in rank and status is Hazrat Rasulullah صَلَّىٱللَّهُعَلَيْهِوَسَلَّمَ.

Not only was Hazrat Rasulullah صَلَّىٱللَّهُعَلَيْهِوَسَلَّمَ sent to this Ummah as the final messenger of Allah تَبَارَكَوَتَعَالَى and the seal of prophethood, but he was also sent as the leader of all the Ambiyaa and Rasuls of the past. The nubuwwat of every Rasul and Nabi of the past was subject to accepting Hazrat Muhammad صَلَّىٱللَّهُعَلَيْهِوَسَلَّمَ as his leader and pledging to support his cause if Hazrat Rasulullah صَلَّى ٱللَّهُ عَلَيْهِ وَسَلَّمَ appeared in his era.[1]

The love that Allah تَبَارَكَ وَتَعَالَى expressed for Hazrat Rasulullah صَلَّى ٱللَّهُ عَلَيْهِ وَسَلَّمَ, which can be clearly gauged from the style of address in the Quraan Majeed, is unique and exclusive to Hazrat Rasulullah صَلَّى ٱللَّهُ عَلَيْهِ وَسَلَّمَ. Likewise, the honour conferred to Hazrat Rasulullah صَلَّى ٱللَّهُ عَلَيْهِ وَسَلَّمَ by Allah تَبَارَكَ وَتَعَالَى on the occasion of Mi'raaj was an honour not enjoyed by any other Messenger of the past.

Furthermore, when Hazrat Rasulullah صَلَّى ٱللَّهُ عَلَيْهِ وَسَلَّمَ will be ushered into the court of Allah تَبَارَكَ وَتَعَالَى on the day of Qiyaamah and will be blessed with the esteemed pedestal of Maqaam-e-Mahmood to intercede for the entire humanity, his distinct position will be envied by all the Ambiyaa and Rasuls عَلَيْهِمُ ٱلسَّلَام and their nations.

The blessings and virtues of Hazrat Rasulullah صَلَّى ٱللَّهُ عَلَيْهِ وَسَلَّمَ are so immense and incredible that it is impossible for anyone to enumerate them all. Suffice to say that he will be the leader of the entire creation of Allah تَبَارَكَ وَتَعَالَى on the day of Qiyaamah.

Hazrat Ibnu Abbaas رَضِيَ ٱللَّهُ عَنْهُمَا reports that a group of Sahaabah رَضِيَ ٱللَّهُ عَنْهُمْ were once sitting (in Musjid Nabawi) when Rasulullah صَلَّى ٱللَّهُ عَلَيْهِ وَسَلَّمَ emerged (from his home) and came towards them. As he drew closer, he

---

[1] وَإِذۡ أَخَذَ ٱللَّهُ مِيثَاقَ ٱلنَّبِيِّنَ لَمَآ ءَاتَيۡتُكُم مِّن كِتَٰبٍ وَحِكۡمَةٍ ثُمَّ جَآءَكُمۡ رَسُولٌ مُّصَدِّقٌ لِّمَا مَعَكُمۡ لَتُؤۡمِنُنَّ بِهِۦ وَلَتَنصُرُنَّهُۥ ۚ قَالَ ءَأَقۡرَرۡتُمۡ وَأَخَذۡتُمۡ عَلَىٰ ذَٰلِكُمۡ إِصۡرِى ۖ قَالُوٓاْ أَقۡرَرۡنَا ۚ قَالَ فَٱشۡهَدُواْ وَأَنَا۠ مَعَكُم مِّنَ ٱلشَّٰهِدِينَ ۝ فَمَن تَوَلَّىٰ بَعۡدَ ذَٰلِكَ فَأُوْلَٰٓئِكَ هُمُ ٱلۡفَٰسِقُونَ (سورة آل عمران: ٨٢)

heard them engaged in a discussion among themselves. One of them said, "Indeed, Allah تَبَارَكَوَتَعَالَى chose Ebrahim عَلَيْهِٱلسَّلَامُ as His khaleel (special friend)." Another said, "Moosa عَلَيْهِٱلسَّلَامُ had the honour of conversing directly with Allah تَبَارَكَوَتَعَالَى." A third said, "Isa عَلَيْهِٱلسَّلَامُ is the kalimah and rooh of Allah تَبَارَكَوَتَعَالَى (i.e. he was born with the command of Allah تَبَارَكَوَتَعَالَى and the rooh was directly inserted into the womb without the medium of a father)." A fourth said, "Allah تَبَارَكَوَتَعَالَى had divinely selected and chosen Aadam عَلَيْهِٱلسَّلَامُ (to be the father of mankind)."

Nabi صَلَّىٱللَّهُعَلَيْهِوَسَلَّمَ then entered their gathering and addressed them saying, "I have overheard your discussion and (I have noticed) your surprise with regard to the esteemed status and lofty positions of the past Ambiyaa عَلَيْهِمُٱلسَّلَامُ. Certainly, Ebrahim عَلَيْهِٱلسَّلَامُ is the khaleel of Allah تَبَارَكَوَتَعَالَى, and there is no doubt in that. Moosa عَلَيْهِٱلسَّلَامُ had the honour of conversing directly with Allah تَبَارَكَوَتَعَالَى - this is an established fact. Isa عَلَيْهِٱلسَّلَامُ is the kalimah and rooh of Allah تَبَارَكَوَتَعَالَى, and this is certainly true. Aadam عَلَيْهِٱلسَّلَامُ has been divinely selected by Allah تَبَارَكَوَتَعَالَى, and undoubtedly, he was such. Behold, I am the habeeb (beloved) of Allah تَبَارَكَوَتَعَالَى and I proclaim it without pride. I will be the bearer of the banner of praise on the day of Qiyaamah (behind which will be Hazrat Aadam عَلَيْهِٱلسَّلَامُ and all those who came after him), and I proclaim this without any pride. I will be the first to intercede and the first whose intercession will be accepted on the day of Qiyaamah, and I proclaim this without pride. I will be the first to shake the chain of the door of Jannah. Thereafter, Allah تَبَارَكَوَتَعَالَى will command that the door be *opened for me and I be made to enter, while with me will be the poor believers, and I proclaim this without pride. I am the noblest of all the former and latter in the sight of Allah تَبَارَكَ وَتَعَالَى, and I say this without pride."* [2]

Undoubtedly, Hazrat Rasulullah صَلَّى ٱللَّهُ عَلَيْهِ وَسَلَّمَ is the greatest human being and the pinnacle of Allah's تَبَارَكَ وَتَعَالَى creation. It is the ultimate honour for every ummati of Hazrat Rasulullah صَلَّى ٱللَّهُ عَلَيْهِ وَسَلَّمَ to be linked to Hazrat Rasulullah صَلَّى ٱللَّهُ عَلَيْهِ وَسَلَّمَ, the Imaam of all the Ambiyaa of Allah تَبَارَكَ وَتَعَالَى.

Hazrat Rasulullah صَلَّى ٱللَّهُ عَلَيْهِ وَسَلَّمَ is the source of hidaayat (guidance) for humanity at large, for it was none other than Hazrat Rasulullah صَلَّى ٱللَّهُ عَلَيْهِ وَسَلَّمَ who was chosen to show us the path of guidance through which we can earn eternal bliss and salvation. The ability to worship and recognize Allah تَبَارَكَ وَتَعَالَى correctly, and simultaneously fulfil the rights of fellow humans, also depends entirely upon emulating the teachings of Hazrat Rasulullah صَلَّى ٱللَّهُ عَلَيْهِ وَسَلَّمَ.

Apart from this, when we study the mubaarak life of Hazrat Rasulullah صَلَّى ٱللَّهُ عَلَيْهِ وَسَلَّمَ, we begin to comprehend and appreciate the

---

عن ابن عباس رضي الله عنهما قال: جلس ناس من أصحاب رسول الله صلى الله عليه وسلم ينتظرونه قال: فخرج حتى إذا دنا منهم سمعهم يتذاكرون فسمع حديثهم فقال بعضهم: عجبا إن الله عز وجل اتخذ من خلقه خليلا اتخذ من إبراهيم خليلا وقال آخر: ماذا بأعجب من كلام موسى كلمه تكليما وقال آخر: فعيسى كلمة الله وروحه وقال آخر: آدم اصطفاه الله فخرج عليهم فسلم وقال: قد سمعت كلامكم وعجبكم إن إبراهيم خليل الله وهو كذلك وموسى نجي الله وهو كذلك وعيسى روحه وكلمته وهو كذلك وآدم اصطفاه الله وهو كذلك ألا وأنا حبيب الله ولا فخر وأنا حامل لواء الحمد يوم القيامة ولا فخر وأنا أول شافع وأول مشفع يوم القيامة ولا فخر وأنا أول من يحرك حلق الجنة فيفتح الله لي فيدخلنيها ومعي فقراء المؤمنين ولا فخر وأنا أكرم الأولين والآخرين ولا فخر (سنن الترمذي، الرقم: ٣٦١٦)

intense love that Hazrat Rasulullah ﷺ possessed, not only for his family and the Sahaabah رضى الله عنهم, but for every ummati until the day of Qiyaamah. The perpetual concern and overwhelming anxiety that Hazrat Rasulullah ﷺ had for every ummati is inconceivable and unimaginable.

In short, his deep love, unwaning concern and unabating worry for every ummati propelled him to patiently bear the numerous atrocities and immense difficulties that had befallen him in the path of propagating Deen – such difficulties which even the most caring and loving mother would not undergo for her one and only child.

The three long years of boycott in the valley of Abu Taalib, his mubaarak shoes being filled with his blessed blood at Taa'if, the blood oozing from his mubaarak face at Uhud etc., are only a few glimpses of what he underwent for the Ummah, to such an extent that Allah تبارك وتعالى pitied him and addressed him in the Quraan Majeed saying:

$$\text{لَعَلَّكَ بَاخِعٌ نَّفْسَكَ أَلَّا يَكُونُوا مُؤْمِنِينَ}$$

Perhaps, [O Muhammad ﷺ], you would kill yourself with grief that they will not be believers.[3]

لَقَدْ جَاءَكُمْ رَسُولٌ مِّنْ أَنْفُسِكُمْ عَزِيزٌ عَلَيْهِ مَا عَنِتُّمْ حَرِيصٌ عَلَيْكُمْ بِالْمُؤْمِنِينَ رَءُوفٌ رَّحِيمٌ

Certainly, a Messenger from amongst yourselves has come to you. It grieves him that you should face difficulty and hardship: ardently anxious is he over your hidaayat, to the believers is he most compassionate and merciful.[4]

Thus, when Hazrat Rasulullah ﷺ is essentially the source of all good in this world and our guide to Paradise, and we are blessed to be his followers, then we can well imagine what rights he has over us and how indebted we are to him.

Among the rights that Hazrat Rasulullah ﷺ has over us is that we obey him in all that he has commanded, we lead a life in conformity to his mubaarak lifestyle, and we continuously recite Durood and Salaam upon him, as instructed by Allah تَبَارَكَ وَتَعَالَى in the Quraan Majeed:

إِنَّ اللَّهَ وَمَلَائِكَتَهُ يُصَلُّونَ عَلَى النَّبِيِّ يَا أَيُّهَا الَّذِينَ آمَنُوا صَلُّوا عَلَيْهِ وَسَلِّمُوا تَسْلِيمًا

Allah and His angels send blessings upon the Nabi ﷺ. O you who believe! Send Durood and Salaam upon him.[5]

Lamentably, on account of our busy schedules and preoccupation with commitments and mundane activities, we have drifted far away from Hazrat Rasulullah ﷺ and lost track of our main

---

[4] سورة التوبة: ١٢٨

[5] سورة الأحزاب: ٥٦

objectives and priorities in life. In view of the present situation, the need was felt to once again rekindle the love of Hazrat Rasulullah ﷺ within our hearts, thereby enabling us to understand and follow the way of his mubaarak sunnah and reach Allah تَبَارَكَ وَتَعَالَى. Hence, this book titled "The Gift of Durood and Salaam" has been prepared which contains the virtues of durood and incidents regarding love for Rasulullah ﷺ.

During the course of preparing this kitaab, I was assisted by a few of Ulamaa who are my close friends. I am indeed appreciative and greatful to them for assisting me. These Ulamaa who had assisted are: Moulana Irfaan Joosab, Moulana Yusuf Mitha, Moulana Abdul Hamid Nana, Moulana Hasan Salejee, Moulana Ebrahim Karodia, Moulana Ebrahim Makada, Moulana Hamza Hassim, Moulana Muhammed Motala, Moulana Waseem Mall, Moulana Luqmaan Mohammedy, Moulana Ebrahim Bobat, Moulana Muaaz Mia, Moulana Fazlur Rahmaan Kadiwala and Moulana Ilyaas Tai. May Allah تَبَارَكَ وَتَعَالَى bestow all these Ulamaa with the best of rewards in this world and the next for their valuable contribution and effort.

We make dua to Allah تَبَارَكَ وَتَعَالَى that He accepts this humble effort and makes it a means of us being blessed with the intercession and mubaarak company of Hazrat Rasulullah ﷺ on the day of Qiyaamah.

(Mufti) Zakariyya Makada

يا رب صل وسلم دائما أبدا على حبيبك خير الخلق كلهم

CHAPTER ONE

The Command of Durood in the Quraan Majeed

The Quraan Majeed contains many verses wherein commands are directed to the servants of Allah تَبَارَكَوَتَعَالَی such as salaah, fasting, hajj, zakaat, etc. Similarly, there are many verses contained in the Quraan Majeed wherein Allah تَبَارَكَوَتَعَالَی honours and praises some of His special servants viz. the Ambiyaa عَلَیْهِمُالسَّلَام, etc.

However, there is no command in the Quraan Majeed wherein Allah تَبَارَكَوَتَعَالَی states that He Himself performs a certain act and thereafter commands the believers to do so as well, besides the command of Durood.

Allah تَبَارَكَوَتَعَالَی says:

اِنَّ اللّٰهَ وَمَلٰٓئِكَتَهٗ يُصَلُّوْنَ عَلَى النَّبِيِّ ۚ يٰٓاَيُّهَا الَّذِيْنَ اٰمَنُوْا صَلُّوْا عَلَيْهِ وَسَلِّمُوْا تَسْلِيْمًا ۝

Allah and His angels send blessings upon the Nabi ﷺ. O you who believe! Send Durood and Salaam upon him.[6]

In this verse, Allah ﷻ has honoured Hazrat Rasulullah ﷺ in a way that He has not honoured any other servant of the creation. This honour is exclusively reserved for the most virtuous of Allah's ﷻ creation, the pride of the children of Nabi Aadam عليه السلام, Nabi Muhammad ﷺ.

After examining the verse, one will find that Allah ﷻ first mentions Salaat alan Nabi coming from Himself, and then from the angels, and lastly, He commands the believers that they too should recite Salaat alan Nabi ﷺ.

In this verse, Allah ﷻ has used the word 'inna' at the beginning of the verse to show emphasis, and Allah ﷻ used the present tense "يصلون" which in the Arabic language denotes continuity.

In other words, the meaning of the verse is that certainly, Allah ﷻ and His angels continuously send Salaat upon Hazrat Rasulullah ﷺ at all times. What greater honour can there be for Hazrat Rasulullah ﷺ that the believers are commanded to join Allah ﷻ and the angels in this blessed act![7]

---

[6] سورة الأحزاب: ٥٦

[7] القول البديع ص ٨٥، فضائل درود ص ٨

A point worthy of note is that in this verse, Allah تَبَارَكَ وَتَعَالَى has referred to Hazrat Rasulullah صَلَّى اللّٰهُ عَلَيْهِ وَسَلَّمَ as "the Nabi" and not by his name, Muhammad صَلَّى اللّٰهُ عَلَيْهِ وَسَلَّمَ, as is the case with the other Ambiyaa عَلَيْهِمُ السَّلَامُ. This too is due to the greatness and honour of Hazrat Rasulullah صَلَّى اللّٰهُ عَلَيْهِ وَسَلَّمَ.[8]

It is also mentioned that the great honour granted to Hazrat Rasulullah صَلَّى اللّٰهُ عَلَيْهِ وَسَلَّمَ far exceeds the honour that was granted to Nabi Aadam عَلَيْهِ السَّلَامُ through the angels making sajdah before him.

The reason is that in the case of Nabi Aadam عَلَيْهِ السَّلَامُ, only the angels were commanded to make sajdah to him, whereas in the case of Hazrat Rasulullah صَلَّى اللّٰهُ عَلَيْهِ وَسَلَّمَ, Allah تَبَارَكَ وَتَعَالَى Himself also sends Salaat alan Nabi صَلَّى اللّٰهُ عَلَيْهِ وَسَلَّمَ, together with the believers and the angels.[9]

THE MEANING OF SALAAT AND SALAAM

It should be borne in mind that Salaat alan Nabi has different meanings. Hence, the Ulama have explained various interpretations of the word 'Salaat' so that the most suitable meaning in reference to Allah تَبَارَكَ وَتَعَالَى, the angels, and the believers can be intended.

---

[8] فضائل درود ص ١٠

[9] القول البديع ص ٨٦

The Ulama state that the meaning of Salaat upon Nabi ﷺ is expressing praise and honour for him together with showing mercy, loving kindness and special affection for him. They also state that the type of praise, honour, mercy, loving kindness and special affection intended is dependent upon the one sending the Salaat.

If the Salaat is from the side of Allah تَبَارَكَ وَتَعَالَى, then it would refer to a different type of praise, honour and mercy, and if the Salaat is from the side of the angels and believers, then it would refer to a different type of praise, honour and mercy.

Hazrat Shaikhul Hadith, Moulana Muhammad Zakariyya Kandhelwi رَحِمَهُ اللّٰه has illustrated this by giving the following example:

We say that a father is kind and affectionate to his son, or the son is kind and affectionate to his father, or a brother is kind and affectionate to his brother. However, one understands that the degree and type of love and kindness which the father shows to the son is different from that which the son shows to his father, or which a brother shows to his brother.

Similar is the case here. Allah تَبَارَكَ وَتَعَالَى also sends Salaat on Hazrat Rasulullah ﷺ. In other words, He honours Hazrat Rasulullah ﷺ with loving kindness and special affection. The angels also recite Salaat, but with a different type of affection, according to their own position and rank. Thereafter, the believers are ordered to recite Salaat upon Hazrat Rasulullah صَلَّى ٱللَّهُ عَلَيْهِ وَسَلَّمَ in accordance with their position. [10]

The author of Rooh-ul-Bayaan writes:

According to some Ulama, the meaning of Allah's تَبَارَكَ وَتَعَالَى mercy on Hazrat Nabi صَلَّى ٱللَّهُ عَلَيْهِ وَسَلَّمَ is that Allah تَبَارَكَ وَتَعَالَى causes him to reach the Maqaam-e-Mahmood – the rank of intercession on behalf of his Ummah (and the entire creation) – and that Salaat alan Nabi by the angels refers to their dua in favour of Hazrat Rasulullah صَلَّى ٱللَّهُ عَلَيْهِ وَسَلَّمَ to be blessed with a higher rank. Salaat alan Nabi by the believers refers to following in his footsteps and expressing love for him (e.g. by reciting Durood and Salaam upon him) and praising with beautiful praises. [11]

Hazrat Moulana Fadhl-ur-Rahmaan Ganj Muraadabaadi رَحْمَةُ ٱللَّهِ has translated Durood as the shower of Allah's تَبَارَكَ وَتَعَالَى love upon Hazrat Rasulullah صَلَّى ٱللَّهُ عَلَيْهِ وَسَلَّمَ. [12]

Hazrat Mufti Mahmood Hasan Gangohi رَحْمَةُ ٱللَّهِ mentioned that the gist of Durood is begging and beseeching Allah تَبَارَكَ وَتَعَالَى to shower His complete and special mercy and peace of both the worlds upon Hazrat Rasulullah صَلَّى ٱللَّهُ عَلَيْهِ وَسَلَّمَ. [13]

---

[10] فضائل درود ص ١١

[11] روح البيان ٧/٢٦٥

[12] مواعظ فقيه الأمة ١/١٥٧

[13] مواعظ فقيه الأمة ١/١٥٨

THE GREATEST DUROOD

Allaamah Sakhaawi رَحِمَهُ ٱللَّٰه has mentioned that when the following verse of the Quraan Majeed was revealed:

اِنَّ ٱللَّٰهَ وَمَلَٰٓئِكَتَهٗ يُصَلُّوْنَ عَلَى ٱلنَّبِيِّ ۚ يَٰٓأَيُّهَا ٱلَّذِيْنَ اٰمَنُوْا صَلُّوْا عَلَيْهِ وَسَلِّمُوْا تَسْلِيْمًا ۝

Allah and His angels send blessings upon the Nabi صَلَّى ٱللَّٰهُ عَلَيْهِ وَسَلَّم. *O you who believe! Send Durood and Salaam upon him.*[14]

The Sahaabah رَضِيَ ٱللَّٰهُ عَنْهُم came to Hazrat Rasulullah صَلَّى ٱللَّٰهُ عَلَيْهِ وَسَلَّم and asked, "O Rasul of Allah صَلَّى ٱللَّٰهُ عَلَيْهِ وَسَلَّم! We know the manner of sending Salaam upon you, as you have taught us how to recite Salaam in the tashahhud of salaah. However, we want to know how to recite Salaat upon you, as Allah تَبَارَكَ وَتَعَالَى has commanded us in the Quraan Majeed to send Salaat upon you."[15]

In reply to this question, Hazrat Rasulullah صَلَّى ٱللَّٰهُ عَلَيْهِ وَسَلَّم taught the Sahaabah رَضِيَ ٱللَّٰهُ عَنْهُم the Durood-e-Ebrahim.

---

[14] سورة الأحزاب: ٥٦

[15] وفي بعض طرق الحديث عند سعيد بن منصور وأحمد والترمذي وإسماعيل القاضي والسراج وأبي عوانة والبيهقي والخلعي والطبراني بسند جيد سبب لهذا السؤال ولفظه لما نزلت {إِنَّ ٱللَّٰهَ وَمَلَائِكَتَهُ يُصَلُّونَ عَلَى ٱلنَّبِيِّ يَا أَيُّهَا ٱلَّذِينَ آمَنُوا صَلُّوا عَلَيْهِ وَسَلِّمُوا تَسْلِيمًا} جاء رجل إلى النبي صلى الله عليه وسلم فقال: يا رسول الله هذا السلام قد عرفناه فكيف الصلاة عليك الحديث (القول البديع صـ ١٠٤)

عن كعب بن عجرة قال: قلنا يا رسول الله هذا السلام قد علمنا فكيف الصلاة عليك قال: قولوا اللهم صل على محمد وعلى آل محمد كما صليت على إبراهيم إنك حميد مجيد وبارك على محمد وعلى آل محمد كما باركت على إبراهيم إنك حميد مجيد (سنن الترمذي، الرقم: ٤٨٣، وقال: حديث كعب بن عجرة حديث حسن صحيح)

اَللّٰهُمَّ صَلِّ عَلٰى مُحَمَّدٍ وَّعَلٰى آلِ مُحَمَّدٍ كَمَا صَلَّيْتَ عَلٰى إِبْرَاهِيْمَ وَعَلٰى آلِ إِبْرَاهِيْمَ إِنَّكَ حَمِيْدٌ مَّجِيْدٌ اَللّٰهُمَّ بَارِكْ عَلٰى مُحَمَّدٍ وَّعَلٰى آلِ مُحَمَّدٍ كَمَا بَارَكْتَ عَلٰى إِبْرَاهِيْمَ وَعَلٰى آلِ إِبْرَاهِيْمَ إِنَّكَ حَمِيْدٌ مَّجِيْدٌ

O Allah ﷻ, shower Your mercy upon Muhammad ﷺ and the family of Muhammad ﷺ, as You showered Your mercy upon Ebrahim ﷺ and the family of Ebrahim ﷺ. Indeed, You are praiseworthy and most glorious. O Allah ﷻ, shower Your blessings upon Muhammad ﷺ and the family of Muhammad ﷺ, as You showered Your blessings upon Ebrahim ﷺ and the family of Ebrahim ﷺ. Indeed, You are praiseworthy and most glorious.

In some narrations, it is recorded that a Sahaabi once came to Rasulullah ﷺ and enquired regarding the manner of sending durood upon Rasulullah ﷺ. In reply, Rasulullah ﷺ mentioned the Durood-e-Ebrahim. It is possible that these are two separate incidents that had occurred. In the first incident a few Sahaabah had come to enquire, and in the second incident, it was one person who came to enquire. On both occasions, Rasulullah ﷺ explained the Durood-e-Ebrahim.[16]

The narration of Bukhaari Shareef reported by Hazrat Abdur Rahmaan bin Abi Layla ﷴ sheds light upon the manner in

---

[16] القول البديع ص ١٠٤

which Hazrat Rasulullah ﷺ taught the Sahaabah رَضِيَ اللهُ عَنْهُمْ the Durood-e-Ebrahim and the great importance and significance that the Sahaabah رَضِيَ اللهُ عَنْهُمْ showed towards the Durood-e-Ebrahim.

Hazrat Abdur Rahmaan bin Abi Layla رَحِمَهُ اللهُ reports:

On one occasion, Hazrat Ka'b bin Ujrah رَضِيَ اللهُ عَنْهُ met me and said, "Shall I not give you a present which I had heard from Rasulullah ﷺ?" I replied, "Yes indeed! Please give it to me!" He then said, "Once, we asked Rasulullah ﷺ, 'O Rasul of Allah ﷺ! How should we recite Salaat upon you? Surely Allah تَبَارَكَ وَتَعَالَى has already taught us how to send Salaam upon you.' Rasulullah ﷺ replied, 'recite the following Durood:

اَللّٰهُمَّ صَلِّ عَلٰى مُحَمَّدٍ وَّعَلٰى آلِ مُحَمَّدٍ كَمَا صَلَّيْتَ عَلٰى إِبْرَاهِيْمَ وَعَلٰى آلِ إِبْرَاهِيْمَ إِنَّكَ حَمِيْدٌ مَّجِيْدٌ اَللّٰهُمَّ بَارِكْ عَلٰى مُحَمَّدٍ وَّعَلٰى آلِ مُحَمَّدٍ كَمَا بَارَكْتَ عَلٰى إِبْرَاهِيْمَ وَعَلٰى آلِ إِبْرَاهِيْمَ إِنَّكَ حَمِيْدٌ مَّجِيْدٌ

O Allah تَبَارَكَ وَتَعَالَى, *shower Your mercy upon Muhammad* ﷺ *and the family of Muhammad* ﷺ, *as You showered Your mercy upon Ebrahim* عَلَيْهِ السَّلَام *and the family of Ebrahim* عَلَيْهِ السَّلَام. *Indeed, You are praiseworthy and most glorious. O Allah* تَبَارَكَ وَتَعَالَى, *shower Your blessings upon Muhammad* ﷺ *and the family of Muhammad* ﷺ, *as You showered Your blessings upon Ebrahim* عَلَيْهِ السَّلَام *and the family of Ebrahim ﻋَﻠَﻴْﻪِ ٱلسَّﻼَﻡُ. Indeed, You are praiseworthy and most glorious.'"* [17]

Hazrat Shaikhul Hadith, Moulana Muhammad Zakariyya ﺭَﺣْﻤَﺔُٱللَّﻪ Kandhelwi mentions that in the above Hadith of Hazrat Ka'b bin Ujrah ﺭَﺿِﻲَٱللَّﻪُﻋَﻨْﻪ, mention is made of gifting a present (the present of Durood-e-Ebrahim). Among the Sahaabah ﺭَﺿِﻲَٱللَّﻪُﻋَﻨْﻬُﻢ, it was a habit to give presents to their guests. Instead of giving them food and drinks or other material things, they rather preferred giving each other the zikr of Hazrat Rasulullah ﺻَﻠَّﻰٱللَّﻪُﻋَﻠَﻴْﻪِﻭَﺳَﻠَّﻢ or his mubaarak Ahaadith. Such things were much more precious in their sight than the material things of the world, and their lives were testimony to this. It is for this reason that Hazrat Ka'b ﺭَﺿِﻲَٱللَّﻪُﻋَﻨْﻪ referred to the Durood-e-Ebrahim as a present. [18]

Allaamah Sakhaawi ﺭَﺣِﻤَﻪُٱللَّﻪ states that the most virtuous Durood is the Durood-e-Ebrahim in view of the fact that Hazrat Rasulullah ﺻَﻠَّﻰٱللَّﻪُﻋَﻠَﻴْﻪِﻭَﺳَﻠَّﻢ taught the Sahaabah ﺭَﺿِﻲَٱللَّﻪُﻋَﻨْﻬُﻢ this Durood when they asked him how they should fulfil the command of Durood mentioned in the Quraan Majeed. [19]

---

[17] حدثني عبد الله بن عيسى "نمع عبد الرحمن بن أبي ليلى قال لقيني كعب بن عجرة فقال ألا أهدي لك هدية سمعتها من النبي صلى الله عليه وسلم فقلت بلى فأهدها لي فقال سألنا رسول الله صلى الله عليه وسلم فقلنا يا رسول الله كيف الصلاة عليكم أهل البيت فإن الله قد علمنا كيف نسلم عليكم قال قولوا اللهم صل على محمد وعلى آل محمد كما صليت على إبراهيم وعلى آل إبراهيم إنك حميد مجيد اللهم بارك على محمد وعلى آل محمد كما باركت على إبراهيم وعلى آل إبراهيم إنك حميد مجيد (صحيح البخاري، الرقم: ٣٣٧٠)

[18] فضائل درود صـ ٥٦

[19] القول البديع صـ ١٤٢

Allaamah Nawawi رَحِمَهُ اللّٰه has mentioned in his kitaab "Rawdah" that if a person takes an oath that he will recite the most virtuous Salaat upon Hazrat Rasulullah صَلَّى اللّٰهُ عَلَيْهِ وَسَلَّم, he will be considered to have fulfilled the oath if he recites the Durood-e-Ebrahim. [20]

The renowned Faqeeh, Allaamah Shaami رَحِمَهُ اللّٰه, reports that Imaam Muhammad رَحِمَهُ اللّٰه (the student of Imaam Abu Hanifah رَحِمَهُ اللّٰه) was once asked, "In which words should we recite Salaat upon Rasulullah صَلَّى اللّٰهُ عَلَيْهِ وَسَلَّم?" He replied by dictating the words mentioned in Durood-e-Ebrahim. [21]

It is for this reason that the Durood-e-Ebrahim is regarded as the most virtuous Durood according to the Hanafi mazhab and it is the Durood that is preferred for recitation in salaah.

It should be borne in mind that there are numerous versions of Durood that are narrated from various Sahaabah رَضِىَ اللّٰهُ عَنْهُم who learnt these Durood directly from Hazrat Rasulullah صَلَّى اللّٰهُ عَلَيْهِ وَسَلَّم. However, when we view these various Durood, we find that they are reported with slight variations in the wording.

Hazrat Shaikhul Hadith, Moulana Muhammad Zakariyya Kandhelwi رَحِمَهُ اللّٰه mentions that the reason for this is that Hazrat Rasulullah صَلَّى اللّٰهُ عَلَيْهِ وَسَلَّم taught different versions to different

---

[20] روضة الطالبين ٨/٥٨

[21] رد المحتار ١/٥١٢

Sahaabah رَضِىَ ٱللّٰهُ عَنْهُمْ so that no specific form of Durood can be considered obligatory.[22]

It is important to note that the duty of reciting Durood is a separate matter and the recitation of a specific version of Durood which has been reported from Hazrat Rasulullah صَلَّى ٱللّٰهُ عَلَيْهِ وَسَلَّمَ is a different matter. Hence, if one recites a Durood which is not reported from Hazrat Rasulullah صَلَّى ٱللّٰهُ عَلَيْهِ وَسَلَّمَ, it will be permissible, though reciting the version reported from Hazrat Rasulullah صَلَّى ٱللّٰهُ عَلَيْهِ وَسَلَّمَ is more virtuous and rewarding.

---

[22] فضائل درود ص ۸۵

CHAPTER TWO

The Rights of Rasulullah ﷺ

If we have to examine the favours of Hazrat Rasulullah ﷺ upon us, we will realize that they are so abundant that it is obligatory upon us to express our gratitude to Hazrat Rasulullah ﷺ. In fact, such is the status of Hazrat Rasulullah ﷺ that the entire universe was created because of him. How wonderful indeed is the statement of the poet:

السلام اے سيد اولاد آدم السلام

السلام اے باعث ايجاد عالم السلام

"Salaam be upon you, O leader of the children of Aadam عَلَيْهِ السَّلَام.

Salaam be upon you, O means of the existence of the universe." [23]

---

[23] مواعظ فقيه الأمة ١٦٠/١

Hazrat Rasulullah ﷺ was the means for us receiving the Quraan Majeed, the means of us receiving the gift of salaah, fasting, zakaat, and hajj. In fact, he was the means of us receiving the entire Deen of Islam and connecting us to our Creator, Allah تَبَارَكَوَتَعَالَى. Therefore, he is the means of us receiving every Deeni bounty bestowed upon us from Allah تَبَارَكَوَتَعَالَى in this world and the next. Hence, Hazrat Rasulullah ﷺ enjoys more rights over us than any other person.

The obligations we owe to Hazrat Rasulullah ﷺ can be categorized into the following four:

1. Love

2. Firm belief

3. Obedience

4. Sending Durood and Salaam upon him

If these four obligations are diligently upheld, then insha Allah, one will be showing loyalty and gratitude to Hazrat Rasulullah ﷺ for the favours that one has received from him, and one will be fulfilling the rights that he owes to Hazrat Rasulullah ﷺ.

The Obligation of Love

The first obligation is that we inculcate true love for Hazrat Rasulullah ﷺ. It is reported in the Hadith that one's imaan will not be perfect unless one loves Hazrat Rasulullah ﷺ more than he loves his parents, children and all the people. [24]

On one occasion, Hazrat Umar رضى الله عنه addressed Hazrat Rasulullah ﷺ saying, "O Rasul of Allah ﷺ! I love you more than everyone, besides myself!" Hazrat Rasulullah ﷺ said to Hazrat Umar رضى الله عنه, "No, by the Being in whose hands my soul lies, (you can never be a perfect believer) until you have more love for me more than your ownself." Thereafter, Hazrat Umar رضى الله عنه mentioned, "O Rasul of Allah ﷺ! I now love you more than everything, including myself." Hazrat Rasulullah ﷺ then said, "O Umar! Now your imaan is perfect." [25]

Without us developing our love for Hazrat Rasulullah ﷺ to this level, where one gives preference to him and his commands over everything else, we will not be successful in reaching Allah تَبَارَكَ وَتَعَالَى.

---

[24] عن أنس قال: قال النبي صلى الله عليه وسلم: لا يؤمن أحدكم حتى أكون أحب إليه من والده وولده والناس أجمعين (صحيح البخاري، الرقم: ١٥)

[25] حدثني أبو عقيل زهرة بن معبد أنه سمع جده عبد الله بن هشام قال: كنا مع النبي صلى الله عليه وسلم وهو آخذ بيد عمر بن الخطاب فقال له عمر يا رسول الله لأنت أحب إلي من كل شيء إلا من نفسي فقال النبي صلى الله عليه وسلم: لا والذي نفسي بيده حتى أكون أحب إليك من نفسك فقال له عمر فإنه الآن والله لأنت أحب إلي من نفسي فقال النبي صلى الله عليه وسلم: الآن يا عمر (صحيح البخاري، الرقم: ٦٦٣٢)

The Obligation of Firm Belief and Confidence

The second obligation is that we have firm belief in Hazrat Rasulullah ﷺ and wholeheartedly accept whatever he informs us of. There were many people of the Quraish who truly loved Hazrat Rasulullah ﷺ, to the extent that they even suffered the boycott with him for three years, however they did not believe in him and accept his Deen. Hence, they failed to attain salvation and passed away on kufr. Therefore, together with having love for Hazrat Rasulullah ﷺ, one should believe in Hazrat Rasulullah ﷺ and have complete confidence in everything that he has said and brought to us.

The Ulama explain that the love which one has for Hazrat Rasulullah ﷺ should assume the form of 'aqeedat'. Aqeedat is for one to believe that Hazrat Rasulullah ﷺ is his greatest benefactor and that everything which Hazrat Rasulullah ﷺ mentioned is the absolute truth and the only path to success. Similarly, he should not equate any person's command to the command of Hazrat Rasulullah ﷺ.

The Obligation of Obedience

The third right that Hazrat Rasulullah ﷺ enjoys over us is the right of obedience. Together with having the greatest love and aqeedat (believing in Hazrat Rasulullah ﷺ and having confidence in everything that he has conveyed to us), one has to inculcate obedience in his life as well. When the highest levels of love and aqeedat are inculcated, automatically the highest levels of obedience and submission will be acquired. One will thereafter live his life in accordance to the mubaarak sunnah of Hazrat Rasulullah ﷺ and make a concerted effort to pass on the mubaarak sunnah to the Ummah.

When we examine the lives of the Sahaabah رَضِيَ اللهُ عَنْهُمْ, we find that Allah تَبَارَكَ وَتَعَالَى had blessed them with the highest levels of love, aqeedat and obedience to Hazrat Rasulullah ﷺ.

The Advice of Hazrat Rasulullah ﷺ to Hazrat Faatimah رَضِيَ اللهُ عَنْهَا

Hazrat Faatimah رَضِيَ اللهُ عَنْهَا was the most beloved daughter of Hazrat Rasulullah ﷺ. The level of her love and aqeedat for Hazrat Rasulullah ﷺ was to the highest standard and degree.

The proof of her love for Hazrat Rasulullah ﷺ can be understood from the Hadith in which Hazrat Rasulullah ﷺ mentioned, "Faatimah is part of me. Whoever harms her, harms me."[26] Similarly, the proof of her aqeedat can be understood from the Hadith wherein Hazrat Rasulullah ﷺ said, "Faatimah is the leader of the women in Jannah." [27]

---

[26] عن المسور بن مخرمة قال: قال رسول الله صلى الله عليه وسلم: إنما فاطمة بضعة مني يؤذيني ما آذاها (صحيح مسلم، الرقم: ٢٤٤٩)

[27] وقال النبي صلى الله عليه وسلم: فاطمة سيدة نساء أهل الجنة (صحيح البخاري ٥٢٦/١)

However, despite the high level of her love and aqeedat for Hazrat Rasulullah صَلَّى اللهُ عَلَيْهِ وَسَلَّم, Hazrat Rasulullah صَلَّى اللهُ عَلَيْهِ وَسَلَّم gave her the following advice, "O Faatimah bintu Muhammad! Ask me for whatever you wish from my wealth, for I will not be able to avail you in the least before Allah تَبَارَكَ وَتَعَالَى (i.e. if you do not follow my teachings, then I will not be able to benefit you in the Hereafter)."[28]

From this, we conclude that it is necessary to have obedience to Hazrat Rasulullah صَلَّى اللهُ عَلَيْهِ وَسَلَّم together with having love and aqeedat for him.

The Obedience of Hazrat Abdullah bin Mas'ood رَضِيَ اللهُ عَنْهُ before Hazrat Rasulullah صَلَّى اللهُ عَلَيْهِ وَسَلَّم

On one occasion, Hazrat Rasulullah صَلَّى اللهُ عَلَيْهِ وَسَلَّم ascended the mimbar and instructed the Sahaabah رَضِيَ اللهُ عَنْهُم to sit down. All the Sahaabah رَضِيَ اللهُ عَنْهُم present in the musjid immediately sat down. At that moment, Hazrat Abdullah bin Mas'ood رَضِيَ اللهُ عَنْهُ was still outside the musjid. However, on account of the instruction of Hazrat Rasulullah صَلَّى اللهُ عَلَيْهِ وَسَلَّم, he immediately sat where he was, without

---

[28] ويا فاطمة بنت محمد سليني ما شئت من مالي لا أغني عنك من الله شيئا (صحيح البخاري، الرقم: ٢٧٥٣)

entering the musjid. In other words, he did not think to himself that this instruction only applied to those in the musjid.[29]

The Sahaabah رَضِىَاللهُعَنْهُمْ always kept death before them. Hence, Hazrat Abdullah bin Mas'ood رَضِىَاللهُعَنْهُ thought to himself that if he had to pass away before entering the musjid, then tomorrow, on the day of Qiyaamah, if Allah تَبَارَكَوَتَعَالَى has to ask him, 'When you heard the instruction of My Nabi ﷺ to sit, then why did you not obey?' then what reply will he have? Hence, he immediately sat down.

Hazrat Rasulullah ﷺ then saw him seated outside the musjid and said to him, "O Ibnu Mas'ood رَضِىَاللهُعَنْهُ, come inside."

This was the level of the Sahaabah's رَضِىَاللهُعَنْهُمْ obedience and submission to Hazrat Rasulullah ﷺ, coupled with the highest levels of love and aqeedat.

The Obligation of Sending Durood and Salaam

Just as a believer must fulfil the obligations of love, aqeedat and obedience for Hazrat Rasulullah ﷺ, he must similarly fulfil the obligation of sending Durood and Salaam upon Hazrat Rasulullah ﷺ.

---

[29] عن جابر قال: لما استوى رسول الله صلى الله عليه وسلم يوم الجمعة قال: اجلسوا فسمع ذلك ابن مسعود فجلس على باب المسجد فرآه رسول الله صلى الله عليه وسلم فقال: تعال يا عبد الله بن مسعود (سنن أبي داود، الرقم: ١٠٩١، المستدرك على الصحيحين للحاكم، الرقم: ١٠٥٦، وقال: هذا حديث صحيح على شرط الشيخين ولم يخرجاه، وقال الذهبي: على شرطهما)

Hazrat Rasulullah ﷺ said, "The people who will be the closest to me on the day of Qiyaamah will be those who would recite the most Durood upon me (in the world)." [30]

A believer should try to daily recite Durood upon Hazrat Rasulullah ﷺ. However, on the blessed day of Friday, one should recite even more Durood as Hazrat Rasulullah ﷺ has exhorted us to increase our Durood on a Friday.

Hazrat Abu Umaamah رضى الله عنه reports that Hazrat Rasulullah ﷺ said, "Recite abundant Durood upon me every Friday, for certainly the Durood of my Ummah are presented before me every Friday. The one who recites the most Durood upon me will be the closest to me (on the day of Qiyaamah)." [31]

The Statement of Haafiz Izzuddeen bin Abdus Salaam رحمه الله

Haafiz Izzuddeen bin Abdus Salaam رحمه الله says:

Our Durood upon Rasulullah ﷺ is by no means to be considered as an intercession by us on his behalf, because we are not in any way fit to intercede on his behalf.

---

[30] عن عبد الله بن مسعود رضي الله عنه أن رسول الله صلى الله عليه وسلم قال: أولى الناس بي يوم القيامة أكثرهم علي صلاة (سنن الترمذي، الرقم: ٤٨٤ وحسنه الإمام الترمذي رحمه الله)

[31] عن أبي أمامة قال: قال رسول الله صلى الله عليه وسلم: أكثروا علي من الصلاة في كل يوم جمعة فإن صلاة أمتي تعرض علي في كل يوم جمعة فمن كان أكثرهم علي صلاة كان أقربهم مني منزلة (شعب الإيمان، الرقم: ٢٧٧٠، وقال الإمام المنذري رحمه الله في الترغيب والترهيب ٣٢٨/٢: رواه البيهقي بإسناد حسن إلا أن مكحولا قيل لم يسمع من أبي أمامة)

In reality, Allah تَبَارَكَوَتَعَالَى has ordered us to repay our benefactor for some of his favours and generosity. No other benefactor has been more generous to us than Nabi ﷺ. Due to the fact that we are unable to repay him for his generosity, Allah تَبَارَكَوَتَعَالَى has seen our weakness and shown us the correct manner of repaying Rasulullah ﷺ, and that is by reciting Durood upon him.

Since we are unable to even fulfil this command of Allah تَبَارَكَوَتَعَالَى in the correct manner, we beg of Allah تَبَارَكَوَتَعَالَى to convey Durood upon Hazrat Rasulullah ﷺ according to His (Allah تَبَارَكَوَتَعَالَى) majesty and exalted position." [32]

The Statement of Allaamah Zarqaani رَحِمَهُ ٱللَّه

Allaamah Zarqaani رَحِمَهُ ٱللَّه writes in "Sharhul Mawaahib" that the main aim and purpose for reciting Durood should be to acquire the pleasure of Allah تَبَارَكَوَتَعَالَى and obey His command (in the Quraan Majeed regarding reciting Durood upon Hazrat Rasulullah ﷺ), as well as fulfilling some of the rights we owe to Rasulullah ﷺ. [33]

---

[32] فضائل درود ص ۱۵

[33] شرح الزرقاني على المواهب ص ۱٦

CHAPTER THREE

The Various Masaail Pertaining to Durood

Reciting Durood upon Hazrat Rasulullah صَلَّى ٱللَّهُ عَلَيْهِ وَسَلَّمَ has been greatly emphasized in the Quraan Majeed and Mubaarak Ahaadith of Hazrat Rasulullah صَلَّى ٱللَّهُ عَلَيْهِ وَسَلَّمَ. There are different commands revealed in relation to Durood upon Hazrat Rasulullah صَلَّى ٱللَّهُ عَلَيْهِ وَسَلَّمَ in regard to various ibaadaat.

1. The Ulama are unanimous on the view that reciting Durood upon Hazrat Rasulullah صَلَّى ٱللَّهُ عَلَيْهِ وَسَلَّمَ once in a lifetime is fardh-e-ain (obligatory) upon every individual. This is due to the injunction of the Quraan Majeed that commands the believers to recite Durood upon Hazrat Rasulullah صَلَّى ٱللَّهُ عَلَيْهِ وَسَلَّمَ.[34]

2. When one hears the mubaarak name of Hazrat Rasulullah صَلَّى ٱللَّهُ عَلَيْهِ وَسَلَّمَ the first time in any gathering, then it is waajib

---

[34] الدر المختار ١/٥١٨

upon him to recite Durood upon Hazrat Rasulullah
صَلَّ ٱللَّهُ عَلَيْهِ وَسَلَّمَ.[34]

3. There are two views of the Fuqahaa in regard to the law of reciting Durood when the blessed name of Hazrat Rasulullah صَلَّ ٱللَّهُ عَلَيْهِ وَسَلَّمَ is repeated several times in a gathering. Is it compulsory to recite Durood every time one hears the mubaarak name of Hazrat Rasulullah صَلَّ ٱللَّهُ عَلَيْهِ وَسَلَّمَ, for example in a bayaan or in a Hadith lesson, or is it sufficient to recite Durood once?

The first view is that it is waajib to recite Durood once. Thereafter, every time one hears the mubaarak name of Hazrat Rasulullah صَلَّ ٱللَّهُ عَلَيْهِ وَسَلَّمَ, reciting Durood is mustahab. This ruling is similar to the ruling of reciting the same aayat of sajdah-e-tilaawat many times in one sitting where it is only waajib to make one sajdah.

The second view is that it is waajib to recite Durood every time one hears the blessed name of Hazrat Rasulullah صَلَّ ٱللَّهُ عَلَيْهِ وَسَلَّمَ in the gathering.

Hazrat Mufti Mahmood Hasan Gangohi رَحَمَهُ ٱللَّهُ mentioned that there is leniency in the first view, while there is caution in the second view. However, the dictates of love and reverence to Hazrat Rasulullah صَلَّ ٱللَّهُ عَلَيْهِ وَسَلَّمَ demand that one should recite

Durood every time one hears the mubaarak name of Hazrat Rasulullah ﷺ.[35]

Hazrat Rasulullah ﷺ said, "That person is a miser who hears my blessed name and does not recite Durood upon me."[36]

4. Apart from this, reciting Durood upon Hazrat Rasulullah ﷺ in salaah is sunnah (i.e. after the tashahhud, before one completes the salaah).[37]

5. In salaah, reciting Durood upon Hazrat Rasulullah ﷺ in any other posture besides tashahhud is makrooh.[37]

6. During the khutbah, when the blessed name of Hazrat Rasulullah ﷺ is mentioned, then one should not verbally recite Durood, but rather one should recite Durood in one's heart.[38]

7. It is permissible to recite Durood even if one does not have wudhu or is in the state of impurity (e.g. haidh, nifaas, janaabah, etc.). However, reciting Durood in the state of wudhu is more rewarding.[39]

---

[35] أحكام القرآن ٤٨٧/٣-٤٨٨، مواعظ فقيه الأمة ١٥٧/١

[36] عن حسين بن علي بن أبي طالب قال: قال رسول الله صلى الله عليه وسلم: البخيل الذي من ذكرت عنده فلم يصل علي (سنن الترمذي الرقم: ٣٥٤٦، وقال: هذا حديث حسن صحيح غريب)

[37] رد المحتار ٥١٨/١

[38] الدر المختار ٥٤٥/١

[39] والمحدث والجنب لا يمنعان عن ذكر الله ما خلا القرآن في حق الجنب (العناية ٥٩/٢)

8. Besides the Ambiyaa عَلَيْهِمُٱلسَّلَامُ and angels, Durood should not be independently recited upon anyone. However, if Durood is recited upon any person after reciting the Durood upon the Ambiyaa عَلَيْهِمُٱلسَّلَامُ and angels, then it will be permissible e.g. one should not say:

اللهم صل على آل محمد

O Allah! Shower Your special mercy upon the family of Muhammad صَلَّىٱللَّهُعَلَيْهِوَسَلَّمَ!

Rather, he should say:

اللهم صل على محمد وعلى آل محمد

O Allah! Shower Your special mercy upon Muhammad صَلَّىٱللَّهُعَلَيْهِوَسَلَّمَ and upon the family of Muhammad صَلَّىٱللَّهُعَلَيْهِوَسَلَّمَ![40]

9. It is forbidden to recite Durood for worldly motives e.g. to promote one's merchandise before the customer.[41]

10. When the blessed name of Hazrat Rasulullah صَلَّىٱللَّهُعَلَيْهِوَسَلَّمَ is written, Durood and Salaam should also be written in full. One should not abbreviate the Durood and Salaam by writing s.a.w, PBUH or in Arabic, صلعم. This is regarded as disrespectful.

Hazrat Moulana Ashraf Ali Thaanwi رَحِمَهُٱللَّهُ has written in his kitaab, Zaadus Sa'eed, that a certain person would not write

---

Durood after writing the blessed name of Hazrat Rasulullah
صَلَّى ٱللَّهُ عَلَيْهِ وَسَلَّمَ. This person would not write the Durood on account
of miserliness as he tried to save on paper. As a consequence,
his right hand had developed an ailment whereby he was
unable to use the hand.

Hazrat Moulana Ashraf Ali Thaanwi رَحِمَهُ ٱللَّهُ has also mentioned
that Shaikh Ibnu Hajar Makki رَحِمَهُ ٱللَّهُ stated that a man would
only write صلى الله عليه without writing وسلم. Once, he had seen
Hazrat Rasulullah صَلَّى ٱللَّهُ عَلَيْهِ وَسَلَّمَ in a dream and Hazrat Rasulullah
صَلَّى ٱللَّهُ عَلَيْهِ وَسَلَّمَ said to him, "Why do you deprive yourself of forty
virtues by not writing the Salaam." In وسلم, there are four
letters, and each letter earns one ten virtues. Hence, reciting
or writing the word وسلم will earn one forty virtues.[42]

11. It is mustahab and an act of great reward to add the word
'sayyiduna' to the blessed name of Hazrat Rasulullah
صَلَّى ٱللَّهُ عَلَيْهِ وَسَلَّمَ when mentioning the blessed name of Hazrat
Rasulullah صَلَّى ٱللَّهُ عَلَيْهِ وَسَلَّمَ.[43]

12. At the time of reciting Durood, one should try and keep his
body and clothing in a clean state.[44]

---

[42] زاد السعيد ص ٢٢

[43] الدر المختار ٥١٣/١

[44] عن عائشة قالت: أمر رسول الله صلى الله عليه وسلم ببناء المساجد في الدور وأن تنظف وتطيب (سنن الترمذي، الرقم: ٥٩٤)

13. The Ulama explain that there are many occasions when reciting Durood upon Hazrat Rasulullah صَلَّى ٱللَّهُ عَلَيْهِ وَسَلَّمَ is mustahab. Among these occasions are the following:

- At the beginning and end of one's dua
- When entering and leaving the musjid
- Upon the completion of the azaan, before reciting the dua after azaan
- After performing wudhu
- When visiting the mubaarak grave of Hazrat Rasulullah صَلَّى ٱللَّهُ عَلَيْهِ وَسَلَّمَ
- When commencing with the writing of a kitaab
- At the beginning of a khutbah
- When awakening for tahajjud
- When faced with difficulties [45]

---

[45] أحكام القرآن ٣/ ٤٩٠

CHAPTER FOUR

Virtues of Durood

Hazrat Shaikhul Hadith, Moulana Muhammad Zakariyya Kandhelwi رَحِمَهُ ٱللّٰه, mentioned the following in his kitaab, Fazaail-e-Durood:

The Ahaadith regarding the virtues of reciting Durood are so numerous that it is difficult to encompass them all in this book. The truth is that even if no virtues are mentioned at all, we would still be obliged to recite Durood in abundance as the favours that Hazrat Rasulullah صَلَّى ٱللّٰهُ عَلَيْهِ وَسَلَّمَ had done to the Ummah can never be counted, let alone repaid.

In view of this, even if any amount of people remain perpetually occupied and engaged in reciting Durood, it will fall far short of fulfilling the rights owed to Hazrat Rasulullaah صَلَّى ٱللّٰهُ عَلَيْهِ وَسَلَّمَ.

Over and above this, Allah تَبَارَكَ وَتَعَالَى has, by His grace and mercy, promised thousands of rewards for the effort of trying to fulfil these rights.

Allaamah Sakhaawi رَحِمَهُ ٱللّٰه has briefly stated the various virtues acquired through reciting Durood. These virtues are listed below:

• Allah تَبَارَكَ وَتَعَالَى confers Durood upon the reciter

• The angels confer Durood upon the reciter

• Hazrat Rasulullah صَلَّى ٱللّٰهُ عَلَيْهِ وَسَلَّم himself confers Durood upon the reciter

• Durood expiates sins

• Durood purifies good deeds

• It elevates the rank of the reciter

• It causes his sins to be forgiven

• It secures forgiveness for the reciter

• It secures the reward of a qeeraat for the reciter's scale of good deeds, with each qeeraat being weightier than Mount Uhud

• It secures a large pan of the scale for his good deeds to be weighed

• All of a person's needs of this world and the Aakhirah will be fulfilled if his duas comprise exclusively of Durood, as stated in the Hadith of Hazrat Ubayy رَضِىَ ٱللّٰهُ عَنْه

• Durood causes sins to be forgiven

• Durood secures the reward of setting slaves free

• Durood secures safety from dangers

- It causes one to benefit from the intercession of Hazrat Rasulullah ﷺ on the day of Qiyaamah

- It earns one the benefit of Hazrat Rasulullah ﷺ becoming a shaahid (a witness) for one (i.e. Hazrat Rasulullah ﷺ bearing witness and testifying for the good deeds which one had done.)

- It secures the pleasure of Allah تَبَارَكَ وَتَعَالَى

- It secures the mercy of Allah تَبَارَكَ وَتَعَالَى

- It grants safety from Allah's تَبَارَكَ وَتَعَالَى wrath

- It will cause the reciter to have shade beneath Allah's تَبَارَكَ وَتَعَالَى Arsh on the day of Qiyaamah

- It will cause the good deeds to outweight the evil deeds on the scale

- It will guarantee one a place by the pond of Kawthar

- It will save one from thirst on the day of Qiyaamah

- It will secure salvation from Jahannum

- It will assist one to cross easily over the bridge of Siraat

- It will cause one to see one's abode in Jannah before death

- It will earn one many spouses in Jannah

- It earns more reward than engaging in jihaad twenty times

- It is sadaqah for the one without wealth

- It is a form of purification

- It attracts blessing in wealth

- It fulfils a hundred and even more needs

- It is a form of ibaadah

- It is most beloved to Allah تَبَارَكَ وَتَعَالَىٰ

- It decorates and beautifies gatherings

- It dispels poverty and neediness

- All means of good can be sought through it

- It will cause the reciter to be close to Hazrat Rasulullah صَلَّى ٱللَّهُ عَلَيْهِ وَسَلَّمَ on the day of Qiyaamah

- It will be a means for the reciter's family, children and grandchildren benefiting from it

- Even the person on whose behalf Durood is recited will benefit likewise and will be brought closer to Hazrat Rasulullah صَلَّى ٱللَّهُ عَلَيْهِ وَسَلَّمَ

- It is a light

- It causes enemies to be defeated

- It purifies the heart from hypocrisy and decay

• It fosters love between the hearts of people

• It causes the reciter to see Hazrat Rasulullah ﷺ in his dreams

• It causes the reciter to remain safe from the sin of gheebah (backbiting)[46]

Durood is an extremely blessed act. It is, in fact, the best of all good deeds and the most beneficial of all deeds, which intelligent people are inclined towards. These will be the people who wish to amass the treasures of the Aakhirah and wish to reap the most benefit from permissible actions.

After stating all these virtues of Durood in brief, Allaamah Sakhaawi رَحِمَهُ ٱللَّهُ proceeds to discuss the details of these virtues from the narrations of Ahadeeth.

After mentioning the narrations, Allaamah Sakhaawi رَحِمَهُ ٱللَّهُ states that all these narrations are a clear proof of the high and lofty status of Durood, as through Durood, Allah تَبَارَكَ وَتَعَالَى multiplies the rewards of the reciter, forgives his sins and also elevates his rank. One should therefore increase in his recitation of Durood upon the guide of all leaders and the fountainhead of all good ﷺ. It is through him that happiness and bounties are achieved and safety is secured from all harm.

---

[46] القول البديع صـ ٢٣٥

The statement of Hazrat Uqlishi رَحِمَهُ ٱللَّه is also quoted, wherein he says:

What medium can be better in securing intercession and what action can be more beneficial than conferring Durood on that being upon whom Allah تَبَارَكَ وَتَعَالَى and His angels confer Durood?

What can be better than the act for which Allah تَبَارَكَ وَتَعَالَى has promised proximity in this world and the Aakhirah? It is a light and a transaction that cannot suffer a loss. Abundant recitation of Durood has always been a regular practice of the pious who remain engaged in it day and night. One should therefore remain steadfast upon it as far as possible since it will save one from deviation, purify one's deeds, fulfil one's expectations and illuminate one's heart. Furthermore, it attracts Allah's تَبَارَكَ وَتَعَالَى pleasure and will guarantee safety on the most difficult and frightful day of Qiyaamah.

CHAPTER FIVE

The Multiple Virtues for Reciting Durood from the Hadith

Virtue One - Glad Tidings from Allah تَبَارَكَوَتَعَالَى for those who Recite Durood

Hazrat Abdur Rahmaan bin Auf رَضِىَاللَّهُعَنْهُ reports: On one occasion, Rasulullah صَلَّىاللَّهُعَلَيْهِوَسَلَّم left his home and I followed him, until he entered a date orchard and fell into prostration. Nabi صَلَّىاللَّهُعَلَيْهِوَسَلَّم made such a lengthy sajdah that I feared that Allah تَبَارَكَوَتَعَالَى had taken away his life. I thus went forward to see if anything had happened to Nabi صَلَّىاللَّهُعَلَيْهِوَسَلَّم. Nabi صَلَّىاللَّهُعَلَيْهِوَسَلَّم then raised his blessed head from sajdah and asked me what the matter was, to which I expressed to him my fear and worry (of him passing away in sajdah). Nabi صَلَّىاللَّهُعَلَيْهِوَسَلَّم replied, "(The reason for me making such a lengthy sajdah was that) Jibraeel عَلَيْهِالسَّلَام came to me and said, 'Shall I not give you the glad tidings that Allah تَبَارَكَوَتَعَالَى says, 'The one who recites Durood upon you, I send My mercy upon him, and the one who recites Salaam upon you, I send peace and blessings upon him.'" [47]

Hazrat Abu Talhah رَضِيَٱللَّهُعَنْهُ relates: One morning, Nabi صَلَّىٱللَّهُعَلَيْهِوَسَلَّمَ came to us in a state of happiness, to such an extent that the joy and happiness beamed from his blessed countenance. The Sahabaah رَضِيَٱللَّهُعَنْهُمْ enquired, "O Rasulullah صَلَّىٱللَّهُعَلَيْهِوَسَلَّمَ, we notice that you are very pleased today. The happiness can be clearly seen on your blessed face." Rasulullah صَلَّىٱللَّهُعَلَيْهِوَسَلَّمَ replied, "Yes indeed, a messenger came to me from my Lord with the following message, 'Whosoever from amongst your Ummah recites Durood upon you once, Allah تَبَارَكَوَتَعَالَى will record for him ten righteous deeds, erase and pardon ten sins, raise his rank in Jannah by ten stages and reply to his Durood in a similar manner (i.e. Allah تَبَارَكَوَتَعَالَى will send ten mercies and blessings upon him).'" [48]

Virtue Two – Receiving Ten Mercies

Hazrat Abu Hurairah رَضِيَٱللَّهُعَنْهُ reports that Hazrat Rasulullah صَلَّىٱللَّهُعَلَيْهِوَسَلَّمَ said, "Whoever sends salutations upon me once, Allah تَبَارَكَوَتَعَالَى will send

---

[47] عن عبد الرحمن بن عوف رضي الله عنه قال خرج رسول الله صلى الله عليه وسلم فاتبعته حتى دخل نخلا فسجد فأطال السجود حتى خفت أو خشيت أن يكون الله قد توفاه أو قبضه قال فجئت أنظر فرفع رأسه فقال ما لك يا عبد الرحمن قال فذكرت ذلك له فقال إن جبريل عليه السلام قال لي ألا أبشرك إن الله عز وجل يقول لك من صلى عليك صليت عليه ومن سلم عليك سلمت عليه (مسند أحمد، الرقم: ١٦٦٢، وقال البيهقي في الخلافيات ١٤٣/٣ (عن طريق لهذه الرواية بنحو هذه الألفاظ): قال أبو عبد الله – رحمه الله –: هذا حديث صحيح)

[48] عن أبي طلحة الأنصاري رضي الله عنه قال أصبح رسول الله صلى الله عليه وسلم يوما طيب النفس يرى في وجهه البشر قالوا يا رسول الله أصبحت اليوم طيب النفس يرى في وجهك البشر قال أجل أتاني آت من ربي عز وجل فقال من صلى عليك من أمتك صلاة كتب الله له عشر حسنات ومحا عنه عشر سيئات ورفع له عشر درجات ورد عليه مثلها (سنن النسائي، الرقم: ١٢٨٣، ورجاله موثقون كما في القول البديع ص ٢٤٨)

salutations (i.e. reward him and shower His mercy) upon him ten times."[49]

Virtue Three – Receiving Ten Blessings

Hazrat Abu Hurairah رَضِيَ اللَّهُ عَنْهُ reports that Hazrat Rasulullah صَلَّى اللَّهُ عَلَيْهِ وَسَلَّمَ said, "Whoever sends salutations upon me once, Allah تَبَارَكَ وَتَعَالَى will write for him ten virtues (in his book of deeds)." [50]

Virtue Four – Ten Ranks Raised

Hazrat Anas bin Maalik رَضِيَ اللَّهُ عَنْهُ reports that Hazrat Rasulullah صَلَّى اللَّهُ عَلَيْهِ وَسَلَّمَ said, "Whoever sends salutations upon me once, Allah تَبَارَكَ وَتَعَالَى will send ten blessings upon him, ten of his sins will be erased and his rank will be raised by ten stages." [51]

Virtue Five – Sins being Expiated

Hazrat Abu Burdah رَضِيَ اللَّهُ عَنْهُ reports that Hazrat Rasulullah صَلَّى اللَّهُ عَلَيْهِ وَسَلَّمَ said, "Whoever from my Ummah conveys one Durood upon me sincerely from his heart, Allah تَبَارَكَ وَتَعَالَى will bless him with ten mercies, elevate his

---

[49] عن أبي هريرة أن رسول الله صلى الله عليه وسلم قال: من صلى علي واحدة صلى الله عليه عشرا (صحيح مسلم، الرقم: ٤٠٨)

[50] عن أبي هريرة قال قال رسول الله صلى الله عليه وسلم من صلى علي مرة واحدة كتب الله عز وجل له بها عشر حسنات (مسند أحمد، الرقم: ٧٥٦١، ورجاله رجال الصحيح غير ربعي بن إبراهيم وهو ثقة مأمون كما في مجمع الزوائد، الرقم: ١٧٢٨٢)

[51] عن أنس بن مالك قال قال رسول الله صلى الله عليه وسلم من صلى علي صلاة واحدة صلى الله عليه عشر صلوات وحطت عنه عشر خطيئات ورفعت له عشر درجات (سنن النسائي، الرقم: ١٢٩٧، وسنده حسن كما في المطالب العالية ١٣/٧٨٥)

status in the Hereafter by ten ranks, record ten righteous deeds in his favour and expiate ten of his sins."[52]

Virtue Six - Earning the Immense Mercy of Allah تَبَارَكَ وَتَعَالَى

Hazrat Abdullah bin Umar رَضِيَ اللّٰهُ عَنْهُمَا *and Hazrat Abu Hurairah* رَضِيَ اللّٰهُ عَنْهُ *narrate that Hazrat Rasulullah* صَلَّى اللّٰهُ عَلَيْهِ وَسَلَّمَ *said, "Send salutations upon me, Allah* تَبَارَكَ وَتَعَالَى *will shower mercy upon you."*[53]

Virtue Seven – Earning the Reward of Freeing Ten Slaves

Hazrat Baraa bin Aazib رَضِيَ اللّٰهُ عَنْهُ *reports that Hazrat Rasulullah* صَلَّى اللّٰهُ عَلَيْهِ وَسَلَّمَ *said, "Whoever recites Durood upon me once, then in lieu of the Durood, Allah* تَبَارَكَ وَتَعَالَى *will record for him ten good deeds, He will erase from him ten sins, He will raise him by ten stages, and the Durood will be a means of him earning the reward of setting free ten slaves."*[54]

<hr>

[52] عن أبي بردة بن نيار رضي الله عنه قال قال رسول الله صلى الله عليه وسلم من صلى علي من أمتي صلاة مخلصا من قلبه صلى الله عليه بها عشر صلوات ورفعه بها عشر درجات وكتب له بها عشر حسنات ومحا عنه بها عشر سيئات (السنن الكبرى للنسائي، الرقم: ٩٨٠٩، ورواته ثقات كما في فتح الباري ١٦٧/١١)

[53] عن ابن عمر وأبي هريرة رضي الله عنهم قالا قال رسول الله صلى الله عليه وسلم صلوا علي صلى الله عليكم (الكامل لابن عدي، الرقم: ١١٠٨٦، وإسناده ضعيف كما في التيسير للمناوي ٩٣/٢)

[54] حدثنا يعقوب بن حميد حدثنا حاتم بن إسماعيل عن محمد بن عبد الله عن مولى البراء بن عازب عن البراء بن عازب أن النبي صلى الله عليه وسلم قال: من صلى علي كتب الله عز وجل له بها عشر حسنات ومحا عنه بها عشر سيئات ورفعه بها عشر درجات وكن به عدل عتق عشر رقاب (الصلاة على النبي لابن أبي عاصم، الرقم: ٥٢، وقد ذكره المنذري في الترغيب والترهيب بلفظة "عن"، إشارة إلى كونه صحيحا أو حسنا أو ما قاربهما عنده كما بين أصله في مقدمة كتابه ١/٥٠)

Virtue Eight – Receiving Seventy Rewards

Hazrat Abdullah bin Amr bin Aas رَضِيَ ٱللَّهُ عَنْهُمَا *reported, "Whoever sends salutations upon Nabi* صَلَّى ٱللَّهُ عَلَيْهِ وَسَلَّمَ *once, Allah* تَبَارَكَ وَتَعَالَى *and His angels will send seventy mercies and blessings upon him in return of his one Durood. Hence, whoever wishes to increase his Durood should increase it, and whoever wishes to decrease his Durood should decrease it (i.e. if he wants to earn great rewards, then he should increase his Durood)."* [55]

Virtue Nine – Earning One Qeeraat of Reward

Hazrat Ali bin Abi Taalib رَضِيَ ٱللَّهُ عَنْهُ *reports that Hazrat Rasulullah* صَلَّى ٱللَّهُ عَلَيْهِ وَسَلَّمَ *said, "Whoever sends Durood upon me once, Allah* تَبَارَكَ وَتَعَالَى *will record one qeeraat of reward for him, and one qeeraat is equal to the mountain of Uhud."* [56]

Virtue Ten - Gaining the Special Proximity of Hazrat Rasulullah صَلَّى ٱللَّهُ عَلَيْهِ وَسَلَّمَ on the Day of Qiyaamah

Hazrat Abdullah bin Mas'ood رَضِيَ ٱللَّهُ عَنْهُ *reports that Hazrat Rasulullah* صَلَّى ٱللَّهُ عَلَيْهِ وَسَلَّمَ *said, "The person who will be closest to me (and most*

---

[55] عن عبد الرحمن بن مريح الخولاني قال سمعت أبا قيس مولى عمرو بن العاصي يقول: سمعت عبد الله بن عمرو يقول: من صلى على رسول الله صلى الله عليه وسلم صلاة صلى الله عليه وملائكته سبعين صلاة فليقل عبد من ذلك أو ليكثر (مسند أحمد، الرقم: ٦٦٠٥، وإسناده حسن وحكمه الرفع إذ لا مجال للإجتهاد فيه كما في القول البديع صـ ٢٣٧)

[56] عن علي بن أبي طالب رضي الله عنه أن رسول الله صلى الله عليه وسلم قال : من صلى علي صلاة كتب الله له قيراطا والقيراط مثل أحد (مصنف عبد الرزاق، الرقم: ١٥٣، وسنده ضعيف كما في القول البديع صـ ٢٦٠)

deserving of my intercession) on the day of Qiyaamah will be the one who used to recite the most Durood upon me in the world." [57]

Hazrat Abu Umaamah ﷺ reports that Hazrat Rasulullah ﷺ said, "Recite abundant Durood upon me every Jumuah, for certainly the Durood of my Ummah are presented before me every Jumuah. The one who recites the most Durood upon me will be the closest to me (on the day of Qiyaamah)." [58]

Virtue Eleven - A Means of Purification from Sins

Hazrat Abu Hurairah ﷺ reports that Hazrat Rasulullah ﷺ said, "Recite Durood upon me, for certainly it is a form of purification for you. Ask Allah ﷻ to grant me the position of "waseelah", which is a rank in the highest stages of Paradise that is reserved for only one person, and I hope that I am the one who is blessed with this honour and position." [59]

---

⁵⁷ عن عبد الله بن مسعود أن رسول الله صلى الله عليه وسلم قال: أولى الناس بي يوم القيامة أكثرهم علي صلاة (سنن الترمذي، الرقم: ٤٨٤، وحسنه الإمام الترمذي رحمه الله)

⁵⁸ عن أبي أمامة رضي الله عنه قال قال رسول الله صلى الله عليه و سلم أكثروا علي من الصلاة في كل يوم جمعة فإن صلاة أمتي تعرض علي في كل يوم جمعة فمن كان أكثرهم علي صلاة كان أقربهم مني منزلة (شعب الإيمان، الرقم: ٢٧٧٠، وإسناده حسن كما في الترغيب والترهيب، الرقم: ٢٥٨٣)

⁵⁹ عن أبي هريرة رضي الله عنه عن النبي صلى الله عليه وسلم قال صلوا علي فإنها زكاة لكم واسألوا الله لي الوسيلة فإنها درجة في أعلى الجنة لا ينالها إلا رجل وأرجو أن أكون أنا هو (مسند أحمد، الرقم: ٨٧٧٠، وفي مجمع الزوائد (الرقم: ١٨٧٧): رواه البزار وفيه داود بن علبة ضعفه ابن معين والنسائي وغيرهما ووثقه ابن نمير وقال موسى بن داود الضبي: حدثنا داود بن علبة وأثنى عليه خيرا وقال ابن عدي: هو في جملة الضعفاء ممن يكتب حديثه)

Virtue Twelve - Securing the Pleasure of Allah تَبَارَكَ وَتَعَالَى

Hazrat Aaishah رَضِيَ اللهُ عَنْهَا reports that Hazrat Rasulullah صَلَّى اللهُ عَلَيْهِ وَسَلَّمَ said, "Whoever wishes to meet Allah تَبَارَكَ وَتَعَالَى while Allah تَبَارَكَ وَتَعَالَى is pleased with him then he should recite abundant Durood upon me." [60]

Virtue Thirteen - Securing the Dua of Hazrat Rasulullah صَلَّى اللهُ عَلَيْهِ وَسَلَّمَ

Hazrat Anas bin Maalik رَضِيَ اللهُ عَنْهُ reports that Hazrat Rasulullah صَلَّى اللهُ عَلَيْهِ وَسَلَّمَ said, "Whoever sends salutations upon me once, his salutations reach me (via the angels) and I make dua for him. Over and above that, ten virtues are recorded for him." [61]

Virtue Fourteen - Assistance on the Bridge of Siraat

Hazrat Abur Rahmaan bin Samurah رَضِيَ اللهُ عَنْهُ reports: On one occasion, Rasulullah صَلَّى اللهُ عَلَيْهِ وَسَلَّمَ came to us and said, "Last night, I saw something extraordinary in a dream. I saw a man from my Ummah who was crossing the pul-siraat (the bridge over Jahannum). At times, he was crawling, at other times, he was dragging himself on his behind, and sometimes, he was hanging onto the siraat (about to fall into Jahannum). Suddenly, his Durood that he would recite upon me in the

<hr>

[60] عن عائشة قالت قال رسول الله صلى الله عليه وسلم من سره أن يلقى الله وهو عليه راض فليكثر الصلاة علي (الكامل في ضعفاء الرجال ٦/٣٢، وإسناده ضعيف كما في القول البديع ص ٢٦٧)

[61] عن أنس بن مالك قال: قال رسول الله صلى الله عليه وسلم: من صلى علي بلغتني صلاته وصليت عليه وكتبت له سوى ذلك عشر حسنات (المعجم الأوسط للطبراني، وسنده لا بأس به كما القول البديع ص ٢٣٩)

world came to him. It then held his hand, helped him to stand up on the siraat and assisted him to cross over it." [62]

Virtue Fifteen - Seeking Goodness from its Source

Hazrat Abu Hurairah رَضِيَٱللَّهُعَنْهُ reports that Hazrat Rasulullah صَلَّىٱللَّهُعَلَيْهِوَسَلَّمَ said, "The one who recites the Quraan Majeed, praises Allah تَبَارَكَوَتَعَالَى, recites Durood upon Rasulullah صَلَّىٱللَّهُعَلَيْهِوَسَلَّمَ and seeks forgiveness from his Rabb has sought goodness from the true source of goodness (i.e. he has carried out actions which are a source of goodness for him)." [63]

---

[62] عن عبد الرحمن بن سمرة قال: خرج رسول الله صلى الله عليه وسلم فقال: إني رأيت البارحة عجبا رأيت رجلا من أمتي قد احتوشته ملائكة فجاءه وضوؤه فاستنقذه من ذلك ورأيت رجلا من أمتي قد احتوشته الشياطين فجاءه ذكر الله فخلصه منهم ورأيت رجلا من أمتي يلهث عطشا من العطش فجاءه صيام رمضان فسقاه ورأيت رجلا من أمتي بين يديه ظلمة ومن خلفه ظلمة وعن يمينه ظلمة وعن شماله ظلمة ومن فوقه ظلمة ومن تحته ظلمة فجاءه حجه وعمرته فاستخرجاه من الظلمة ورأيت رجلا من أمتي جاءه ملك الموت يقبض روحه فجاءه بره بوالديه فرد عنه ورأيت رجلا من أمتي يكلم المؤمنين ولا يكلموه فجاءته صلة الرحم فقالت إن هذا كان واصلا لرحمه فكلمهم وكلموه وصار معهم ورأيت رجلا من أمتي يأتي الناس وهم حلق فكلما أتى على حلقة طرد فجاءه اغتساله من الجنابة فأخذه بيده فأجلسه معهم ورأيت رجلا من أمتي جاءته زبانية العذاب فجاءه أمره بالمعروف ونهيه عن المنكر فاستنقذه من ذلك ورأيت رجلا من أمتي هوى في النار فجاءته دموعه التي بكى من خشية الله فأخرجته من النار ورأيت رجلا من أمتي قد هوت صحيفته إلى شماله فجاءه خوفه من الله فأخذ صحيفته فجعلها في يمينه ورأيت رجلا من أمتي يرعد كما ترعد السعفة فجاءه حسن ظنه بالله فسكن رعدته ورأيت رجلا من أمتي يزحف على الصراط مرة ويحبو مرة ويتعلق مرة فجاءته صلاته علي فأخذت بيده فأقامته على الصراط حتى جاوز ورأيت رجلا من أمتي انتهى إلى أبواب الجنة فغلقت الأبواب دونه فجاءته شهادة أن لا إله إلا الله فأخذته بيده فأدخلته الجنة (الأحاديث الطوال للطبراني ص ٢٧٣، وإسناده ضعيف كما في مجمع الزوائد، الرقم: ١١٧٦٤)

[63] عن أبي هريرة قال: قال رسول الله صلى الله عليه وسلم: من قرأ القرآن وحمد الرب وصلى على النبي صلى الله عليه وسلم واستغفر ربه فقد طلب الخير مكانه (شعب الإيمان، الرقم: ٢٠٨٤، وسنده ضعيف كما في القول البديع ص ٢٨٠)

Virtue Sixteen – Reward for the One who recites Durood when Hearing the Blessed Name of Hazrat Rasulullah ﷺ

Hazrat Anas bin Maalik رَضِيَ اللّٰهُ عَنْهُ reports that Hazrat Rasulullah ﷺ said, "The person in whose presence my name is taken should send salutations upon me, and certainly whoever sends salutations upon me once, Allah تَبَارَكَ وَتَعَالَى will send ten blessings upon him." [64]

Virtue Seventeen - Earning the Special Dua of the Angels

Hazrat Aamir bin Rabee'ah رَضِيَ اللّٰهُ عَنْهُ reports that Hazrat Rasulullah ﷺ said, "Whoever recites Durood upon me, the angels continuously send Salaat upon him (i.e. make dua for him) so long as he is engaged in Durood. Therefore, it is left to one to decide whether he wishes to recite a little Durood or abundant Durood."[65]

Virtue Eighteen - Special Reward for Reciting One Hundred Durood

Hazrat Abu Hurairah رَضِيَ اللّٰهُ عَنْهُ reports that Hazrat Rasulullah ﷺ said, "Whoever sends salutations upon me ten times, Allah تَبَارَكَ وَتَعَالَى will

---

[64] عن أنس بن مالك قال: قال رسول الله صلى الله عليه وسلم: من ذكرت عنده فليصل علي فإنه من صلى علي مرة صلي عليه عشرا (المعجم الأوسط للطبراني، الرقم: ٢٧٦٧، ورجاله رجال الصحيح كما في القول البديع صـ ٢٣٧)

[65] عن عامر بن ربيعة رضي الله عنه عن النبي صلى الله عليه و سلم قال: ما من مسلم يصلي علي إلا صلت عليه الملائكة ما صلى علي فليقلَّ العبد من ذلك أو ليكثر (سنن ابن ماجة، الرقم: ٩٠٧، وإسناده ضعيف كما في مصباح الزجاجة ١١٢/١)

send salutations upon him one hundred times, and whoever sends salutations upon me one hundred times, Allah تَبَارَكَ وَتَعَالَى will send salutations upon him one thousand times, and whoever increases (salutations upon me) out of love (for me) and eagerness (for gaining reward), I will intercede and testify for him on the day of Qiyaamah.”[66]

Virtue Nineteen – One Hundred Needs Being Fulfilled

Hazrat Jaabir رَضِيَ ٱللَّهُ عَنْهُ reports that Hazrat Rasulullah صَلَّى ٱللَّهُ عَلَيْهِ وَسَلَّمَ said, “Whoever recites Durood upon me one hundred times daily, Allah تَبَارَكَ وَتَعَالَى will fulfil one hundred of his needs, seventy of the Hereafter and thirty of this world.” [67]

Virtue Twenty – All Worldly and Deeni Needs being Sufficed

Hazrat Habbaan bin Munqiz رَحِمَهُ ٱللَّهُ reports that a certain Sahaabi once asked Hazrat Rasulullah صَلَّى ٱللَّهُ عَلَيْهِ وَسَلَّمَ, “O Rasul of Allah صَلَّى ٱللَّهُ عَلَيْهِ وَسَلَّمَ, should I devote one-third of the time I have allocated for dua to recite Durood upon you?” Rasulullah صَلَّى ٱللَّهُ عَلَيْهِ وَسَلَّمَ replied, “Yes, if you wish.” The Sahaabi then asked, “Should I devote two-thirds of that time for reciting Durood upon you?” Rasulullah صَلَّى ٱللَّهُ عَلَيْهِ وَسَلَّمَ again replied, “Yes, if

---

عن أبي هريرة رضي الله عنه عن النبي صلى الله عليه وسلم قال من صلى علي عشرا صلى الله عليه مئة ومن صلى علي مئة صلى الله عليه ألفا ومن زاد صبابة وشوقا كنت له شفيعا وشهيدا يوم القيامة (أخرجه أبو موسى المديني بسند قال الشيخ مغلطاى لا بأس به، كذا في القول البديع صـ ٢٣٦)

عن جابر رضي الله عنه قال قال رسول الله صلى الله عليه وسلم من صلى علي في كل يوم مائة مرة قضى الله له مائة حاجة سبعين منها لآخرته و ثلاثين منها لدنياه (أخرجه ابن منده وقال الحافظ أبو موسى المديني: إنه غريب حسن، كذا في القول البديع صـ ٢٧٧)

you wish." The Sahaabi then asked, "Should I devote all of that time for reciting Durood upon you?" Rasulullah ﷺ responded, "If you do so, Allah تَبَارَكَوَتَعَالَى will suffice you of every need which you have (and you would have asked for in your dua), whether it relates to your dunya or your Aakhirah." [68]

Virtue Twenty One – Being Relieved of all Worries

Hazrat Ubayy bin Ka'b رَضِىَاللهُعَنْهُ reports: I once asked Rasulullah ﷺ, "O Rasulullah ﷺ, I wish to increase my Durood upon you, so from the time I allocate for dua, how much should I reserve for sending Durood upon you?" Rasulullah ﷺ replied, "As much as you desire." I asked, "One quarter (i.e. one quarter of the time)?" Rasulullah ﷺ replied, "If you so wish, and if you increase it, it will be better for you." I then asked, "One half?" Rasulullah ﷺ replied, "As much as you desire, and if you increase it, it will be better for you." I then asked, "Two thirds?" Rasulullah ﷺ replied, "If you so wish, and if you increase it, it will be better for you." I finally said, "O Rasulullah ﷺ, in that case, I resolve to devote all the time I have allocated for dua to convey Durood upon you." Rasulullah ﷺ mentioned, "Allah تَبَارَكَوَتَعَالَى will make it a means of relieving

---

[68] عن محمد بن يحيى بن حبان عن أبيه عن جده حبان بن منقذ أن رجلا قال: يا رسول الله أجعل ثلث صلاتي عليك قال: نعم إن شئت قال: الثلثين قال: نعم قال: فصلاتي كلها قال رسول الله صلى الله عليه وسلم: إذن يكفيك الله ما أهمك من أمر دنياك وآخرتك (المعجم الكبير للطبراني، الرقم: ٣٥٧٤، وإسناده حسن كما في الترغيب والترهيب للمنذري، الرقم: ٢٥٧٨)

you from all your worries (and problems), and a means of atonement for your sins." [69]

Note: In this Hadith, the Sahaabi explained to Hazrat Rasulullah ﷺ that he had reserved some time during the day or night to engage in making special dua. He further asked Hazrat Rasulullah ﷺ whether it would be better for him to dedicate that entire time to reciting Durood, to which Hazrat Rasulullah ﷺ informed him that he would receive the reward of the Durood as well as have his duas answered for the needs that he would have begged Allah تَبَارَكَ وَتَعَالَى for had he engaged in dua.

It should be borne in mind that this Hadith in no way shows that the Sahaabi was intending to abandon the sunnah of dua, as dua is made after every fardh salaah as well as after the tahajjud salaah and nafl salaah that one performs. Hence, this Sahaabi would have been making dua at these other times as well. However, he only asked Hazrat Rasulullah ﷺ if he could recite Durood during a separate time that he had allocated for dua.

Furthermore, the meaning of this Hadith is supported by the Hadith-e-Qudsi in which Allah تَبَارَكَ وَتَعَالَى says:

---

[69] عن أبي بن كعب رضي الله عنه قال قلت يا رسول الله إني أكثر الصلاة عليك فكم أجعل لك من صلاتي ؟ فقال ما شئت قال قلت الربع قال ما شئت فإن زدت فهو خير لك قلت النصف قال ما شئت فإن زدت فهو خير لك قال قلت فالثلثين قال ما شئت فإن زدت فهو خير لك قلت أجعل لك صلاتي كلها قال إذا تكفى همك ويغفر لك ذنبك (سنن الترمذي الرقم ٢٤٥٧: وقال هذا حديث حسن)

من شغله ذكري عن مسألتي أعطيته أفضل ما أعطي السائلين

The one who My remembrance occupies him from making dua to Me and asking of Me, I will give him better than that which I give to the people who make dua to Me and ask of Me. [70]

Virtue Twenty Two - Making Musaafahah with Hazrat Rasulullah ﷺ on the Day of Qiyaamah

It is reported that Hazrat Rasulullah ﷺ said, "Whoever recites Durood upon me fifty times daily, I will make musaafahah (shake hands) with him on the day of Qiyaamah." [71]

Virtue Twenty Three – Seeing One's Abode in Paradise

Hazrat Anas رضي الله عنه reports that Hazrat Rasulullah ﷺ said, "The one who recites Durood upon me one thousand times on the day of Friday, will not pass away until he is shown his abode in Paradise." [72]

---

[70] عن عمرو بن مرة رفعه قال: من شغله ذكري عن مسألتي أعطيته فوق ما أعطي السائلين (المصنف لابن أبي شيبة، الرقم: ٢٩٨٨٣، قال الربعي في تخريج أحاديث الكشاف (٢٢٠/٣): وفي الصحيح من شغله ذكري عن مسألتي أعطيته أفضل ما أعطي السائلين)

[71] قال النبي صلى الله عليه وسلم من صلى علي في يوم خمسين مرة صافحته يوم القيامة (القربة لابن بشكوال، الرقم: ٨٧، وقد سكت عنه السخاوي في القول البديع صـ ٢٨٩، ويفهم من سكوته أن الحديث معمول به عنده، ولذلك ذكره في كتابه)

[72] عن أنس بن مالك قال: قال رسول الله صلى الله عليه وسلم: من صلى علي في يوم الجمعة ألف مرة لم يمت حتى يرى مقعده من الجنة (أخرجه ابن شاهين بسند ضعيف كذا في القول البديع صـ ٣٩٧)

Virtue Twenty Four – Receiving the Certificate of Freedom from Hypocrisy and the Fire of Jahannum

Hazrat Anas رَضِيَ اللَّهُ عَنْهُ *reports that Hazrat Rasulullah* صَلَّى اللَّهُ عَلَيْهِ وَسَلَّمَ *said, "Whoever sends salutations upon me once, then as a reward for it, Allah* تَبَارَكَ وَتَعَالَى *will send salutations (i.e. reward him and shower His mercy) upon him ten times, and whoever sends salutations upon me ten times, Allah* تَبَارَكَ وَتَعَالَى *will send salutations (i.e. reward him and shower His mercy) upon him one hundred times, and whoever sends salutations upon me one hundred times, Allah* تَبَارَكَ وَتَعَالَى *will write for him (a certificate of) emancipation, between his eyes, from hypocrisy, and (a certificate of) emancipation from the fire of Jahannum, and Allah* تَبَارَكَ وَتَعَالَى *will honour him to be with the martyrs on the day of Qiyaamah."* [73]

Virtue Twenty Five - The Reward of Sadaqah through Reciting Durood

Hazrat Abu Sa'eed Khudri رَضِيَ اللَّهُ عَنْهُ *reports that Hazrat Rasululah* صَلَّى اللَّهُ عَلَيْهِ وَسَلَّمَ *said, "Whichever Muslim does not have anything to give in sadaqah, he should recite the following Durood in his dua as it will be a*

---

[73] عن أنس بن مالك قال: قال رسول الله صلى الله عليه وآله وسلم: من صلى علي صلاة واحدة صلى الله عليه عشرا ومن صلى علي عشرا صلى الله عليه مائة ومن صلى علي مائة كتب الله له بين عينيه براءة من النفاق وبراءة من النار وأسكنه الله يوم القيامة مع الشهداء (المعجم الصغير للطبراني، الرقم: ٨٩٩، وقال الهيثمي في مجمع الزوائد (الرقم: ١٨٢٩٨): رواه الطبراني في الصغير والأوسط وفيه إبراهيم بن سالم بن شبل الهجيمي ولم أعرفه وبقية رجاله ثقات، وقال المنذري في الترغيب والترهيب (الرقم: ٢٥٦٠): وفي إسناده إبراهيم بن سالم بن شبل الهجعي لا أعرفه بجرح ولا عدالة)

means of him receiving the reward of sadaqah and it will purify him of his sins."

اَللّٰهُمَّ صَلِّ عَلٰى مُحَمَّدٍ عَبْدِكَ وَرَسُوْلِكَ وَصَلِّ عَلَى الْمُؤْمِنِيْنَ وَالْمُؤْمِنَاتِ وَالْمُسْلِمِيْنَ وَالْمُسْلِمَاتِ

O Allah تَبَارَكَ وَتَعَالٰى! Send Durood (i.e. shower Your mercy) upon Muhammad صَلَّى اللّٰهُ عَلَيْهِ وَسَلَّمَ, Your slave and Rasul, and shower Your mercy upon all the mu'mineen and muslimeen, males and females.

Hazrat Rasulullah صَلَّى اللّٰهُ عَلَيْهِ وَسَلَّمَ thereafter said, "A believer continues to do good and is never fully satisfied with the good that he carries out until he finally (passes away on imaan and) reaches Jannah."[74]

Virtue Twenty Six - A source of Noor (Light) on the Day of Qiyaamah

Hazrat Ibnu Umar رَضِيَ اللّٰهُ عَنْهُمَا reports that Hazrat Rasulullah صَلَّى اللّٰهُ عَلَيْهِ وَسَلَّمَ said, "Adorn your gatherings with the recitation of Durood upon me, because on the day of Qiyaamah, the Durood will be a noor (a means of light) for you."[75]

---

[74] عن أبي سعيد الخدري رضي الله عنه عن رسول الله صلى الله عليه وسلم قال أيما رجل مسلم لم تكن عنده صدقة فليقل في دعائه اللهم صل على محمد عبدك ورسولك وصل على المؤمنين والمؤمنات والمسلمين والمسلمات فإنها زكاة وقال لا يشبع مؤمن خيرا حتى يكون منتهاه الجنة (صحيح ابن حبان، الرقم: ٩٠٣، وإسناده حسن كما في مجمع الزوائد، الرقم: ١٧٢٣١)

[75] عن ابن عمر رضي الله عنهما قال قال رسول الله صلى الله عليه وسلم زينوا مجالسكم بالصلاة علي فإن صلاتكم علي نور لكم يوم القيامة (الفردوس بمأثور الخطاب، الرقم: ٣٣٣٠، وإسناده ضعيف كما في القول البديع صـ ٢٧٨)

Virtue Twenty Seven – Increase in Sustenance

Hazrat Sahl bin Sa'd رَضِيَٱللَّهُعَنْهُ reports that on one occasion, a Sahaabi came to Hazrat Rasulullah صَلَّىٱللَّهُعَلَيْهِوَسَلَّمَ and complained of poverty and difficulty in earning a livelihood. Hazrat Rasulullah صَلَّىٱللَّهُعَلَيْهِوَسَلَّمَ said to this Sahaabi, "When you enter your home then make Salaam, regardless of whether there is anyone in the home or not. Thereafter, send Salaam upon me and recite Qul-Huwallah (Surah Ikhlaas) once." The Sahaabi did as instructed by Hazrat Rasulullah صَلَّىٱللَّهُعَلَيْهِوَسَلَّمَ, and Allah تَبَارَكَوَتَعَالَ blessed him with such abundant sustenance that he even began to spend upon his neighbors and relatives. [76]

Virtue Twenty Eight – Acceptance of Duas

Hazrat Umar رَضِيَٱللَّهُعَنْهُ narrates, "Duas remain suspended between the heavens and the Earth. They do not proceed towards the heavens as long as Durood on Nabi صَلَّىٱللَّهُعَلَيْهِوَسَلَّمَ has not been recited (i.e. there is no guarantee for their acceptance)." [77]

---

[76] عن سهل بن سعد رضي الله عنه قال: جاء رجل إلى النبي صلى الله عليه وسلم فشكا إليه الفقر وضيق العيش أو المعاش فقال له رسول الله صلى الله عليه وسلم: إذا دخلت منزلك فسلم إن كان فيه أحد أو لم يكن فيه أحد ثم سلم علي واقرأ قل هو الله أحد مرة واحدة ففعل الرجل فأدَرَّ الله عليه الرزق حتى أفاض على جيرانه وقراباته (أبو موسى المديني وسنده ضعيف كما في القول البديع ص ٢٧٩)

[77] عن عمر بن الخطاب قال: إن الدعاء موقوف بين السماء والأرض لا يصعد منه شيء حتى تصلي على نبيك صلى الله عليه وسلم (سنن الترمذي، الرقم: ٤٨٦)

ويتقوى ذلك بما أخرجه الترمذي عن عمر موقوفا الدعاء موقوف بين السماء والأرض لا يصعد منه شيء حتى يصلي على النبي صلى الله عليه وسلم (فتح الباري ١٦٤/١١، وقد التزم الحافظ في الأحاديث التي سكت عنها في الفتح ألا تقل درجتها عن الحسن فقد قال في مقدمته المسماة هدي الساري (ص ٧): ثم أستخرج ثانيا ما يتعلق به غرض صحيح في ذلك الحديث من الفوائد المتنية والاسنادية من تتمات وزيادات وكشف غامض وتصريح مدلس بسماع ومتابعة سامع من شيخ اختلط قبل ذلك منتزعا كل ذلك من أمهات المسانيد والجوامع والمستخرجات والأجزاء والفوائد بشرط الصحة أو الحسن فيما أورده من ذلك)

Virtue Twenty Nine – Eradication of Poverty

Hazrat Samurah Suwaai رَضِىَٱللَّهُعَنْهُ, *the father of Hazrat Jaabir* رَضِىَٱللَّهُعَنْهُ, *reports: We were once in the company of Rasulullah* صَلَّىٱللَّهُعَلَيْهِوَسَلَّمَ *when a man came to Rasulullah* صَلَّىٱللَّهُعَلَيْهِوَسَلَّمَ *and asked, "O Rasulullah* صَلَّىٱللَّهُعَلَيْهِوَسَلَّمَ*! Which action is most pleasing to Allah* تَبَارَكَوَتَعَالَ*?" Rasulullah* صَلَّىٱللَّهُعَلَيْهِوَسَلَّمَ *replied, "Truthful speech and fulfilling of trusts." I said, "O Rasulullah* صَلَّىٱللَّهُعَلَيْهِوَسَلَّمَ*! Please give us further advice (regarding actions that are pleasing to Allah* تَبَارَكَوَتَعَالَ*)!" Rasulullah* صَلَّىٱللَّهُعَلَيْهِوَسَلَّمَ *said, "Performing salaah during the night and fasting during hot days." I then said, "O Rasulullah* صَلَّىٱللَّهُعَلَيْهِوَسَلَّمَ*! Please give us further advice!" Rasulullah* صَلَّىٱللَّهُعَلَيْهِوَسَلَّمَ *said, "Engaging in abundant zikr and conveying Durood upon me eradicates poverty." I again asked, "O Rasulullah* صَلَّىٱللَّهُعَلَيْهِوَسَلَّمَ*! Please give us further advice!" Rasulullah* صَلَّىٱللَّهُعَلَيْهِوَسَلَّمَ *remarked, "The one who leads the people in salaah should perform a concise salaah, because among the congregation are the old, the ill, the young and people who have some need."* [78]

Virtue Thirty – Earning the Intercession of Hazrat Rasulullah صَلَّىٱللَّهُعَلَيْهِوَسَلَّمَ

Hazrat Abu Dardaa رَضِىَٱللَّهُعَنْهُ *reports that Hazrat Rasulullah* صَلَّىٱللَّهُعَلَيْهِوَسَلَّمَ *said, "Whoever recites ten Durood upon me in the morning and ten*

---

[78] وعن سمرة السوائي والد جابر رضي الله عنهما قال: كنا عند النبي – صلى الله عليه وسلم – إذ جاءه رجل فقال يا رسول الله ما أقرب الأعمال إلى الله قال صدق الحديث وأداء الأمانة، قلت يا رسول الله زدنا قال صلاة الليل وصوم الهواجر قلت يا رسول الله زدنا قال كثرة الذكر والصلاة علي تنفي الفقر قلت يا رسول الله زدنا قال من أم قوماً فليخفف فإن فيهم الكبير والعليل والصغير وذا الحاجة (معرفة الصحابة لأبي نعيم، الرقم: ٣٥٧٢، وسنده ضعيف كما في القول البديع صـ ٢٧٨)

Durood upon me in the evening, he will receive my intercession on the day of Qiyaamah." [79]

Hazrat Ruwaifi' bin Thaabit Al-Ansaari ﵁ narrates that Hazrat Rasulullah ﷺ said, "Whoever recites the following (Durood), my intercession will be binding for him."

اَللّٰهُمَّ صَلِّ عَلٰى مُحَمَّدٍ وَأَنْزِلْهُ الْمَقْعَدَ الْمُقَرَّبَ عِنْدَكَ يَوْمَ الْقِيَامَة

O Allah ﵎! Send salutations upon Muhammad ﷺ and grant him the position of proximity to You on the day of Qiyaamah. [80]

Note: According to some Muhadditheen, the "position of proximity" mentioned in this Hadith refers to the honour of interceding on behalf of the entire creation for the reckoning to commence on the day of Qiyaamah (Maqaam-e-Mahmood). According to other Muhadditheen, it refers to an extremely esteemed and exalted position in Jannah, according to the status of Hazrat Rasulullah ﷺ.

Virtue Thirty One – Hazrat Rasulullah ﷺ Making Dua for One's Forgiveness

Hazrat Umar bin Khattaab ﵁ reports that Hazrat Rasulullah ﷺ said, "Increase your recitation of Durood upon me on the

⁷⁹ عن أبي الدرداء قال: قال رسول الله صلى الله عليه وسلم: من صلى علي حين يصبح عشرا وحين يمسي عشرا أدركته شفاعتي يوم القيامة (رواه الطبراني بإسنادين وإسناد أحدهما جيد ورجاله وثقوا كذا في مجمع الزوائد، الرقم: ١٧٠٢٢)

⁸⁰ عن رويفع بن ثابت قال: قال رسول الله صلى الله عليه وسلم: من صلى على محمد وقال: اللهم أنزله المقعد المقرب عندك يوم القيامة، وجبت له شفاعتي (المعجم الكبير للطبراني، الرقم: ٤٤٨٠، وإسناده حسن كما في مجمع الزوائد، الرقم: ١٧٣٠٤)

night and day of Jumuah as your Durood is presented to me. I then make dua for you and ask Allah تَبَارَكَوَتَعَالَى to forgive your sins." [81]

Virtue Thirty Two - Needs of the Dunya and Aakhirah Fulfilled through Reciting Durood on a Jumuah

Hazrat Anas bin Maalik رَضِىَاللهُعَنْهُ reports that Hazrat Rasulullah صَلَّىاللهُعَلَيْهِوَسَلَّمَ said, "Those of you who recite the most Durood upon me in the dunya will be closest to me on the day of Qiyaamah, at every juncture. The one who recites Durood upon me during the night of Jumuah and the day of Jumuah, Allah تَبَارَكَوَتَعَالَى will fulfill one hundred of his needs; seventy needs of the Aakhirah and thirty needs of the dunya. After the Durood is recited, Allah تَبَارَكَوَتَعَالَى will entrust it to an angel who will bring it to me in my grave, just as your gifts are brought to you. The angel informs me of the person who recited the Durood by telling me his name and his family lineage. I then keep the Durood by me on a white scroll." [82]

Note: Imaam Bayhaqi رَحِمَهُاللهُ has reported this Hadith under the chapter of the Ambiyaa عَلَيْهِمُالسَّلَامُ being alive in their graves.

---

[81] عن أبي هريرة قال: قال رسول الله صلى الله عليه وسلم: أكثروا الصلاة علي في الليلة الزهراء واليوم الأزهر فإن صلاتكم تعرض علي (المعجم الأوسط، الرقم: ٢٤١، وسنده ضعيف لكن يتقوى بشواهده كما في القول البديع صـ ٣٢٥)

[82] عن أنس بن مالك خادم النبي صلى الله عليه وسلم قال: قال النبي صلى الله عليه وسلم: إن أقربكم مني يوم القيامة أكثركم علي صلاة في الدنيا من صلى علي في يوم الجمعة وليلة الجمعة قضى الله له مائة حاجة سبعين من حوائج الآخرة وثلاثين من حوائج الدنيا ثم وكل الله بذلك ملكا يدخله في قبره كما يدخل عليكم الهدايا يخبرني من صلى علي باسمه ونسبه إلى عشيرته فأثبته عندي في صحيفة بيضاء (شعب الإيمان، الرقم: ٢٧٧٣، وسنده ضعيف كما في القول البديع صـ ٣٢٩)

Virtue Thirty Three – Seventy Angels recording the Reward for a Thousand Days

Hazrat Ibnu Abbaas صَلَّى اللَّهُ عَلَيْهِ وَسَلَّمَ *narrates that Hazrat Rasulullah* صَلَّى اللَّهُ عَلَيْهِ وَسَلَّمَ *said, "Whoever recites the following (Durood), he will (engage and) tire seventy angels (in recording the reward of the Durood recited) for a thousand days."*

جَزَى اللّٰهُ عَنَّا مُحَمَّدًا صَلَّى اللّٰهُ عَلَيْهِ وَسَلَّمَ بِمَا هُوَ أَهْلُهُ

May Allah تَبَارَكَ وَتَعَالَى *reward Muhammad* صَلَّى اللَّهُ عَلَيْهِ وَسَلَّمَ *on our behalf as he is worthy (i.e. a reward that befits his esteemed position).*[83]

Virtue Thirty Four - Durood being Weighed on the Scale of Full Measure

Hazrat Abu Hurairah رَضِيَ اللَّهُ عَنْهُ *narrates that Hazrat Rasulullah* صَلَّى اللَّهُ عَلَيْهِ وَسَلَّمَ *said, "The one who wishes that his Durood be weighed on the scale that weighs in full (thereby receiving full reward for the Durood) when he recites Durood upon us, the Ahlul Bayt, then he should recite the following Durood:*

اَللّٰهُمَّ صَلِّ عَلَى مُحَمَّدٍ النَّبِيِّ الْأُمِّيِّ وَأَزْوَاجِهِ أُمَّهَاتِ الْمُؤْمِنِيْنَ وَذُرِّيَّتِهِ وَأَهْلِ بَيْتِهِ كَمَا صَلَّيْتَ عَلَى آلِ إِبْرَاهِيْمَ إِنَّكَ حَمِيْدٌ مَجِيْدٌ

---

[83] عن ابن عباس قال: قال رسول الله صلى الله عليه وسلم: من قال جزى الله عنا محمدا صلى الله عليه وسلم بما هو أهله أتعب سبعين كاتبا ألف صباح (حلية الأولياء ٢٠٦/٣، وفي سنده هاني بن المتوكل وهو ضعيف كما في القول البديع ص ١١٦)

O Allah تَبَارَكَ وَتَعَالَى! Send salutations upon Muhammad صَلَّى ٱللَّهُ عَلَيْهِ وَسَلَّمَ, the unlettered Nabi, his wives, the Mothers of the Believers, his progeny and his household, as You sent salutations upon the family of Ebrahim عَلَيْهِ ٱلسَّلَامُ, indeed You are most worthy of praise, most exalted. [84]

---

[84] عن أبي هريرة رضي الله عنه قال قال رسول الله صلى الله عليه وسلم من سره أن يكتال بالمكيال الأوفى إذا صلى علينا أهل البيت فليقل اللهم صل على محمد النبي الأمي وأزواجه أمهات المؤمنين وذريته وأهل بيته كما صليت على آل إبراهيم إنك حميد مجيد (سنن أبي داود، الرقم: ٩٨٢، وسكت عليه هو والمنذري في مختصره، الرقم: ٩٨١)

CHAPTER SIX

The Angels Conveying the Durood and Salaam of the Ummah

There are many Ahaadith that have been reported regarding the Durood and Salaam of the Ummah being conveyed to Rasulullah صَلَّى ٱللَّهُ عَلَيْهِ وَسَلَّمَ. Allah تَبَارَكَ وَتَعَالَى has deputed an entire group of angels that are dedicated for this great task of collecting the Durood and Salaam of the Ummah and conveying it to Hazrat Rasulullah صَلَّى ٱللَّهُ عَلَيْهِ وَسَلَّمَ.

It is reported in the Hadith that Hazrat Rasulullah صَلَّى ٱللَّهُ عَلَيْهِ وَسَلَّمَ said, "When you recite Durood at my grave, then I hear your Durood, and when you recite Durood from afar, then your Durood is conveyed to me (via the angels)." [85] In one Hadith, Hazrat

---

[85] وعنه أيضا (أي: أبي هريرة رضي الله عنه) قال: قال رسول الله صلى الله عليه وسلم من صلى علي عند قبري سمعته ومن صلى علي من بعيد أعلمته (أخرجه أبو الشيخ في الثواب له من طريق أبي معاوية عن الأعمش عن أبي صالح عنه ومن طريقه الديلمي وقال ابن القيم إنه غريب قلت: وسنده جيد كما أفاده شيخنا كذا في القول البديع ص ٣٢٥)

Rasulullah ﷺ mentioned, "Whenever any person makes Salaam to me, then Allah تَبَارَكَوَتَعَالَى allows my soul to be returned to my body until I reply to the Salaam." [86]

Hazrat Anas رَضِىَاللهُعَنْهُ reports that Hazrat Rasulullah ﷺ said, "Whoever recites Durood upon me, his Durood reaches me (via the angels), and I reply to his Durood, and ten good deeds are written for him."[87]

In yet another Hadith, Hazrat Rasulullah ﷺ said, "The one who comes to my grave and conveys Salaam, I will intercede for him on the Day of Qiyaamah." [88]

Apart from the group of angels collecting and conveying the Durood of the Ummah to Hazrat Rasulullah ﷺ, it is also reported in some Ahaadith that Allah تَبَارَكَوَتَعَالَى has appointed an angel to stand at the blessed grave of Hazrat Rasulullah ﷺ and convey the Durood and Salaam of the entire Ummah to Hazrat Rasulullah ﷺ. This angel has been blessed with the power of hearing the Durood of every ummati, wherever he may be in the world. The angel conveys the Durood and Salaam of the

---

[86] عن أبي هريرة أن رسول الله صلى الله عليه وسلم قال: ما من أحد يسلم علي إلا رد الله علي روحي حتى أرد عليه السلام (سنن أبي داود، الرقم: ٢٠٤١، وسنده جيد كما قال العراقي في المغني عن حمل الأسفار في الأسفار ص ٣٦٧)

[87] عن أنس بن مالك رضي الله عنه عن النبي صلى الله عليه وسلم من صلى علي بلغتني صلاته وصليت عليه وكتبت له سوى ذلك عشر حسنات (المعجم الأوسط، الرقم: ١٦٤٢، وسنده لا بأس به كما في الترغيب والترهيب للمنذري، الرقم: ٢٥٧٢)

[88] عن ابن عمر قال قال رسول الله صلى الله عليه و سلم: من زار قبري وجبت له شفاعتي (سنن الدارقطني، الرقم: ١٩٤، وسنده جيد كما في البدر المنير ٢٩٧/٦)

Ummah to Hazrat Rasulullah ﷺ saying, "O Rasulullah ﷺ! So-and-so, the son of so-and-so, has conveyed Durood and Salaam upon you."

Hazrat Ammaar bin Yaasir رضي الله عنه reports that Hazrat Rasulullah ﷺ said, "Indeed, Allah تبارك وتعالى has appointed an angel whom He has given the ability to hear the voices of the entire creation. This angel remains standing at my blessed grave since the time I passed away. There is no person who recites Durood upon me once except that this angel says, "O Muhammad ﷺ! So-and-so, the son of so-and-so, has recited Durood upon you." Allah تبارك وتعالى then showers ten mercies upon that person in exchange of every Durood that he recites."[89]

Below are some Ahaadith regarding the Durood and Salaam that are conveyed to Hazrat Rasulullah ﷺ by the angels.

Angels Travelling the Earth to Collect Durood

Hazrat Abdullah bin Mas'ood رضي الله عنه reports that Hazrat Rasulullah ﷺ said, "Indeed, Allah تبارك وتعالى has a group of angels that roam (throughout the earth so that they may search for the

[89] عن عمار بن ياسر رضي الله عنه قال : قال رسول الله صلى الله عليه وسلم : إن لله ملكا أعطاه أسماع الخلائق، فهو قائم على قبري إذا مت، فليس أحد يصلي علي صلاة إلا قال : يا محمد صلى عليك فلان ابن فلان، قال : فيصلي الرب تبارك وتعالى على ذلك الرجل بكل واحدة عشرا (رواه الطبراني، ونعيم بن ضمضم ضعيف وابن الحميري اسمه عمران قال البخاري: لا يتابع على حديثه وقال صاحب الميزان: لا يعرف، وبقية رجاله رجال الصحيح كذا في مجمع الزوائد، الرقم: ١٧٢٩٢)

gatherings of Durood) and convey the Durood of my Ummah to me." [90]

The Angel that Stands at the Blessed Grave of Hazrat Rasulullah ﷺ to Convey the Durood of the Ummah

Hazrat Ammaar bin Yaasir رضى الله عنه reports that Hazrat Rasulullah ﷺ said, "Allah تبارك وتعالى has appointed an angel to remain by my grave, such an angel whom Allah تبارك وتعالى gave the knowledge of the names (and in some narrations, the ability of hearing the voices) of the creation. Thus, no person will send Durood upon me until the day of Qiyaamah, except that he conveys it to me with his name and the name of his father. (He will say,) This is so-and-so the son of so-and-so, who has recited Durood upon you.'" [91]

---

[90] عن عبد الله قال: قال رسول الله صلى الله عليه وسلم: إن لله ملائكة سياحين في الأرض يبلغوني من أمتي السلام (سنن النسائي، الرقم: ١٢٨٢، صحيح ابن حبان، الرقم: ٩١٣)

[91] عن عمار بن ياسر رضي الله عنه قال قال رسول الله صلى الله عليه و سلم إن الله وكل بقبري ملكا أعطاه الله أسماء الخلائق فلا يصلي على أحد إلى يوم القيامة إلا أبلغني باسمه واسم أبيه هذا فلان بن فلان قد صلى عليك (رواه البزار كما في الترغيب والترهيب، الرقم: ٢٥٧٤، قال الهيثمي: رواه البزار وفيه ابن الحميري واسمه عمران يأتي الكلام عليه بعده ... قال البخاري: لا يتابع على حديثه وقال صاحب الميزان: لا يعرف ونعيم بن ضمضم ضعفه بعضهم، وبقية رجاله الصحيح كذا في مجمع الزوائد، الرقم: ١٧٢٩١)

عن عمار بن ياسر رضي الله عنه قال : قال رسول الله صلى الله عليه وسلم : إن الله ملكا أعطاه أسماع الخلائق، فهو قائم على قبري إذا مت، فليس أحد يصلي علي صلاة إلا قال : يا محمد صلى عليك فلان ابن فلان، قال : فيصلي الرب تبارك وتعالى على ذلك الرجل بكل واحدة عشرا (رواه الطبراني، ونعيم بن ضمضم ضعيف وابن الحميري اسمه عمران قال البخاري: لا يتابع على حديثه وقال صاحب الميزان: لا يعرف، وبقية رجاله الصحيح كذا في مجمع الزوائد، الرقم: ١٧٢٩٢)

Salaat and Salaam Being Conveyed to Hazrat Rasulullah صَلَّى ٱللَّهُ عَلَيْهِ وَسَلَّمَ via the Angels

Hazrat Ibnu Abbaas رَضِيَ ٱللَّهُ عَنْهُمَا *once mentioned the following, "There is no person from the Ummah of Rasulullah* صَلَّى ٱللَّهُ عَلَيْهِ وَسَلَّمَ *who recites Salaat or Salaam upon Rasulullah* صَلَّى ٱللَّهُ عَلَيْهِ وَسَلَّمَ *except that it is conveyed to him (via the angels) and he is told, 'So-and-so has recited Salaat upon you, and so-and-so has recited Salaam upon you.'"* [92]

The Durood of the Ummah reaching Hazrat Rasulullah صَلَّى ٱللَّهُ عَلَيْهِ وَسَلَّمَ

Hazrat Hasan bin Ali رَضِيَ ٱللَّهُ عَنْهُمَا *reports that Hazrat Rasulullah* صَلَّى ٱللَّهُ عَلَيْهِ وَسَلَّمَ *said, "Recite Durood upon me wherever you may be, as your Durood is conveyed to me (via the angels)."* [93]

Hazrat Abu Hurairah رَضِيَ ٱللَّهُ عَنْهُ *reports that Hazrat Rasulullah* صَلَّى ٱللَّهُ عَلَيْهِ وَسَلَّمَ *said, "Do not make your homes into graveyards (i.e. enliven your homes with righteous aa'maal e.g. salaah, reciting the Quraan Majeed, etc, so that your homes do not become like the graveyard which is void of aa'maal), and do not make my grave a place of festivity, and recite*

---

[92] عن ابن عباس قال: ليس أحد من أمة محمد يصلي على محمد أو يسلم عليه يبلغه يصلي عليك فلان ويسلم عليك فلان (مسند إسحاق بن راهويه، الرقم: ٩١١، رجاله ثقات إلا أبا يحيى القتات، ففيه ضعف.

[93] عن الحسن بن علي رضي الله عنهما أن رسول الله صلى الله عليه و سلم قال حيثما كنتم فصلوا علي فإن صلاتكم تبلغني (المعجم الكبير للطبراني، الرقم: ٢٧٢٩، وإسناده حسن كما في الترغيب والترهيب للمنذري، الرقم: ٢٥٧١)

Durood upon me, for certainly your Durood reaches me (through the angels) from wherever you may be." [94]

---

[94] عن أبي هريرة قال قال رسول الله صلى الله عليه وسلم لا تجعلوا بيوتكم قبورا ولا تجعلوا قبري عيدا وصلوا علي فإن صلاتكم تبلغني حيث كنتم (سنن أبي داود، الرقم: ٢٠٤٢، وإسناده جيد كما في البدر المنير ٢٩٠/٥)

The Virtues of Gatherings of Zikr and Durood

Hazrat Anas رَضِيَ ٱللَّهُ عَنْهُ reports that Hazrat Rasulullah صَلَّى ٱللَّهُ عَلَيْهِ وَسَلَّمَ said, "There is a group of angels of Allah تَبَارَكَ وَتَعَالَى that continue to roam throughout the earth, searching for the gatherings of zikr (gatherings of the remembrance of Allah تَبَارَكَ وَتَعَالَى). When they find such a gathering, they throng around it. Thereafter, they send the leading angels among them to the sky (to report to Allah تَبَارَكَ وَتَعَالَى). These angels say to Allah تَبَارَكَ وَتَعَالَى, "O our Lord! We have come to a group of Your servants who regard Your favours as a great bounty upon them, recite Your kitaab, send Durood upon Your Nabi صَلَّى ٱللَّهُ عَلَيْهِ وَسَلَّمَ and they beg You for their needs relating to the Aakhirah and dunya." Allah تَبَارَكَ وَتَعَالَى replies, "Envelop them in My mercy." The angels then submit, "O Lord! Among them is so-and-so, who is a great sinner, and he only arrived at the ending of the gathering." Allah تَبَارَكَ وَتَعَالَى says, "Envelop all the people of this gathering (including him) in My mercy, for the people in this gathering are such that no person who joins them will be unfortunate and deprived of My mercy." [95]

---

[95] عن أنس رضي الله عنه عن النبي صلى الله عليه وسلم قال: إن لله سيارة من الملائكة يطلبون حلق الذكر فإذا أتوا عليهم حفوا بهم ثم بعثوا رائدهم إلى السماء إلى رب العزة تبارك وتعالى فيقولون ربنا أتينا على عباد من عبادك يعظمون آلاءك ويتلون كتابك ويصلون على نبيك صلى الله

Angels Thronging to Gatherings of Zikr

Hazrat Uqbah bin Aamir رَضِيَٱللَّهُعَنْهُ *reports that Hazrat Rasulullah* صَلَّىٱللَّهُعَلَيْهِوَسَلَّمَ *said, "Indeed, the masaajid have 'pegs' (i.e. people who remain committed to the musjid, engaged in ibaadah, just as pegs are fixed to the ground). The angels remain seated with such people. If they are absent from the musjid, the angels miss them, and if they are sick, the angels visit them, and if the angels see them, they welcome them, and if they have any need, the angels assist them to fulfill their need. When they sit (in the musjid to engage in the remembrance of Allah* تَبَارَكَوَتَعَالَى*, recitation of Durood, etc.), the angels throng around them from their feet until the sky. These angels have pages of silver and pens of gold in their hands with which they record the Durood upon Rasulullah* صَلَّىٱللَّهُعَلَيْهِوَسَلَّمَ *(which is recited by these people). The angels say to them, "Continue engaging in the zikr of Allah* تَبَارَكَوَتَعَالَى*, may Allah* تَبَارَكَوَتَعَالَى *have mercy on you! Increase (your zikr and Durood), may Allah* تَبَارَكَوَتَعَالَى *increase you (in good)!" When these people commence making the zikr of Allah* تَبَارَكَوَتَعَالَى*, the doors of the sky are opened for them, their duas are answered, the damsels of Jannah peer down at them, and Allah* تَبَارَكَوَتَعَالَى *focuses His special mercy towards them so long as they do not engage in any other activity and they do not depart. When they depart from the musjid, the angels rise and search for the gatherings of zikr."* [96]

عليه وسلم ويسئلونك لآخرتهم ودنياهم فيقول تبارك وتعالى: غشوهم رحمتي فيقولون يا رب إن فهم فلانا الخطاء إنما أعتقناهم إعناق فيقول تبارك وتعالى: غشوهم رحمتي فهم الجلساء لا يشقى بهم جليسهم (مسند البزار، الرقم: ٦٤٩٤ وسنده حسن كما في القول البديع صـ ٢٦٧)

[96] عن عقبة بن عامر رضي الله عنه قال : قال رسول الله صلى الله عليه وسلم : إن للمساجد أوتادا جلساؤهم الملائكة إن غابوا فقدوهم وإن مرضوا عادوهم وإن رأوهم رحبوا بهم وإن طلبوا حاجة أعانوهم فإذا جلسوا حفت بهم الملائكة من لدن أقدامهم إلى عنان السماء بأيديهم قراطيس

الفضة وأقلام الذهب يكتبون الصلاة على النبي صلى الله عليه وسلم ويقولون : اذكروا رحمكم الله زيدوا زادكم الله فإذا استفتحوا الذكر فتحت لهم أبواب السماء واستجيب لهم الدعاء وتطلع عليهم الحور العين وأقبل الله عز وجل عليهم بوجهه ما لم يخوضوا في حديث غيره ويتفرقوا فإذا تفرقوا أقام الزوار يلتمسون حلق الذكر

الفضة وأقلام الذهب يكتبون الصلاة على النبي صلى الله عليه وسلم ويقولون : اذكروا رحمكم الله زيدوا زادكم الله فإذا استفتحوا الذكر فتحت لهم أبواب السماء واستجيب لهم الدعاء وتطلع عليهم الحور العين وأقبل الله عز وجل عليهم بوجهه ما لم يخوضوا في حديث غيره ويتفرقوا فإذا تفرقوا أقام الزوار يلتمسون حلق الذكر (القربة لابن بشكوال، الرقم: ١١٥، وسنده ضعيف كما في القول البديع ص ٢٥٧)

CHAPTER SEVEN

Warnings for those who Neglect to Recite Durood

One will generally express gratitude to a person in proportion to the favour he has received from him. Hence, the greater the favour that one enjoys, the more gratitude one will express.

Without doubt, Hazrat Rasulullah صَلَّى ٱللَّهُ عَلَيْهِ وَسَلَّمَ is the greatest benefactor of every ummati, as he brought us Deen, guided us to Allah تَبَارَكَ وَتَعَالَى and showed us the path of salvation. Hence, when his favour upon us is the greatest, then we should show him the highest gratitude from all people – even more than we show to our own parents. Thus, no matter how much Durood we convey upon Hazrat Rasulullah صَلَّى ٱللَّهُ عَلَيْهِ وَسَلَّمَ, we can never repay him for his favour upon us.

Apart from this, Allah تَبَارَكَ وَتَعَالَى has blessed Hazrat Rasulullah صَلَّى ٱللَّهُ عَلَيْهِ وَسَلَّمَ with the highest rank from the creation, and has commanded us to send Durood upon Hazrat Rasulullah صَلَّى ٱللَّهُ عَلَيْهِ وَسَلَّمَ and show gratitude to him for the favours we received through him. Hence, when a child is born and the azaan and iqaamah are called out in his ears, we are commanded to take the name of Hazrat Rasulullah ﷺ with the name of Allah تَبَارَكَ وَتَعَالَى.

Accordingly, when the azaan and iqaamah are called out for salaah, during the khutbahs of Jumuah, the two Eids and even the khutbah of nikaah, at the time of making dua and when reciting the kalimah at the time of death, the name of Hazrat Rasulullah ﷺ is taken with the name of Allah تَبَارَكَ وَتَعَالَى

Since the virtue of Durood is so great, Hazrat Rasulullah ﷺ has informed the Ummah of the great loss of those who neglect to recite Durood upon him.

Hazrat Abu Sa'eed Khudri ﵁ reports that Hazrat Rasulullah ﷺ said, "People do not sit in any gathering in which they do not recite Durood upon Rasulullah ﷺ except that it will be a means of regret for them (on the day of Qiyaamah), even though they may enter Jannah, on account of them seeing the reward (which they failed to acquire by neglecting to recite Durood)."[97]

<hr>

[97] عن أبي سعيد الخدري عن النبي صلى الله عليه وسلم قال: لا يجلس قوم مجلسا لا يصلون فيه على رسول الله صلى الله عليه وسلم إلا كان عليهم حسرة وإن دخلوا الجنة لما يرون من الثواب (شعب الإيمان، الرقم: ١٤٧٠، وهو حديث صحيح كما في القول البديع صـ ٣١٧)

The Real Miser

Hazrat Husain رَضِيَٱللَّهُعَنْهُ reports that Hazrat Rasulullah صَلَّىٱللَّهُعَلَيْهِوَسَلَّمَ said, "The real miser is the one in whose presence my name is mentioned, yet he does not recite Durood upon me." [98]

A Sign of being Ill-Mannered and Ungrateful

Hazrat Qataadah رَحِمَهُٱللَّهُ reports that Hazrat Rasulullah صَلَّىٱللَّهُعَلَيْهِوَسَلَّمَ said, "It is a sign of a person being ill-mannered (and ungrateful) that my name is mentioned in his presence, yet he neglects reciting Durood upon me." [99]

Leaving out an Action Leading One to Jannah

Hazrat Husain bin 'Ali رَضِيَٱللَّهُعَنْهَا reports that Hazrat Rasulullah صَلَّىٱللَّهُعَلَيْهِوَسَلَّمَ said, "The one in whose presence my name is mentioned, and he does not send salutations upon me, he has left out an action which leads to Jannah." [100]

---

[98] عن حسين بن علي بن أبي طالب قال: قال رسول الله صلى الله عليه وسلم: البخيل الذي من ذكرت عنده فلم يصل علي (سنن الترمذي، الرقم: ٣٥٤٦، وقال هذا حديث حسن صحيح غريب)

[99] عن قتادة قال: قال رسول الله صلى الله عليه وسلم: من الجفاء أن أذكر عند الرجل فلا يصلي علي (الإعلام بفضل الصلاة على النبي صلى الله عليه وسلم للنميري، الرقم: ٢٠٩، ورواته ثقات كما في القول البديع صـ ٣١١)

[100] عن حسين بن علي رضي الله عنهما قال قال رسول الله صلى الله عليه وسلم من ذكرت عنده فخطىء الصلاة علي خطىء طريق الجنة (المعجم الكبير للطبراني، الرقم: ٢٨٨٧، وقال المناوي في فيض القدير (٦/٢٣٢) تحت حديث من نسي الصلاة علي خطئ طريق الجنة. لكن انتصر له ابن الملقن فقال: حديث ضعيف لكنه تقوى بما رواه الطبراني عن الحسن بن علي مرفوعا: من ذكرت عنده فخطئ الصلاة علي خطئ طريق الجنة، وتبعه الحافظ ابن حجر فقال: خرجه ابن ماجه عن ابن عباس والبيهقي في الشعب عن أبي هريرة والطبراني عن الحسين بن علي قال: وهذه الطرق يشد بعضها بعضا)

The Curse of Hazrat Jibreel عَلَيْهِ السَّلَام and Hazrat Rasulullah صَلَّى اللهُ عَلَيْهِ وَسَلَّمَ

Hazrat Ka'b bin Ujrah رَضِيَ اللهُ عَنْهُ reports the following: On one occasion, Rasulullah صَلَّى اللهُ عَلَيْهِ وَسَلَّمَ called out to the Sahaabah رَضِيَ اللهُ عَنْهُمْ, "Come to the mimbar." When we assembled around the mimbar, Rasulullah صَلَّى اللهُ عَلَيْهِ وَسَلَّمَ ascended the first step and said, "Aameen." He then ascended the second step and said, "Aameen." Then, Rasulullah صَلَّى اللهُ عَلَيْهِ وَسَلَّمَ ascended the third step and said, "Aameen." After delivering the khutbah, when Rasulullah صَلَّى اللهُ عَلَيْهِ وَسَلَّمَ descended from the mimbar, we asked, "O Rasul of Allah صَلَّى اللهُ عَلَيْهِ وَسَلَّمَ! We heard you say something today that we did not hear you say before (i.e. saying aameen thrice while ascending the mimbar)." Rasulullah صَلَّى اللهُ عَلَيْهِ وَسَلَّمَ replied, "(When I ascended the first step,) Jibreel عَلَيْهِ السَّلَام appeared before me and said, 'Woe to him who witnessed the blessed month of Ramadhaan, yet he let it pass without gaining forgiveness (i.e. he did not fulfill the rights of this month).' I said aameen to this dua. When I ascended the second step, he said, 'Woe to him before whom your name is mentioned, yet he does not send Durood upon you.' I said aameen to this dua. When I ascended the third step, he said, "Woe to him in whose presence both of his parents or one of them attain old age, yet (due to not serving them,) they do not become the means for him to enter Jannah. I said aameen to this dua."[101]

---

١٠١ عن كعب بن عجرة قال: قال رسول الله صلى الله عليه وسلم: احضروا المنبر فحضرنا فلما ارتقى درجة قال: آمين فلما ارتقى الدرجة الثانية قال: آمين فلما ارتقى الدرجة الثالثة قال: آمين فلما نزل قلنا: يا رسول الله لقد سمعنا منك اليوم شيئا ما كنا نسمعه قال: إن جبريل عليه الصلاة

The Outcome of a Gathering Devoid of Zikr and Durood

Hazrat Jaabir رَضِيَٱللَّهُعَنْهُ *reports that Hazrat Rasulullah* صَلَّىٱللَّهُعَلَيْهِوَسَلَّمَ *said,
"Whenever a group of people gather, and thereafter terminate their
gathering and depart without remembering Allah* تَبَارَكَوَتَعَالَى *or sending
Durood upon Rasulullah* صَلَّىٱللَّهُعَلَيْهِوَسَلَّمَ *in the gathering, it is as though
they have gathered around a foul smelling corpse and thereafter
departed (i.e. the gathering which is void of Allah's* تَبَارَكَوَتَعَالَى
remembrance and Durood upon Rasulullah صَلَّىٱللَّهُعَلَيْهِوَسَلَّمَ *is so
reprehensible that it is compared to a foul smelling corpse which no
person wishes to go near)."* [102]

والسلام عرض لي فقال: بعدا لمن أدرك رمضان فلم يغفر له قلت: آمين فلما رقيت الثانية قال: بعدا لمن ذكرت عنده فلم يصل عليك قلت: آمين

فلما رقيت الثالثة قال: بعدا لمن أدرك أبواه الكبر عنده أو أحدهما فلم يدخلاه الجنة قلت: آمين (المستدرك على الصحيحين للحاكم، الرقم:

٧٢٥٦، وقال: هذا حديث صحيح الإسناد ولم يخرجاه وأقره الذهبي)

١٠٢ عن جابر قال: قال رسول الله صلى الله عليه وسلم: ما اجتمع قوم ثم تفرقوا عن غير ذكر الله وصلاة على النبي صلى الله عليه وسلم إلا قاموا

عن أنتن جيفة (مسند أبي داود الطيالسي، الرقم: ١٨٦٣، ورواته ثقات كما في إتحاف الخيرة المهرة، الرقم: ٦٠٦٢)

CHAPTER EIGHT

Occasions for Reciting Durood and Salaam

1. RECITING DUROOD IN THE MORNING AND EVENING

Reciting Ten Durood in the Morning and Evening

Hazrat Abu Dardaa رَضِىَ اللّٰهُ عَنْهُ *reports that Hazrat Rasulullah* صَلَّى اللّٰهُ عَلَيْهِ وَسَلَّمَ *said, "Whoever recites ten Durood upon me in the morning and ten Durood upon me in the evening, he will receive my intercession on the day of Qiyaamah."* [103]

Reciting One Hundred Durood after Fajr and Maghrib

Hazrat Jaabir رَضِىَ اللّٰهُ عَنْهُ *reports that Hazrat Rasulullah* صَلَّى اللّٰهُ عَلَيْهِ وَسَلَّمَ *said, "The one who recites one hundred Durood upon me immediately after*

---

[103] عن جابر قال: قال رسول الله صلى الله عليه وسلم: ما اجتمع قوم ثم تفرقوا عن غير ذكر الله وصلاة على النبي صلى الله عليه وسلم إلا قاموا عن أنتن جيفة (مسند أبي داود الطيالسي، الرقم: ١٨٦٣، ورواته ثقات كما في إتحاف الخيرة المهرة، الرقم: ٦٠٦٢)

performing the Fajr Salaah, before speaking, Allah تَبَارَكَ وَتَعَالَى will fulfill one hundred of his needs. Allah تَبَارَكَ وَتَعَالَى will hasten the fulfillment of thirty needs (in this world), and Allah تَبَارَكَ وَتَعَالَى will keep the fulfillment of seventy in store for the Hereafter, and similar will be the case if one recites the Durood after the Maghrib Salaah (i.e. one will receive the same virtue)." The Sahaabah رَضِيَ اللهُ عَنْهُمْ enquired, "How should we recite Durood upon you, O Rasul of Allah صَلَّى اللهُ عَلَيْهِ وَسَلَّمَ?" Rasulullah صَلَّى اللهُ عَلَيْهِ وَسَلَّمَ instructed the Sahaabah رَضِيَ اللهُ عَنْهُمْ to recite the following Durood one hundred times:[104]

إِنَّ اللهَ وَمَلَئِكَتَهُ يُصَلُّوْنَ عَلَى النَّبِيِّ يأَيُّهَا الَّذِيْنَ آمَنُوْا صَلُّوْا عَلَيْهِ وَسَلِّمُوْا تَسْلِيْمًا اَللَّهُمَّ صَلِّ عَلى مُحَمَّد

2. RECITING DUROOD WHEN ENTERING AND EXITING THE MUSJID

Hazrat Faatimah رَضِيَ اللهُ عَنْهَا reports that when Rasulullah صَلَّى اللهُ عَلَيْهِ وَسَلَّمَ would enter the musjid, he would first recite Durood and thereafter recite the following dua:

رَبِّ اغْفِرْ لِيْ ذُنُوْبِيْ وَافْتَحْ لِيْ أَبْوَابَ رَحْمَتِك

O my Rabb, forgive my sins and open for me the doors of Your mercy.

When Rasulullah ﷺ would leave the musjid, he would recite Durood and thereafter recite the following dua:

رَبِّ اغْفِرْ لِيْ ذُنُوْبِيْ وَافْتَحْ لِيْ أَبْوَابَ فَضْلِكَ

O my Rabb, forgive my sins and open for me the doors of Your bounties. [105]

Hazrat Abu Humaid or Abu Usaid رَضِيَ اللّٰهُ عَنْهُمَا reports that Hazrat Rasulullah ﷺ said, "Whenever anyone enters the musjid, he should recite Durood upon Rasulullah ﷺ and then recite the following dua:

اَللّٰهُمَّ افْتَحْ لِيْ أَبْوَابَ رَحْمَتِكَ

O Allah تَبَارَكَ وَتَعَالَى, open for me the doors of Your mercy.

And when he leaves the musjid, he should recite Durood upon Rasulullah ﷺ and then recite the following dua:

اَللّٰهُمَّ إِنِّيْ أَسْأَلُكَ مِنْ فَضْلِكَ

---

١٠٥ عن فاطمة رضي الله عنها قالت: ٰكان رسول الله صلى الله عليه وسلم إذا دحل المسجد صلى على محمد وسلم وقال رب اغفر لي ذنوبي وافتح لي أبواب رحمتك وإذا خرج صلى على محمد وسلم وقال رب اغفر لي ذنوبي وافتح لي أبواب فضلك (سنن الترمذي، الرقم: ٣١٤، وحسنه)

O Allah, I ask You for Your bounties. [106]

3. RECITING DUROOD IN SALAAH AND AFTER SALAAH

Hazrat Abdullah bin Umar ﷺ *reports, "Rasulullah* ﷺ *would teach us the dua of tashahhud of salaah, and thereafter, Rasulullah* ﷺ *said that (after one completes the tashahhud of salaah,) one should recite Durood."* [107]

Hazrat Abu Ummamah ﷺ *reports that Hazrat Rasulullah* ﷺ *said, "Whoever recites the following words after every fardh salaah, my intercession becomes incumbent upon him on the day of Qiyaamah:*

اَللّٰهُمَّ أَعْطِ مُحَمَّدًا الْوَسِيلَةَ وَاجْعَلْهُ فِي الْمُصْطَفَيْنَ مَحَبَّتَهُ وَفِي الْعَالِيْنَ دَرَجَتَهُ وَفِي الْمُقَرَّبِيْنَ دَارَهُ

---

[106] عن أبي حميد أو أبي أسيد الأنصاري رضي الله عنه قال قال رسول الله صلى الله عليه وسلم إذا دخل أحدكم المسجد فليسلم على النبي صلى الله عليه وسلم ثم ليقل اللهم افتح لي أبواب رحمتك فإذا خرج فليقل اللهم إني أسألك من فضلك (سنن أبي داود، الرقم: ٤٦٥، وسكت عليه هو والمنذري في مختصره، الرقم: ٤٦٥)

[107] عن ابن عمر قال: كان رسول الله صلى الله عليه وسلم يعلمنا التشهد التحيات الطيبات الزاكيات لله السلام عليك أيها النبي ورحمة الله وبركاته السلام علينا وعلى عباد الله الصالحين أشهد أن لا إله إلا الله وحده لا شريك له وأن محمدا عبده ورسوله ثم يصلي على النبي صلى الله عليه وسلم (سنن الدارقطني، الرقم: ١٣٣٠، وفيه موسى بن عبيدة الربذي وهو ضعيف كما في القول البديع ص ٣٦٥، وفي شرح ابن ماجة للمغلطاي ص ١٥٢٣: وفي حديث موسى بن عبيدة وخارجة وهما ضعيفان: كان رسول الله صلى الله عليه وسلم يعلمنا التشهد التحيات الطيبات الزاكيات لله السلام عليك أيها النبي ورحمة الله وبركاته السلام علينا وعلى عباد الله الصالحين أشهد أن لا إله إلا الله وحده لا شريك له وأن محمدا عبده ورسوله ثم يصلي على النبي صلى الله عليه وسلم وفي العلل الكبير للترمذي: سألت محمدا عن هذا الحديث فقال: روى شعبة عن أبي بشر عن مجاهد عن ابن عمر وروى سفيان عن مجاهد عن أبي معمر عن أبي مسعود وهو المحفوظ عندي)

O Allah تَبَارَكَ وَتَعَالَى! Grant Muhammad صَلَّى اللّٰهُ عَلَيْهِ وَسَلَّم waseelah (the right of intercession on the day of Qiyaamah), and place his love in the (hearts of) your chosen ones, and place him among the high ranking people, and make his abode among the beloved and close servants. [108]

4. RECITING DUROOD WHEN AWAKENING FOR TAHAJJUD SALAAH

Hazrat Abdullah bin Mas'ood رَضِيَ اللّٰهُ عَنْهُ mentioned, "Allah تَبَارَكَ وَتَعَالَى becomes pleased with two people. The first is the person who encounters the enemy while mounted on the best of horses among his companions. His companions are then defeated while he remains firm and he perseveres. If he is killed then he attains martyrdom, and if he survives then he is the person with whom Allah تَبَارَكَ وَتَعَالَى is pleased. The second is the person who stands during the night (before Allah تَبَارَكَ وَتَعَالَى to perform tahajjud salaah) without anyone aware of him awakening to perform salaah. He performs a complete and perfect wudhu and thereafter praises Allah تَبَارَكَ وَتَعَالَى and glorifies Him, and recites Durood upon Rasulullah صَلَّى اللّٰهُ عَلَيْهِ وَسَلَّم. He then commences the recitation of the Quraan Majeed. This is the person with whom Allah تَبَارَكَ وَتَعَالَى becomes pleased. Allah

<hr>

108 عن أبي أمامة عن النبي صلى الله عليه وسلم قال: من دعا بهؤلاء الدعوات في دبر كل صلاة مكتوبة حلت له الشفاعة مني يوم القيامة اللهم أعط محمدا الوسيلة واجعله في المصطفين محبته، وفي العالين درجته وفي المقربين داره (المعجم الكبير للطبراني، الرقم: ٧٩١٦، وفيه مطرح بن يزيد وهو ضعيف كما في مجمع الزوائد، الرقم: ١٦٩٨١، وقد تحرفت كلمة العالين إلى العالمين في المعجم الكبير ومجمع الزوائد كما نبه عليه الشيخ محمد عوامة في حاشيته على القول البديع صـ ٣٦٣)

تَبَارَكَوَتَعَالَى says regarding him, 'Look at My servant who is standing (in salaah) while nobody is seeing him (perform salaah) besides Me.'"[109]

5. RECITING DUROOD ON THE NIGHT AND DAY OF JUMUAH

Increasing the Recitation of Durood on a Jumuah

Hazrat Abu Hurairah رَضِىَاللهُعَنهُ reports that Hazrat Rasulullah صَلَّىاللهُعَلَيهِوَسَلَّم said, "Increase the recitation of Durood upon me on the night of Jumuah and the day of Jumuah, as your Durood is presented to me."[110]

Hazrat Aws bin Aws رَضِىَاللهُعَنهُ reports that Hazrat Rasulullah صَلَّىاللهُعَلَيهِوَسَلَّم said, "The most virtuous of days is the day of Jumuah. Therefore, recite abundant Durood upon me on this day, for indeed your Durood are presented to me. The Sahaabah رَضِىَاللهُعَنهُم asked, "How will our Durood be presented to you after your demise when your bones would have decayed?" Rasulullah صَلَّىاللهُعَلَيهِوَسَلَّم replied, "Certainly Allah تَبَارَكَوَتَعَالَى has

---

[109] عن عبد الله بن مسعود قال يضحك الله إلى رجلين رجل لقي العدو وهو على فرس من أمثل خيل أصحابه فاهزموا وثبت فإن قتل استشهد وان بقي فذلك الذي يضحك الله إليه ورجل قام في جوف الليل لا يعلم به أحد فتوضأ فأسبغ الوضوء ثم حمد الله ومجده وصلى على النبي صلى الله عليه وسلم واستفتح القرآن فذلك الذي يضحك الله إليه يقول انظروا إلى عبدى قائما لا يراه أحد غيري (عمل اليوم والليلة، الرقم: ٨٦٧، وسنده صحيح كما في القول البديع صـ ٣٧٦)

[110] عن أبي هريرة رضي الله عنه قال : قال رسول الله صلى الله عليه وسلم : أكثروا الصلاة علي في الليلة الزهراء واليوم الأغر فإن صلاتكم تعرض علي (المعجم الاوسط للطبراني وسنده ضعيف لكن يتقوى بشواهده كما في القول البديع صـ ٣٢٥)

prohibited the earth from consuming the bodies of the Ambiyaa عَلَيْهِمُالسَّلَامُ.""""[111]

The Great Virtue of Reciting Durood on a Jumuah

Hazrat Aws bin Aws صَلَّىاللَّهُعَلَيْهِعَنْهُ reports that Hazrat Rasulullah صَلَّىاللَّهُعَلَيْهِوَسَلَّمَ said, "Among the best of your days is the day of Friday. On Friday, Aadam عَلَيْهِالسَّلَامُ, was created, on Friday, he passed away, on Friday, the trumpet will be blown, and on Friday, the creation will fall unconscious, so increase your Durood upon me on the day of Friday as your Durood is presented to me." The Sahaabah رَضِيَاللَّهُعَنْهُمْ enquired, 'O Rasul of Allah صَلَّىاللَّهُعَلَيْهِوَسَلَّمَ! How will our Durood be presented to you, whereas your body will have decomposed in the grave?' Rasulullah صَلَّىاللَّهُعَلَيْهِوَسَلَّمَ replied, 'Indeed, Allah تَبَارَكَوَتَعَالَى has prohibited the earth from consuming the bodies of the Ambiyaa عَلَيْهِمُالسَّلَامُ.""[112]

From 'Qoot-ul-Quloob', Allaamah Sakhaawi رَحَمَهُاللَّهُ quotes that 'abundant Durood' mentioned in the above Hadith, refers to reciting Durood at least three hundred times daily. [113] Hazrat Moulana Rashid Ahmad Gangohi رَحَمَهُاللَّهُ also instructed his

---

[111] عن أوس بن أوس رضي الله عنه قال قال رسول الله صلى الله عليه وسلم إن من أفضل أيامكم يوم الجمعة فأكثروا علي من الصلاة فيه فإن صلاتكم معروضة علي قال: فقالوا: يا رسول الله، وكيف تعرض صلاتنا عليك، وقد أرمت قال: يقولون بليت قال: إن الله تبارك وتعالى حرم على الأرض أجساد الأنبياء صلى الله عليهم (سنن أبي داود، الرقم: ١٥٣١، وإسناده صحيح كما في خلاصة الأحكام للنووي ٤٤١/١)

[112] عن أوس بن أوس قال: قال رسول الله صلى الله عليه وسلم: إن من أفضل أيامكم يوم الجمعة فيه خلق آدم وفيه قبض وفيه النفخة وفيه الصعقة فأكثروا علي من الصلاة فيه فإن صلاتكم معروضة علي قال: قالوا: يا رسول الله وكيف تعرض صلاتنا عليك وقد أرمت يقولون بليت فقال: إن الله عز وجل حرم على الأرض أجساد الأنبياء (سنن أبي داود، الرقم: ١٠٤٧، وقال الحاكم في مستدركه، الرقم: ١٠٢٩: هذا حديث صحيح على شرط البخاري ولم يخرجاه وأقره الذهبي)

[113] القول البديع ص ٣٤٦

followers to recite Durood upon Nabi ﷺ three hundred times daily. [114]

Hazrat Zainul Aabideen, Ali bin Husain رَحِمَهُ ٱللَّٰه, once said, "The salient feature of those affiliated to the Ahlus Sunnah wal Jamaa'ah is the recitation of abundant Durood upon Nabi ﷺ." [115]

Earning the Dua of Hazrat Rasulullah ﷺ through Reciting Durood on a Jumuah

Hazrat Umar bin Khattaab رَضِىَ ٱللَّٰهُ عَنْهُ reports that Hazrat Rasulullah ﷺ said, "Increase your recitation of Durood upon me on the night and day of Jumuah as your Durood is presented to me. I then make dua for you and ask Allah تَبَارَكَ وَتَعَالَىٰ to forgive your sins." [116]

Reciting Durood One Thousand times on Friday

Hazrat Anas رَضِىَ ٱللَّٰهُ عَنْهُ reports that Hazrat Rasulullah ﷺ said, "The one who recites Durood upon me one thousand times on the day of Friday, will not pass away until he is shown his abode in Paradise." [117]

---

[114] فضائل درود ص ٢٧

[115] الترغيب والترهيب لقوام السنة ٣٣٣/٢، القول البديع صـ ١٣٢

[116] عن عمر بن الخطاب رضي الله عنه أن رسول الله صلى الله عليه وسلم قال: أكثروا الصلاة علي في الليلة الزهراء واليوم الأغر فإن صلاتكم تعرض علي فأدعو لكم وأستغفر (القربة لابن بشكوال، الرقم: ١٠٧، وسنده ضعيف كما في القول البديع صـ ٣٣٥)

[117] عن أنس بن مالك قال: قال رسول الله صلى الله عليه وسلم: من صلى علي في يوم الجمعة ألف مرة لم يمت حتى يرى مقعده من الجنة

(أخرجه ابن شاهين بسند ضعيف كذا في القول البديع صـ ٣٩٧)

Eighty Years of Sins Forgiven, and Eighty Years of Ibaadah Recorded through Reciting Durood Eighty Times on a Friday

Hazrat Abu Hurairah رَضِىَاللَّهُعَنْهُ reports that Hazrat Rasulullah صَلَّىاللَّهُعَلَيْهِوَسَلَّمَ said, "The one who performs Asr Salaah on Friday and thereafter recites the following Durood eighty times before standing up from his place, eighty years of sins are forgiven for him and eighty years of (nafl) ibaadah are recorded for him:

اَللّٰهُمَّ صَلِّ عَلٰى مُحَمَّدٍ النَّبِيِّ الْأُمِّيِّ وَعَلٰى آلِهِ وَسَلِّمْ تَسْلِيْمًا

O Allah, shower your choicest Durood and abundant peace upon Muhammad صَلَّىاللَّهُعَلَيْهِوَسَلَّمَ the unlettered Nabi, and on his family. [118]

It is reported by Hazrat Sahl bin Abdullah رَضِىَاللَّهُعَنْهُ, "Whosoever recites the following Durood eighty times after asr salaah on Friday, his sins of eighty years will be forgiven

اللّٰهُمَّ صَلِّ عَلٰى مُحَمَّدٍ النَّبِيِّ الْأُمِّيِّ وَعَلٰى آلِهِ وَسَلِّمْ

O Allah, shower your choicest Durood and peace upon Muhammad صَلَّىاللَّهُعَلَيْهِوَسَلَّمَ the unlettered Nabi, and on his family. [119]

---

١١٨ عن أبي هريرة رضي الله عنه قال: قال رسول الله صلى الله عليه وسلم: من صلى صلاة العصر من يوم الجمعة فقال قبل أن يقوم من مكانه اللهم صل على محمد النبي الأمي وعلى آله وسلم تسليما غفرت له ذنوب ثمانين عاما وكتبت له عبادة ثمانين سنة (القول البديع ص ٣٩٩)

١١٩ وعن سهل بن عبد الله قال من قال في يوم الجمعة بعد العصر اللهم صل على محمد النبي الأمي وعلى إله وسلم ثمانين مرة غفرت له ذنوب ثمانين عاماً أخرجه ابن بشكوال وقد تقدم قريباً في حديث أبي هريرة معناه (القول البديع ص ٤٠٠)

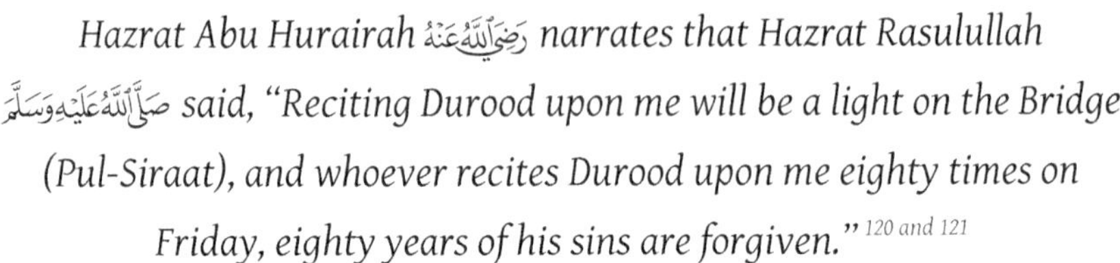

Hazrat Abu Hurairah رَضِىَ اللهُ عَنْهُ narrates that Hazrat Rasulullah صَلَّى اللهُ عَلَيْهِ وَسَلَّمَ said, "Reciting Durood upon me will be a light on the Bridge (Pul-Siraat), and whoever recites Durood upon me eighty times on Friday, eighty years of his sins are forgiven." [120 and 121]

١٢٠ عن أبي هريرة رضي الله عنه قال: قال رسول الله صلى الله عليه وسلم: الصلاة علي نور على الصراط ومن صلى علي يوم الجمعة ثمانين مرة غفرت له ذنوب ثمانين عاماً أخرجه ابن شاهين في الأفراد وغيرها وابن بشكوال من طريقه وأبو الشيخ والضياء من طريق الدارقطني في الأفراد أيضاً والديلمي في مسند الفردوس وأبو نعيم وسنده ضعيف وهو عند الأزدي في الضعفاء من حديث أبي هريرة أيضاً لكنه من وجه آخر ضعيف أيضاً وأخرجه أبو سعيد في شرف المصطفى من حديث أنس والله أعلم (القول البديع صه ٣٩٨)

¹²¹ **The Practice of Eighty Durood after Asr on Friday**

Q: Is the eighty durood that is recited after Asr on Friday a practice which is established in Deen? Does it have a source in the Hadith of Rasulullah صَلَّى اللهُ عَلَيْهِ وَسَلَّمَ?

A: The practice of reciting eighty durood after Asr on Friday is established in Deen. This practice is established from the following Hadith of Hazrat Abu Hurairah رَضِىَ اللهُ عَنْهُ:

وعن أبي هريرة رضي الله عنه قال قال رسول الله صلى الله عليه وسلم من صلى صلاة العصر من يوم الجمعة فقال قبل أن يقوم من مكانه اللهم صل على محمد النبي الأمي وعلى آله وسلم تسليماً ثمانين مرة غفرت له ذنوب ثمانين عاماً وكتبت له عبادة ثمانين سنة (القول البديع عن ابن بشكوال صه ٣٩٩)

Hazrat Abu Hurairah رَضِىَ اللهُ عَنْهُ reports that Rasulullah صَلَّى اللهُ عَلَيْهِ وَسَلَّمَ said, "The one who performs Asr Salaah on Friday and thereafter recites eighty times before standing up from his place,

اللهم صل على محمد النبي الأمي وعلى آله وسلم تسليماً

eighty years of sins are forgiven for him and eighty years of (nafl) ibaadat are written for him."

Allaamah Sakhaawi رَحِمَهُ اللهُ quoted this Hadith in his famous book القول البديع and did not declare it to be unworthy for practise, (as is his style in his book regarding Ahaadith which are not worthy for practise). Therefore, we understand that this Hadith is worthy for practise as Allaamah Sakhaawi رَحِمَهُ اللهُ clearly mentioned in the introduction of his book القول البديع that he will only include such Ahaadith in his book which are worthy for practise

Allaamah Sakhaawi رَحِمَهُ اللهُ mentioned at the end of his book that he had personally examined the chains of the Ahaadith which he had qouted from Allaamah Ibnu Bashkuwaal رَحِمَهُ اللهُ in his book, (and among these Ahaadith is the Hadith which establishes the practice of eighty Durood after Asr on Friday). Therefore, when this great Muhaddith, who was an expert in the science of authenticating Ahaadith, included this Hadith in his book on Durood and regarded it worthy of practise, one may practise upon it.

Many of our Akaabir and Buzrugaan-e-Deen used to diligently recite the eighty durood after Asr on Friday. Among them were the likes of Hazrat Shaikhul Hadith Moulana Muhammad Zakariyya رَحِمَهُ اللهُ, Hazrat Mufti Mahmood Hasan Gangohi Saheb رَحِمَهُ اللهُ and Hazrat Moulana Yusuf Motala Saheb رَحِمَهُ اللهُ.

In reply to a query regarding the practice of eighty durood after Asr on Friday, Hazrat Moulana Aaqil Saheb (a senior Muhaddith of India) had prepared a detailed response, establishing the practice of eighty durood after Asr on Friday.

Shaikh Muhammad Awwaamah حفظه الله, a senior ranking Muhaddith of this era, has also approved of this practice and regarded it to be established.

From among the senior ranking Muhadditheen and Ulamaa of the past and present who encouraged this practice or included it in their compilations are:

1. Allaamah Ibnu Bashkuwaal, a Muhaddith of the sixth century (d.578) رَحِمَهُ ٱللَّهُ, mentioned the above practice in his book, القربة إلى رب العالمين بالصلاة على سيد العالمين صلى الله عليه وعلى آله وصحبه أجمعين

2. Allaamah Abu Muhammad Jabr bin Muhammad bin Jabr bin Hishaam Al-Qurtubee, an Aalim and Faqeeh of the seventh century (d.630) رَحِمَهُ ٱللَّهُ, the student of Allaamah Ibnu Bashkuwaal, mentioned the above practice in his book, مطالع الأنوار ومسالك الأبرار في فضائل الصلاة على النبي المختار

3. The author of Al-Qaamus, Allaamah Majdud-Deen Fayruz-Aabaadee, a Muhaddith of the ninth century (d.817) رَحِمَهُ ٱللَّهُ, mentioned the above practice in his book, الصلات والبشر على خير البشر ص ١٣٠

4. Allaamah Alamud-Deen Saalih bin Umar Al-Bulqeenee, a Muhaddith of the ninth century (d.868) رَحِمَهُ ٱللَّهُ mentioned the above practice in his book, التذكرة البلقينية ص ٤٤

5. Allaamah Sakhaawi, a Muhaddith of the tenth century (d.902) رَحِمَهُ ٱللَّهُ, mentioned the above practice in his book, القول البديع ص ٣٩٩

6. Allaamah Ibnu Hajar Makki, a Muhaddith of the tenth century (d.974) رَحِمَهُ ٱللَّهُ mentioned the above practice in his book, الدر المنضود في الصلاة والسلام على صاحب المقام المحمود ص ٢١٣

7. Allaamah Muhammad Khalil Al-Muraadee رَحِمَهُ ٱللَّهُ mentioned in his book, سلك الدرر في أعيان القرن الثاني عشر ص ٨٠ regarding Allaamah Ahmad Al-Jibaali (d. 1147) رَحِمَهُ ٱللَّهُ that he would advise his disciples to recite the eighty Durood after Asr on Friday.

8. Allaamah Yusuf bin Isma'eel Nabhaani, an Aalim of the fourteenth century (d.1350) رَحِمَهُ ٱللَّهُ mentioned the above practice in his book, أفضل الصلوات على سيد السادات ص ٢٥

9. Shaikhul Hadith Moulana Muhammad Zakariyya Kandhelwi (d.1402) رَحِمَهُ ٱللَّهُ mentioned the above practice in his book, فضائل درود ص 70

10. Mufti Mahmood Hasan Gangohi Saheb (d.1417) رَحِمَهُ ٱللَّهُ. Hazrat Mufti Saheb would recite the eighty Durood after Asr on Friday and encourage others to do so as recorded in Hayaat-e-Mahmood 1/411.

11. Moulana Yusuf Motala Saheb (d.1441) رَحِمَهُ ٱللَّهُ. Hazrat Moulana would encourage people to practise on this and he himself remained committed to it until the end of his life.

12. Shaikh Muhammad Awwaamah حفظه الله a senior ranking Muhaddith of this era, has also approved of this practice.

13 Hazrat Moulana Aaqil Saheb, a senior Muhaddith of India, had prepared a detailed response, establishing the practice of eighty durood after Asr on Friday.

Alhamdulillah, with the grace of Allah تَبَارَكَ وَتَعَالَى, we have prepared a book on this topic titled "The Practice of Eighty Durood After Asr on Friday."

The kitaab provides insight into this issue and expels the doubts that people have regarding the practice of reciting eighty Durood after Asr on Friday being an innovation in Deen.

The kitaab may be may be downloaded from: http://ihyaauddeen.co.za/?p=10118
http://muftionline.co.za/node/23786

6. RECITING DUROOD WHEN IN A GATHERING

Hazrat Abdullah bin Umar رَضِيَ ٱللَّهُ عَنْهُمَا *reports that Hazrat Rasulullah* صَلَّى ٱللَّهُ عَلَيْهِ وَسَلَّمَ *said, "Beautify your gatherings by reciting Durood upon me, for your Durood upon me will be a noor for you on the day of Qiyaamah."* [122]

7. RECITING DUROOD AFTER HEARING THE AZAAN

- After the azaan, one should recite Durood upon Hazrat Rasulullah صَلَّى ٱللَّهُ عَلَيْهِ وَسَلَّمَ and thereafter recite the following dua:

اللّٰهُمَّ رَبَّ هٰذِهِ الدَّعْوَةِ التَّامَّةِ وَالصَّلَاةِ الْقَائِمَةِ آتِ مُحَمَّدَانِ الْوَسِيْلَةَ وَالْفَضِيلَةَ وَابْعَثْهُ مَقَامًا مَّحْمُودَانِ الَّذِيْ وَعَدْتَّهُ إِنَّكَ لَا تُخْلِفُ الْمِيْعَادْ

O Allah تَبَارَكَ وَتَعَالَى, *Rabb of this perfect call and of the established salaah, bestow upon Muhammad* صَلَّى ٱللَّهُ عَلَيْهِ وَسَلَّمَ *the 'waseelah' (an extremely high stage in Jannah) and 'fadheelah' (a lofty position that is above all the creation), and grant him the "Maqaam-e-Mahmood" (i.e the honour of interceding to Allah* تَبَارَكَ وَتَعَالَى *to commence the reckoning for the entire*

---

[122] عن ابن عمر رضي الله عنهما قال قال رسول الله صلى الله عليه وسلم زينوا مجالسكم بالصلاة علي فإن صلاتكم علي نور لكم يوم القيامة

(الفردوس بمأثور الخطاب، الرقم: ٣٣٣٠، وإسناده ضعيف كما في القول البديع ص ٢٧٨)

creation on the day of Qiyaamah) which You have promised him, indeed You do not go against Your promise.

Hazrat Abdullah bin Amr bin Aas رَضِىَ اللّٰهُ عَنْهَا reports that he heard Hazrat Rasulullah صَلَّى اللّٰهُ عَلَيْهِ وَسَلَّمَ saying, "When you hear the muazzin call out the azaan, then repeat the words of the azaan after him and thereafter recite Durood upon me (before reciting the dua of azaan). Verily, whoever recites Durood upon me once, Allah تَبَارَكَ وَتَعَالَى sends ten blessings on him. Then (recite the dua after the azaan in which you) supplicate to Allah تَبَارَكَ وَتَعَالَى to bless me with the honour of 'waseelah' which is a lofty position and rank in Jannah which will be exclusively granted to one of Allah's تَبَارَكَ وَتَعَالَى special servants. I earnestly hope that I am granted that position, and whoever supplicates to Allah تَبَارَكَ وَتَعَالَى to grant me the 'waseelah', he will receive my intercession on the day of Qiyaamah." [123]

Hazrat Jaabir رَضِىَ اللّٰهُ عَنْهُ reports that Hazrat Rasulullah صَلَّى اللّٰهُ عَلَيْهِ وَسَلَّمَ said, "Whosoever recites the following dua after azaan, he will receive my intercession on the day of Qiyaamah." [124]

---

[123] عن عبد الله بن عمرو بن العاص رضي الله عنهما أنه سمع النبي صلى الله عليه وسلم يقول إذا سمعتم المؤذن فقولوا مثل ما يقول ثم صلوا علي فإنه من صلى علي صلاة صلى الله عليه بها عشرا ثم سلوا الله لي الوسيله فإنها منزلة في الجنة لا تنبغي إلا لعبد من عباد الله وأرجو أن أكون أنا هو فمن سأل لي الوسيلة حلت له الشفاعة (صحيح مسلم، الرقم: ٣٨٤)

[124] عن جابر رضي الله عنه قال قال رسول الله صلى الله عليه وسلم من قال حين يسمع النداء اللهم رب هذه الدعوة التامة والصلاة القائمة آت محمدا الوسيلة والفضيلة وابعثه مقاما محمودا الذي وعدته حلت له شفاعتي يوم القيامة (صحيح البخاري، الرقم: ٦١٤، وأما زيادة إنك لا تخلف الميعاد فقد ذكرها البيهقي في السنن الكبرى، الرقم: ١٩٣٣، وقال عنها السخاوي في المقاصد الحسنة ص ٣٤٣: وهو عند البيهقي في سننه فزاد في آخره مما ثبت عند الكشميهني في البخاري نفسه إنك لا تخلف الميعاد)

اللَّهُمَّ رَبَّ هٰذِهِ الدَّعْوَةِ التَّامَّةِ وَالصَّلَاةِ الْقَائِمَةِ آتِ مُحَمَّدَانِ الْوَسِيلَةَ وَالْفَضِيلَةَ وَابْعَثْهُ مَقَامًا مَحْمُودًانِ الَّذِيْ وَعَدْتَّهُ (إِنَّكَ لَاتُخْلِفُ الْمِيْعَادْ)

- The following duas of azaan may also be recited:

اللَّهُمَّ رَبَّ هٰذِهِ الدَّعْوَةِ التَّامَّةِ وَالصَّلَاةِ الْقَائِمَةِ صَلِّ عَلَى مُحَمَّدٍ وَأَعْطِهِ سُؤْلَهُ يَوْمَ الْقِيَامَةِ

O Allah تَبَارَكَوَتَعَالَى *! Rabb of this perfect call and established salaah! Send salutations upon Muhammad* صَلَّىٰ اللَّهُ عَلَيْهِ وَسَلَّمَ *(shower Your mercy upon him) and grant him his request (of interceding for all the creation) on the day of Qiyaamah.* [125]

اللَّهُمَّ رَبَّ هٰذِهِ الدَّعْوَةِ التَّامَّةِ وَالصَّلَاةِ الْقَائِمَةِ صَلِّ عَلَى عَبْدِكَ وَرَسُوْلِكَ وَاجْعَلْنَا فِيْ شَفَاعَتِهِ يَوْمَ الْقِيَامَةِ

O Allah تَبَارَكَوَتَعَالَى *! Rabb of this perfect call and established salaah! Send salutations upon Your slave and Your Rasul* صَلَّىٰ اللَّهُ عَلَيْهِ وَسَلَّمَ *(shower Your mercy upon him), and make us among those who will receive his intercession on the day of Qiyaamah.* [126]

---

[125] عن أبي الدرداء رضي الله عنه أن رسول الله صلى الله عليه وسلم كان يقول إذا سمع المؤذن اللهم رب هذه الدعوة التامة والصلاة القائمة صل على محمد وأعطه سؤله يوم القيامة وكان يسمعها من حوله ويحب أن يقولوا مثل ذلك إذا سمعوا المؤذن قال ومن قال مثل ذلك إذا سمع المؤذن وجبت له شفاعة محمد صلى الله عليه وسلم يوم القيامة (رواه الطبراني في الكبير وفيه صدقة بن عبد الله السمين ضعفه أحمد والبخاري ومسلم وغيرهم ووثقه دحيم وأبو حاتم وأحمد بن صالح المصري كما في مجمع الزوائد، الرقم: ١٨٧٨)

[126] عن عبد الله بن ضمرة السلولي قال: سمعت أبا الدرداء يقول: كان رسول الله صلى الله عليه وسلم إذا سمع النداء قال: اللهم رب هذه الدعوة التامة والصلاة القائمة صل على محمد عبدك ورسولك واجعلنا في شفاعته يوم القيامة قال رسول الله صلى الله عليه وسلم: من قال هذا عند النداء

اللّٰهُمَّ رَبَّ هٰذِهِ الدَّعْوَةِ الْقَائِمَةِ وَالصَّلَاةِ النَّافِعَةِ صَلِّ عَلَى مُحَمَّدٍ وَارْضَ عَنِّيْ رِضَاءً لَا سَخَطَ بَعْدَهُ

O Allah ﷿! Rabb of this established call and beneficial salaah! Send salutations (shower Your mercy) upon Muhammad ﷺ and grant me Your pleasure after which You will never be displeased with me.[127]

It is reported in the Hadith that if one recites the above dua and thereafter makes dua to Allah ﷿, his dua will be accepted.

Another Dua to be Recited after Azaan

Hazrat Abdullah bin Mas'ood ﵁ reports that Hazrat Rasulullah ﷺ said, "Whichever Muslim hears the azaan being called out, and replies to the takbeer of the muazzin by reciting takbeer, and replies to the shahaadat of the muazzin by reciting shahaadat, and thereafter

---

جعله الله في شفاعتي يوم القيامة (المعجم الأوسط للطبراني، الرقم: ٣٦٦٢، وفيه صدقة بن عبد الله السمين ضعفه أحمد والبخاري ومسلم وغيرهم ووثقه دحيم وأبو حاتم وأحمد بن صالح المصري كما في مجمع الزوائد، الرقم: ١٨٧٩)

[127] عن جابر رضي الله عنه أن رسول الله صلى الله عليه وسلم قال حين ينادي المنادي اللهم رب هذه الدعوة القائمة والصلاة النافعة صل على محمد وارض عني رضاء لا سخط بعده استجاب الله له دعوته رواه أحمد والطبراني في الأوسط وفيه ابن لهيعة وفيه صعف (جمع الزوائد، الرقم: ١٨٧٥)

عن جابر أن رسول الله صلى الله عليه وسلم قال: من قال حين ينادي المنادي: اللهم رب هذه الدعوة التامة والصلاة القائمة صل على محمد وارض عنه رضا لا سخط بعده استجاب الله له دعوته (مسند أحمد، الرقم: ١٤٦١٩)

عن جابر أن رسول الله صلى الله عليه وسلم قال: من قال حين ينادي المنادي: اللهم رب هذه الدعوة التامة والصلاة القائمة صل على محمد وارض عنه رضا لا سخط بعده استجاب الله له دعوته (المعجم الأوسط، الرقم: ١٩٤)

he recites the following dua, he will be granted the intercession of Rasulullah ﷺ on the day of Qiyaamah:

اللّٰهُمَّ أَعْطِ مُحَمَّدًا الْوَسِيلَةَ وَاجْعَلْ فِيْ عِلِّيِّينَ دَرَجَتَهُ وَفِيْ الْمُصْطَفَيْنَ مَحَبَّتَهُ وَفِيْ الْمُقَرَّبِيْنَ دَارَهُ

O Allah تَبَارَكَ وَتَعَالَى, bless Muhammad ﷺ with waseelah (the right of interceding for the entire creation on the day of Qiyaamah), and elevate his stage to the highest stage in illiyeen (in Paradise), and bless the hearts of Your chosen servants with his special love, and bless the extremely pious of Your servants with his companionship in the Hereafter. [128]

8. WRITING DUROOD WHEN WRITING THE BLESSED NAME OF HAZRAT RASULULLAH ﷺ

Hazrat Abu Hurairah رضى الله عنه reports that Hazrat Rasulullah ﷺ said, "Whoever sends Durood upon me through writing the Durood in a

---

[128] عن عبد الله بن مسعود رضي الله عنه أن رسول الله صلى الله عليه وسلم قال : ما من مسلم يقول إذا سمع النداء فيكبر المنادي فيكبر ثم يشهد أن لا إله إلا الله وأن محمدا رسول الله فيشهد على ذلك ثم يقول اللهم أعط محمدا الوسيلة واجعل في عليين درجته وفي المصطفين محبته وفي المقربين داره إلا وجبت له شفاعة النبي صلى الله عليه و سلم يوم القيامة (شرح معاني الآثار، الرقم: ٨٩٤)

يحيى النيسابوري شيخ البخاري ومسلم وأبو عمر البزار اسمه حفص بن سليمان الأسدي ويعرف بحفيص ضعيف جدا حتى كذبه بعضهم ولكن كان ثبتا في القراءة والبزار الباء الموحدة المفتوحة وتشديد الزاي المعجمة وفي آخره زاي معجمة وقيس بن مسلم الجدلي العدواني أحد مشايخ أبي حنيفة روى له الجماعة وطارق بن شهاب بن عبد شمس البجلي الأحمسي (نخب الأفكار ١٢٢/٣)

وقال الإمام الترمذي – رحمه الله –: وحفص بن سليمان أبو عمر بزاز كوفي يضعف في الحديث (سنن الترمذي ١٧١/٥)

kitaab, the angels continue seeking forgiveness on his behalf as long as my name remains in that kitaab." [129]

9. RECITING DUROOD BEFORE MAKING DUA

Hazrat Abdullah bin Mas'ood رَضِىَاللهُعَنْهُ has mentioned, "When any of you intends to make dua to Allah تَبَارَكَوَتَعَالَ, then he should commence his dua by praising and glorifying Allah تَبَارَكَوَتَعَالَ with praises that are befitting His majesty and honour. He should then send Durood (salutations) upon Nabi صَلَّىاللهُعَلَيْهِوَسَلَّمَ, and he should thereafter make dua, as (through following this method of making dua,) it is more likely that he will be successful (in his dua being answered)." [130]

Duas are Suspended until Durood is Recited

Hazrat Umar رَضِىَاللهُعَنْهُ narrates, "Duas remain suspended between the heavens and the Earth. They do not proceed towards the heavens as long

---

١٢٩ عن أبي هريرة قال: قال رسول الله صلى الله عليه وسلم: من صلى علي في كتاب لم تزل الملائكة تستغفر له ما دام اسمي في ذلك الكتاب (المعجم الأوسط للطبراني، الرقم: ١٨٣٥، وسنده ضعيف كما في كشف الخفاء، الرقم: ٢٠١٨)

١٣٠ عن عبد الله بن مسعود قال إذا أراد أحدكم أن يسأل فليبدأ بالمدحة والثناء على الله بما هو أهله ثم ليصل على النبي صلى الله عليه وسلم ثم ليسأل بعد فإنه أجدر أن ينجح (المعجم الكبير للطبراني، الرقم: ٨٧٨٠، ورجاله رجال الصحيح إلا أن أبا عبيدة لم يسمع من أبيه كما في مجمع الزوائد، الرقم: ١٧٢٥٥)

as Durood on Nabi ﷺ has not been recited (i.e. there is no guarantee for their acceptance)."[131]

Reciting Durood before Making Dua

Hazrat Fadhaalah bin Ubaid رَضِىَٱللَّهُعَنْهُ mentions that on one occasion, while Rasulullah ﷺ was seated (in the musjid), a certain person entered and performed salaah. After performing salaah, the person made dua saying, "O Allah تَبَارَكَوَتَعَالَ! Forgive me and shower Your mercy upon me!" Observing the manner in which this person had made dua, Rasulullah ﷺ addressed him saying, "You have hastened (in asking Allah تَبَارَكَوَتَعَالَ for your need), O musalli! After performing salaah, when you are seated to make dua, commence by first praising Allah تَبَارَكَوَتَعَالَ as He is worthy of being praised. Thereafter, recite Durood upon me, and then present your need to Allah تَبَارَكَوَتَعَالَ." Thereafter, another person performed salaah. After performing salaah, he praised Allah تَبَارَكَوَتَعَالَ, recited Durood upon Rasulullah ﷺ (and then commenced making dua). Observing this person (and him adhering to

---

^{١٣١} عن عمر بن الخطاب قال: إن الدعاء موقوف بين السماء والأرض لا يصعد منه شيء حتى تصلي على نبيك صلى الله عليه وسلم (سنن الترمذي، الرقم: ٤٨٦)

ويتقوى ذلك بما أخرجه الترمذي عن عمر موقوفا الدعاء موقوف بين السماء والأرض لا يصعد منه شيء حتى يصلي على النبي صلى الله عليه وسلم (فتح الباري ١١/١٦٤)، وقد التزم الحافظ في الفتح ألا تقل درجة الحديث عن الحسن فقال في مقدمته المسماة بهدي الساري (ص ٧): ثم أستخرج ثانيا ما يتعلق به غرض صحيح في ذلك الحديث من الفوائد المتنية والاسنادية من تمات وزيادات وكشف غامض وتصريح مدلس بسماع ومتابعة سامع من شيخ اختلط قبل ذلك منتزعاكل ذلك من أمهات المسانيد والجوامع والمستخرجات والأجزاء والفوائد بشرط الصحة أو الحسن فيما أورده من ذلك)

the etiquettes of dua), Rasulullah ﷺ said to him, "O Musalli! Make dua, for your dua will be accepted!" [132]

10. Reciting Durood when Meeting

Hazrat Anas bin Maalik ﷺ reports that Hazrat Rasulullah ﷺ said, "When two muslims who love one another (for the sake of Allah تَبَارَكَ وَتَعَالَى) meet each other and send Durood (salutations) upon Rasulullah ﷺ, then before they depart from one another, their future and past (minor) sins are forgiven." [133]

11. Reciting Durood when Forgetting Something

Hazrat Anas ﷺ reports that Hazrat Rasulullah ﷺ said, "If you forget something, then recite Durood upon me, you will remember it if Allah تَبَارَكَ وَتَعَالَى wills." [134]

---

[132] عن فضالة بن عبيد قال: بينا رسول الله صلى الله عليه وسلم قاعد إذ دخل رجل فصلى فقال: اللهم اغفر لي وارحمني فقال رسول الله صلى الله عليه وسلم: عجلت أيها المصلي إذا صليت فقعدت فاحمد الله بما هو أهله وصل علي ثم ادعه قال: ثم صلى رجل آخر فحمد الله وصلى على النبي صلى الله عليه وسلم فقال له النبي صلى الله عليه وسلم: أيها المصلي ادع تجب (سنن الترمذي، الرقم: ٣٤٧٦ وقال: هذا حديث حسن)

[133] عن أنس عن النبي صلى الله عليه وسلم قال: ما من عبدين متحابين في الله يستقبل أحدهما صاحبه فيصافحه ويصليان على النبي صلى الله عليه وسلم إلا لم يفترقا حتى تغفر ذنوبهما ما تقدم منهما وما تأخر (مسند أبي يعلى الموصلي، الرقم: ٢٩٦٠، وفيه درست بن حمزة وهو ضعيف كما في مجمع الزوائد، الرقم: ١٧٩٨٧)

[134] عن أنس رضي الله عنه قال: قال رسول الله صلى الله عليه وسلم: إذا نسيتم شيئا فصلوا علي تذكروه إن شاء الله تعالى (أخرجه أبو موسى المديني بسند ضعيف كما في القول البديع ص ٤٤٨)

12. Reciting Durood in Places where People are Negligent

Hazrat Abu Waa'il رَضِيَ ٱللَّهُ عَنْهُ mentions, "I have not seen Abdullah bin Mas'ood رَضِيَ ٱللَّهُ عَنْهُ attending any gathering or invitation, except that he would praise and glorify Allah تَبَارَكَ وَتَعَالَى and recite Durood upon Rasulullah صَلَّى ٱللَّهُ عَلَيْهِ وَسَلَّمَ. If he had to go to the market place, where he found people negligent of the remembrance of Allah تَبَارَكَ وَتَعَالَى, he would praise Allah تَبَارَكَ وَتَعَالَى and recite Durood in those places." [135]

---

[135] عن أبي وائل قال : ما شهد عبد الله مجمعا ولا مأدبة فيقوم حتى يحمد الله ويصلي على النبي صلى الله عليه وسلم وإن كان مما يتبع أغفل مكان في السوق فيجلس فيه فيحمد الله ويصلي على النبي صلى الله عليه وسلم (المصنف لابن أبي شيبة، الرقم: ٣٠٤٢٩، ورواته ثقات)

CHAPTER NINE

Wordings of Durood and Salaam

WORDINGS OF DUROOD AND SALAAM ESTABLISHED IN THE AHAADITH

Durood-e-Ebrahim

Abdur Rahmaan ibnu Abi Layla رَضِىَ اللهُ عَنْهُ *reports:*

Hazrat Ka'b bin Ujrah رَضِىَ اللهُ عَنْهُ *once met me and asked, "Should I not gift you with something that I acquired from Rasulullah* صَلَّى اللهُ عَلَيْهِ وَسَلَّمَ*?" I replied, "Yes, indeed. Please do gift it to me." He said, "On one occasion, we asked Rasulullah* صَلَّى اللهُ عَلَيْهِ وَسَلَّمَ*, 'O Rasul of Allah* صَلَّى اللهُ عَلَيْهِ وَسَلَّمَ*, what is the manner of reciting Salaat upon you and your family, for indeed Allah* تَبَارَكَ وَتَعَالَى *has taught us (through you) how to recite Salaam upon you?'" Rasulullah* صَلَّى اللهُ عَلَيْهِ وَسَلَّمَ *replied, "Say,*

اَللّٰهُمَّ صَلِّ عَلٰى مُحَمَّدٍ وَعَلٰى آلِ مُحَمَّدٍ كَمَا صَلَّيْتَ عَلٰى إِبْرَاهِيْمَ وَعَلٰى آلِ إِبْرَاهِيْمَ إِنَّكَ حَمِيْدٌ مَجِيْدٌ اَللّٰهُمَّ بَارِكْ عَلٰى مُحَمَّدٍ وَعَلٰى آلِ مُحَمَّدٍ كَمَا بَارَكْتَ عَلٰى إِبْرَاهِيْمَ وَعَلٰى آلِ إِبْرَاهِيْمَ إِنَّكَ حَمِيْدٌ مَجِيْدٌ

'O Allah صَلَّى ٱللَّهُ عَلَيْهِ وَسَلَّمَ*, shower Your mercy upon Muhammad* صَلَّى ٱللَّهُ عَلَيْهِ وَسَلَّمَ *and the family of Muhammad* صَلَّى ٱللَّهُ عَلَيْهِ وَسَلَّمَ*, as You showered Your mercy upon Ebrahim* عَلَيْهِ ٱلسَّلَامُ *and the family of Ebrahim* عَلَيْهِ ٱلسَّلَامُ*. Indeed, You are praiseworthy and most glorious. O Allah, shower Your blessings upon Muhammad* صَلَّى ٱللَّهُ عَلَيْهِ وَسَلَّمَ *and the family of Muhammad* عَلَيْهِ ٱلسَّلَامُ*, as You showered Your blessings upon Ebrahim* صَلَّى ٱللَّهُ عَلَيْهِ وَسَلَّمَ *and the family of Ebrahim* عَلَيْهِ ٱلسَّلَامُ*. Indeed, You are praiseworthy and most glorious.'"* [136]

The Special Durood of Hazrat ibnu Mas'ood رَضِيَ ٱللَّهُ عَنْهُ

Hazrat Abdullah bin Mas'ood رَضِيَ ٱللَّهُ عَنْهُ *reports, "When you recite Durood upon Rasulullah* صَلَّى ٱللَّهُ عَلَيْهِ وَسَلَّمَ*, then recite Durood in the best of manners (i.e. with complete devotion, concentration, love and respect), for certainly you do not know that perhaps that Durood of yours will be presented before him." The students of Hazrat Abdullah bin Mas'ood* رَضِيَ ٱللَّهُ عَنْهُ *asked, "Teach us how to recite Durood on Rasulullah*

---

[136] عن عبد الرحمن بن أبي ليلى قال لقيني كعب بن عجرة فقال ألا أهدي لك هدية سمعتها من النبي صلى الله عليه وسلم فقلت بلى فأهدها لي فقال سألنا رسول الله صلى الله عليه وسلم فقلنا يا رسول الله كيف الصلاة عليكم أهل البيت فإن الله قد علمنا كيف نسلم عليكم قال قولوا اللهم صل على محمد وعلى آل محمد كما صليت على إبراهيم وعلى آل إبراهيم إنك حميد مجيد اللهم بارك على محمد وعلى آل محمد كما باركت على إبراهيم وعلى آل إبراهيم إنك حميد مجيد (صحيح البخاري، الرقم: ٣٣٧٠)

صَلَّ ٱللَّهُ عَلَيْهِ وَسَلَّمَ ." Hazrat Abdullah bin Mas'ood رَضِىَ ٱللَّهُ عَنْهُ replied, "Recite the following:

اَللّٰهُمَّ اجْعَلْ صَلَوَاتِكَ وَرَحْمَتَكَ وَبَرَكَاتِكَ عَلَى سَيِّدِ الْمُرْسَلِيْنَ وَإِمَامِ الْمُتَّقِيْنَ وَخَاتَمِ النَّبِيِّيْنَ مُحَمَّدٍ عَبْدِكَ وَرَسُوْلِكَ إِمَامِ الْخَيْرِ وَقَائِدِ الْخَيْرِ وَرَسُوْلِ الرَّحْمَةِ اَللّٰهُمَّ ابْعَثْهُ مَقَامًا مَّحْمُوْدًا يَغْبِطُهُ فِيْهِ الْأَوَّلُوْنَ وَالْآخِرُوْنَ اَللّٰهُمَّ صَلِّ عَلَى مُحَمَّدٍ وَعَلَى آلِ مُحَمَّدٍ كَمَا صَلَّيْتَ عَلَى إِبْرَاهِيْمَ وَعَلَى آلِ إِبْرَاهِيْمَ إِنَّكَ حَمِيْدٌ مَجِيْدٌ اَللّٰهُمَّ بَارِكْ عَلَى مُحَمَّدٍ وَعَلَى آلِ مُحَمَّدٍ كَمَا بَارَكْتَ عَلَى إِبْرَاهِيْمَ وَعَلَى آلِ إِبْرَاهِيْمَ إِنَّكَ حَمِيْدٌ مَجِيْدٌ

O Allah تَبَارَكَ وَتَعَالَى, shower your special blessings and mercies and upon the leader of the Messengers, the Imaam of all the pious servants, and the seal of the Ambiyaa عَلَيْهِمُ ٱلسَّلَامُ, Muhammad صَلَّ ٱللَّهُ عَلَيْهِ وَسَلَّمَ, Your servant and messenger, the Imaam of all good and virtue and the messenger of mercy. O Allah تَبَارَكَ وَتَعَالَى, elevate him to the highest of positions, and make him worthy of the position of Maqaam-e-Mahmood, in such a way that the former and the latter of the entire creation will all envy him. O Allah تَبَارَكَ وَتَعَالَى, shower Your mercy upon Muhammad صَلَّ ٱللَّهُ عَلَيْهِ وَسَلَّمَ and the family of Muhammad صَلَّ ٱللَّهُ عَلَيْهِ وَسَلَّمَ, as You showered Your mercy upon Ebrahim عَلَيْهِ ٱلسَّلَامُ and the family of Ebrahim عَلَيْهِ ٱلسَّلَامُ. Indeed, You are praiseworthy and most glorious. O Allah, shower Your blessings upon Muhammad صَلَّ ٱللَّهُ عَلَيْهِ وَسَلَّمَ and the family of Muhammad صَلَّ ٱللَّهُ عَلَيْهِ وَسَلَّمَ, as You showered Your blessings upon Ebrahim عَلَيْهِ ٱلسَّلَامُ and the family of Ebrahim عَلَيْهِ ٱلسَّلَامُ. Indeed, You are praiseworthy and most glorious. [137]

---

١٣٧ عن عبد الله بن مسعود قال: إذا صليتم على رسول الله صلى الله عليه وسلم فأحسنوا الصلاة عليه فإنكم لا تدرون لعل ذلك يعرض عليه قال: فقالوا له: فعلمنا قال: قولوا: اللهم اجعل صلواتك ورحمتك وبركاتك على سيد المرسلين وإمام المتقين وخاتم النبيين محمد عبدك ورسولك إمام

The Special Durood of Hazrat Ibnu Abbaas رَضِيَٱللَّهُعَنْهُ

Hazrat Ibnu Abbaas رَضِيَٱللَّهُعَنْهُمَا *reports that when he used to recite Durood upon Hazrat Rasulullah* صَلَّىٱللَّهُعَلَيْهِوَسَلَّمَ*, he would recite it in the following words:*

اَللّٰهُمَّ تَقَبَّلْ شَفَاعَةَ مُحَمَّدٍ الْكُبْرٰى وَارْفَعْ دَرَجَتَهُ الْعُلْيَا وَآتِهِ سُؤْلَهُ فِي الْآخِرَةِ وَالْأُوْلٰى كَمَا آتَيْتَ إِبْرَاهِيْمَ وَمُوْسٰى

O Allah تَبَارَكَوَتَعَالَى*, accept the intercession of Muhammad* صَلَّىٱللَّهُعَلَيْهِوَسَلَّمَ *(i.e. the intercession at the time when all the nations will be in difficulty on the plains of resurrection) and raise him to the highest rank, and grant him what he desires in the Aakhirah and this world, as You granted Ebrahim and Moosa* عَلَيْهِمَاٱلسَّلَامُ*.* [138]

A Special Durood upon Hazrat Rasulullah صَلَّىٱللَّهُعَلَيْهِوَسَلَّمَ

Hazrat Abu Hurairah رَضِيَٱللَّهُعَنْهُ *narrates that Hazrat Rasulullah* صَلَّىٱللَّهُعَلَيْهِوَسَلَّمَ *said, "Whoever recites the following (Durood), I will bear testimony on his behalf on the day of Qiyaamah and I will intercede for him."*

الخير وقائد الخير ورسول الرحمة اللهم ابعثه مقاما محمودا يغبطه به الأولون والآخرون اللهم صل على محمد وعلى آل محمد كما صليت على إبراهيم وآل إبراهيم إنك حميد مجيد اللهم بارك على محمد وعلى آل محمد كما باركت على إبراهيم وآل إبراهيم إنك حميد مجيد (سنن ابن ماجة، الرقم: ٩٠٦، وإسناده حسن كما في الترغيب و الترهيب، الرقم: ٢٥٨٨)

١٣٨ عن ابن عباس أنه كان يقول: اللهم تقبل شفاعة محمد الكبرى وارفع درجته العليا وآته سؤله في الآخرة والأولى كما آتيت إبراهيم وموسى (مصنف عبد الرزاق، الرقم: ٣١٠٤، وإسناده جيد قوي صحيح كما في القول البديع صـ ١٢٢)

اَللّٰهُمَّ صَلِّ عَلٰى مُحَمَّدٍ وَعَلٰى آلِ مُحَمَّدٍ كَمَا صَلَّيْتَ عَلٰى إِبْرَاهِيْمَ وَعَلٰى آلِ إِبْرَاهِيْمَ

وَبَارِكْ عَلٰى مُحَمَّدٍ وَعَلٰى آلِ مُحَمَّدٍ كَمَا بَارَكْتَ عَلٰى إِبْرَاهِيْمَ وَعَلٰى آلِ إِبْرَاهِيْمَ

وَتَرَحَّمْ عَلٰى مُحَمَّدٍ وَعَلٰى آلِ مُحَمَّدٍ كَمَا تَرَحَّمْتَ عَلٰى إِبْرَاهِيْمَ وَعَلٰى آلِ إِبْرَاهِيْمَ

O Allah تَبَارَكَ وَتَعَالٰى! *Send salutations upon Muhammad* صَلَّى ٱللَّهُ عَلَيْهِ وَسَلَّمَ *and the family of Muhammad* صَلَّى ٱللَّهُ عَلَيْهِ وَسَلَّمَ, *as You have sent salutations upon Ebrahim* عَلَيْهِ ٱلسَّلَامُ *and the family of Ebrahim* عَلَيْهِ ٱلسَّلَامُ, *and shower blessings upon Muhammad* صَلَّى ٱللَّهُ عَلَيْهِ وَسَلَّمَ *and the family of Muhammad* صَلَّى ٱللَّهُ عَلَيْهِ وَسَلَّمَ, *as You have showered blessings upon Ebrahim* عَلَيْهِ ٱلسَّلَامُ *and the family of Ebrahim* عَلَيْهِ ٱلسَّلَامُ, *and shower mercy upon Muhammad* صَلَّى ٱللَّهُ عَلَيْهِ وَسَلَّمَ *and the family of Muhammad* صَلَّى ٱللَّهُ عَلَيْهِ وَسَلَّمَ, *as You have showered mercy upon Ebrahim* عَلَيْهِ ٱلسَّلَامُ *and the family of Ebrahim* عَلَيْهِ ٱلسَّلَامُ.[139]

Sending Durood upon Hazrat Rasulullah صَلَّى ٱللَّهُ عَلَيْهِ وَسَلَّمَ with the other Ambiyaa عَلَيْهِمُ ٱلسَّلَامُ

Hazrat Qataadah رَحِمَهُ ٱللَّهُ *reports that Hazrat Rasulullah* صَلَّى ٱللَّهُ عَلَيْهِ وَسَلَّمَ *said,* "*When you send salutations upon the Ambiyaa* عَلَيْهِمُ ٱلسَّلَامُ *then send*

salutations upon me with them, as I am (also) a Rasul from among the Rasuls of Allah." [140]

In this Hadith, Hazrat Rasulullah ﷺ has taught us that whenever we send salutations on the Ambiyaa عَلَيْهِمُ ٱلسَّلَام, we should send Durood and salutations on him as well. Hence, when we take the name of any Nabi, we should try to recite the following:

عَلَيْهِ وَعَلٰى نَبِيِّنَا الصَّلَاةُ وَالسَّلَامُ

May peace and salutations descend upon him and upon our Nabi ﷺ as well.

Sending Durood upon the other Ambiyaa عَلَيْهِمُ ٱلسَّلَام with Hazrat Rasulullah ﷺ

Hazrat Anas رَضِيَ ٱللَّهُ عَنْهُ reports that Hazrat Rasulullah ﷺ said, "Jibreel عَلَيْهِ ٱلسَّلَام just departed from me now. He had come to inform me that Allah تَبَارَكَ وَتَعَالَى said, 'There is no Muslim on the earth who recites Durood upon you (i.e. on Hazrat Rasulullah ﷺ) once, except that I and My angels send Durood upon him (i.e. I shower ten mercies on him and My angels seek forgiveness for him ten times).' Thus, recite abundant Durood upon me on the day of Jumuah, and when you recite

---

١٤٠ عن قتادة عن أنس قال: قال رسول الله صلى الله عليه وسلم: إذا صليتم على المرسلين فصلوا علي معهم فإني رسول من المرسلين (الصلاة على النبي لابن أبي عاصم، الرقم: ٦٩، وإسناده حسن جيد لكنه مرسل كما في القول البديع ص ١٣٤)

Durood upon me, then send salutations upon the Ambiyaa عَلَيْهِمُٱلسَّلَامُ, as I am a Nabi among the Ambiyaa عَلَيْهِمُٱلسَّلَامُ." [141]

In this Hadith, Hazrat Rasulullah صَلَّىٱللَّهُعَلَيْهِوَسَلَّمَ has taught us that whenever we send Durood on him, we should send salutations on the Ambiyaa عَلَيْهِمُٱلسَّلَامُ as well. Hence, when we recite Durood on Hazrat Rasulullah صَلَّىٱللَّهُعَلَيْهِوَسَلَّمَ, we should add the following at the end:

وَعَلَى الْمُرْسَلِيْن

And on the Ambiyaa عَلَيْهِمُٱلسَّلَامُ as well.

'[141] عن أنس رضي الله عنه قال : قال رسول الله صلى الله عليه وسلم : خرج جبريل عليه السلام من عندي آنفا يخبرني عن ربه عز وجل : ما على الأرض مسلم صلى عليك واحدة إلا صليت عليه أنا وملائكتي عشرا، فأكثروا علي من الصلاة يوم الجمعة، وإذا صليتم علي فصلوا على المرسلين، فإني رجل من المرسلين (فوائد أبي يعلى الصابوني كما في القول البديع صـ ٢٥٠)

Wordings of Durood and Salaam from the Pious

Drinking from the Howdh-e-Kawthar of Mustafa صَلَّى اللّٰهُ عَلَيْهِ وَسَلَّم with the cup of full measure

Hazrat Hasan Basri رَحِمَهُ اللّٰه mentioned, "Whoever wishes to drink from the Howdh-e-Kawthar of Mustafa صَلَّى اللّٰهُ عَلَيْهِ وَسَلَّم with the cup of full measure, then he should recite the following Durood:

اَللّٰهُمَّ صَلِّ عَلٰى مُحَمَّدٍ وَعَلٰى اٰلِهٖ وَأَصْحَابِهٖ وَأَوْلَادِهٖ وَأَزْوَاجِهٖ وَذُرِّيَّتِهٖ وَأَهْلِ بَيْتِهٖ وَأَصْهَارِهٖ وَأَنْصَارِهٖ وَأَشْيَاعِهٖ وَمُحِبِّيْهِ وَأُمَّتِهٖ وَعَلَيْنَا مَعَهُمْ أَجْمَعِيْنَ يَا أَرْحَمَ الرَّاحِمِيْنَ

O Allah تَبَارَكَ وَتَعَالٰى*! Send salutations upon Muhammad* صَلَّى اللّٰهُ عَلَيْهِ وَسَلَّم*, his family, his Sahaabah* رَضِيَ اللّٰهُ عَنْهُم*, his children, his wives, his progeny, his household, his relatives through marriage, his helpers (the Ansaar* رَضِيَ اللّٰهُ عَنْهُم*), his followers, those who love him, his Ummah, and upon us all with them, O Most Merciful of those who show mercy.* [142]

The Five Duroods of Imaam Shaafi'ee رَحِمَهُ اللّٰه

It is mentioned that after the demise of Imaam Shaafi'ee رَحِمَهُ اللّٰه, someone had seen him in a dream and asked him the reason for being pardoned by Allah تَبَارَكَ وَتَعَالٰى. Imaam Shaafi'ee رَحِمَهُ اللّٰه replied, "It is because of these five Durood upon Rasulullah صَلَّى اللّٰهُ عَلَيْهِ وَسَلَّم that I used to recite every Friday night (i.e. the night preceding Friday)."

<hr>

١٤٢ الشفا بتعريف حقوق المصطفى ٧٢/٢

اَللّٰهُمَّ صَلِّ عَلٰى مُحَمَّدٍ عَدَدَ مَنْ صَلّٰى عَلَيْهِ وَصَلِّ عَلٰى مُحَمَّدٍ بِعَدَدِ مَنْ لَّمْ يُصَلِّ عَلَيْهِ وَصَلِّ عَلٰى مُحَمَّدٍ كَمَا اَمَرْتَ اَنْ يُّصَلّٰى عَلَيْهِ وَصَلِّ عَلٰى مُحَمَّدٍ كَمَا تُحِبُّ اَنْ يُّصَلّٰى عَلَيْهِ وَصَلِّ عَلٰى مُحَمَّدٍ كَمَا تَنْبَغِيْ الصَّلَاةُ عَلَيْهِ

O Allah تَبَارَكَوَتَعَالَی, shower Your choicest mercy and blessings on the master of the worlds, Muhammad صَلَّیاللهُعَلَیهِوَسَلَّم, according to the number of people who recited Durood upon Nabi صَلَّیاللهُعَلَیهِوَسَلَّم. And shower Your choicest mercy and blessings on the master of the worlds, Muhammad صَلَّیاللهُعَلَیهِوَسَلَّم, according to the number of people who did not recite Durood upon Nabi صَلَّیاللهُعَلَیهِوَسَلَّم. And shower Your choicest mercy and blessings on the master of the worlds, Muhammad صَلَّیاللهُعَلَیهِوَسَلَّم, in the manner that You have commanded that Durood be recited upon him. And shower Your choicest mercy and blessings on the master of the worlds, Muhammad صَلَّیاللهُعَلَیهِوَسَلَّم, in the most befitting manner which pleases You. And shower Your choicest mercy and blessings on the master of the worlds, Muhammad صَلَّیاللهُعَلَیهِوَسَلَّم, in the manner he should be remembered and Durood be recited upon him. [143]

The Special Durood of Imaam Shaafi'ee رَحِمَهُاللهُ

Hazrat Ibnu Bunaan Asbahaani رَحِمَهُاللهُ says:

I once saw Rasulullah صَلَّیاللهُعَلَیهِوَسَلَّم in a dream and asked him, "O Rasulullah صَلَّیاللهُعَلَیهِوَسَلَّم, has any special honour been granted to Muhammad bin Idrees Shaafi'ee رَحِمَهُاللهُ, who is the son of your 'uncle'? ('Uncle' has been mentioned because Imaam Shaafi'ee's

---

[143] ذكره الإمام البيهقي رحمه الله كما في القول البديع ص ٤٩١

رَحِمَهُ ٱللَّهُ ancestory meets Hazrat Rasulullah's صَلَّى ٱللَّهُ عَلَيْهِ وَسَلَّمَ ancestory at Abd Yazeed bin Hishaam, whose father, Hishaam, was the great-grandfather of Hazrat Rasulullah صَلَّى ٱللَّهُ عَلَيْهِ وَسَلَّمَ).”

Rasulullah صَلَّى ٱللَّهُ عَلَيْهِ وَسَلَّمَ replied, “Yes indeed. I have supplicated to Allah تَبَارَكَ وَتَعَالَى for him to be saved from the reckoning on the day of Qiyaamah.” I then asked, “O Rasulullah صَلَّى ٱللَّهُ عَلَيْهِ وَسَلَّمَ, on account of which deed did he become worthy of such a favour?” Rasulullah صَلَّى ٱللَّهُ عَلَيْهِ وَسَلَّمَ replied, “It is because he has recited such a Durood upon me that no one else had ever recited.” I then enquired, “O Rasulullah صَلَّى ٱللَّهُ عَلَيْهِ وَسَلَّمَ, what is that Durood?” Rasulullah صَلَّى ٱللَّهُ عَلَيْهِ وَسَلَّمَ replied:

اَللَّهُمَّ صَلِّ عَلَى مُحَمَّدٍ كُلَّمَا ذَكَرَهُ الذَّاكِرُوْنَ وَصَلِّ عَلَى مُحَمَّدٍ كُلَّمَا غَفَلَ عَنْ ذِكْرِهِ الْغَافِلُوْنَ

O Allah تَبَارَكَ وَتَعَالَى! *Bestow special mercy upon Muhammad* صَلَّى ٱللَّهُ عَلَيْهِ وَسَلَّمَ *equivalent to the number of times that all those remember him, and bestow special mercy upon Muhammad* صَلَّى ٱللَّهُ عَلَيْهِ وَسَلَّمَ *equivalent to the number of times that all those forget to remember him.*[144]

Another Special Durood of Imaam Shaafi'ee رَحِمَهُ ٱللَّهُ

In “Rowdhatul Ahbaab”, Imaam Isma'eel bin Ebrahim Muzani رَحِمَهُ ٱللَّهُ (one of Imaam Shaafi'ee's رَحِمَهُ ٱللَّهُ famous students) reports:

I once saw Imaam Shaafi'ee رَحِمَهُ ٱللَّهُ in a dream after his death and asked him, “How did Allah تَبَارَكَ وَتَعَالَى treat you?” Imaam Shaafi'ee

---

[144] طبقات الشافعية الكبرى للسبكي ١٨٨/١

رَحِمَهُ ٱللَّهُ replied, "Allah تَبَارَكَوَتَعَالَى has pardoned me and commanded that I be escorted into Paradise with honour and respect. I have acquired all this through the blessings of one particular Durood which I used to recite upon Nabi صَلَّى ٱللَّهُ عَلَيْهِ وَسَلَّمَ." I enquired, "Which Durood is that?" Imaam Shaafi'ee رَحِمَهُ ٱللَّهُ replied:

اَللّٰهُمَّ صَلِّ عَلٰى مُحَمَّدٍ كُلَّمَا ذَكَرَهُ الذَّاكِرُوْنَ وَكُلَّمَا غَفَلَ عَنْ ذِكْرِهِ الْغَافِلُوْنَ

O Allah تَبَارَكَوَتَعَالَى*! Bestow mercy upon Muhammad* صَلَّى ٱللَّهُ عَلَيْهِ وَسَلَّمَ *equivalent to the number of times that people remember him, and bestow mercy upon Muhammad* صَلَّى ٱللَّهُ عَلَيْهِ وَسَلَّمَ *equivalent to the number of times that people forget to remember him.* [145]

The Durood which is the cure for all diseases

The following story is related in "Nuzhah":

There was once a pious person who had fallen seriously ill due to the inability to pass urine. One night, he had a dream in which he was complaining to Shaikh Shahaabuddeen bin Raslaan رَحِمَهُ ٱللَّهُ (who was a very famous saint and scholar) about the difficulty he was going through. In the dream, the Shaikh told him, "How is it that you are ignorant of the cure for all diseases? Commence reciting Durood upon Rasulullah صَلَّى ٱللَّهُ عَلَيْهِ وَسَلَّمَ and Allah تَبَارَكَوَتَعَالَى will bless you with shifaa." The Shaikh then told him to recite the following Durood:

---

[145] فضائل درود ص ١٥١، المنامات للبرداني كما في القول البديع ص ٤٨٩

اَللّٰهُمَّ صَلِّ وَسَلِّمْ عَلَى رُوْحِ سَيِّدِنَا مُحَمَّدٍ فِي الْأَرْوَاحْ وَصَلِّ وَسَلِّمْ عَلَى قَلْبِ سَيِّدِنَا مُحَمَّدٍ فِي الْقُلُوْبِ وَصَلِّ وَسَلِّمْ عَلَى جَسَدِ سَيِّدِنَا مُحَمَّدٍ فِي الْأَجْسَادْ وَصَلِّ وَسَلِّمْ عَلَى قَبْرِ سَيِّدِنَا مُحَمَّدٍ فِي الْقُبُوْرْ

O Allah تَبَارَكَ وَتَعَالَى, from all souls (You have created), bestow Your special mercy, peace and blessings on the mubaarak soul of Sayyiduna Muhammad صَلَّى اللّٰهُ عَلَيْهِ وَسَلَّمَ, and from all the hearts (You have created), bestow Your special mercy and peace on the heart of Sayyiduna Muhammad صَلَّى اللّٰهُ عَلَيْهِ وَسَلَّمَ, and from all the bodies (You have created), bestow Your special mercy and peace upon the body of Sayyiduna Muhammad صَلَّى اللّٰهُ عَلَيْهِ وَسَلَّمَ, and from all the graves (of the creation), bestow Your special mercy and peace upon the grave of Sayyiduna Muhammad صَلَّى اللّٰهُ عَلَيْهِ وَسَلَّمَ.

Upon awakening, the man commenced reciting this Durood, and through reciting it abundantly, his illness had soon disappeared.[146]

The Most Virtuous of Praises and Durood

It has been narrated that Abu Muhammad, Abdullah Al-Mowsili رَحِمَهُ اللّٰهُ, who was well known by the title 'Ibnul Mushtahir' and was a pious person, mentioned the following:

"Whoever wishes to praise Allah تَبَارَكَ وَتَعَالَى in a manner more excellent than any creation of Allah تَبَارَكَ وَتَعَالَى has ever praised Him, from the people who came first and those who will come last, the

---

[146] نزهة المجالس ٢/٨٥

close angels and the dwellers of the heavens and the earth, and he wishes to send salutations upon Nabi Muhammad ﷺ in a manner more excellent than anybody else has remembered him (and sent salutations upon him), and he wishes to ask Allah تَبَارَكَ وَتَعَالَى for something which is more excellent than anybody else from the creation has asked Allah تَبَارَكَ وَتَعَالَى, then he should recite the following:

اَللّٰهُمَّ لَكَ الْحَمْدُ كَمَا أَنْتَ أَهْلُهُ فَصَلِّ عَلَى مُحَمَّدٍ كَمَا أَنْتَ أَهْلُهُ وَافْعَلْ بِنَا مَا أَنْتَ أَهْلُهُ فَإِنَّكَ أَهْلُ التَّقْوَى وَأَهْلُ الْمَغْفِرَةِ

O Allah تَبَارَكَ وَتَعَالَى*! To You alone belongs all praise as befits You, thus send salutations upon Muhammad* ﷺ *as befits You, and deal with us as befits You, as You are indeed the Lord who is most worthy of being feared and the Lord who is most worthy of forgiving His servants.* [147]

The Durood of Shaikh Shibli رَحِمَهُ اللّٰه after Every Salaah

Allaamah Sakhaawi رَحِمَهُ اللّٰه relates the following incident. Abu Bakr bin Muhammad رَحِمَهُ اللّٰه mentioned:

While I was once in the presence of Shaikh Abu Bakr bin Mujaahid رَحِمَهُ اللّٰه, and it so happened that Shaikh Shibli رَحِمَهُ اللّٰه arrived, Abu Bakr bin Mujaahid رَحِمَهُ اللّٰه rose from his seat, stepped forward, embraced the saint and kissed his forehead in honour. I asked him, "How is it that you bestow such honour on Shaikh Shibli رَحِمَهُ اللّٰه when you and all the Ulama of Baghdaad are of the opinion that

<hr>

he is a mad man?" Abu Bakr bin Mujaahid ﷫ replied, "I have only done that which I saw Rasulullah ﷺ do to him."

He then related the following dream: I had seen Rasulullah ﷺ in a dream and Shaikh Shibli ﷫ appeared. Rasulullah ﷺ rose and kissed him on his forehead. When I asked the reason for this great honour, Rasulullah ﷺ replied, "After every salaah, this man used to recite the following verse:

$$لَقَدْ جَآءَكُمْ رَسُوْلٌ مِّنْ اَنْفُسِكُمْ عَزِيْزٌ عَلَيْهِ مَا عَنِتُّمْ حَرِيْصٌ عَلَيْكُمْ بِالْمُؤْمِنِيْنَ رَءُوْفٌ رَّحِيْمٌ ﴿١٢٨﴾$$

Verily the Messenger ﷺ has come to you from among yourselves, it greatly causes him pain that you fall into distress and hardship, who is extremely anxious for your welfare, for the believers he is full of compassion and mercy.

He would thereafter recite the following Durood:

$$صَلَّى اللهُ عَلَيْكَ يَا مُحَمَّد صَلَّى اللهُ عَلَيْكَ يَا مُحَمَّد صَلَّى اللهُ عَلَيْكَ يَا مُحَمَّد$$

Hazrat Abu Bakr ﷫ continues: After having seen this dream, I met Shibli ﷫ and asked him, "What Durood do you recite upon Rasulullah ﷺ after salaah?" When he told me the durood then it was the exact durood that I had been informed of in the dream." [148]

---

[148] ساقها ابن بشكوال وأبو موسى المديني وعبد الغني بن سعيد كما في القول البديع صـ ٣٦٢

The Durood for Safety – Durood Tunjeenaa

Hazrat Moosa Zareer رَحِمَهُ ٱللّٰه was a great, saintly personality. He once related an incident regarding his personal experience. He says:

I was once travelling on a boat which was about to sink. At that crucial moment I was overcome with slumber. In a vision, I had seen Rasulullah صَلَّى ٱللّٰهُ عَلَيْهِ وَسَلَّم who taught me the following Durood and instructed me to tell all the passengers of that boat to recite the Durood one thousand times. The passengers began reciting the Durood and had not yet reached three hundred times when the condition normalised and the boat was saved. This was all through the barakah of the Durood that Rasulullah صَلَّى ٱللّٰهُ عَلَيْهِ وَسَلَّم had taught me.

اَللّٰهُمَّ صَلِّ عَلٰى سَيِّدِنَا مُحَمَّدٍ وَّعَلٰى آلِ سَيِّدِنَا مُحَمَّدٍ صَلٰوةً تُنْجِيْنَا بِهَا مِنْ جَمِيْعِ الْأَهْوَالِ وَالْآفَاتِ وَتَقْضِيْ لَنَا بِهَا جَمِيْعَ الْحَاجَاتِ وَتُطَهِّرُنَا بِهَا مِنْ جَمِيْعِ السَّيِّئَاتِ وَتَرْفَعُنَا بِهَا عِنْدَكَ أَعْلَى الدَّرَجَاتِ وَتُبَلِّغُنَا بِهَا أَقْصَى الْغَايَاتِ مِنْ جَمِيْعِ الْخَيْرَاتِ فِيْ الْحَيٰوةِ وَبَعْدَ الْمَمَاتِ (إِنَّكَ عَلٰى كُلِّ شَيْءٍ قَدِيْرٌ)

O Allah تَبَارَكَ وَتَعَالَى, bestow Your special mercy upon Hazrat Muhammad صَلَّى ٱللّٰهُ عَلَيْهِ وَسَلَّم and upon his family, such mercy that will save us from all calamites and misfortunes, and that will be a means of fulfilling all our needs and requirements, and that will cleanse us from all evil and sin, and that will raise us to high, lofty positions by You (in the Hereafter), and that will cause us to reach all our desired righteous aims and goals, in this world and the next. Certainly, You have power over everything. [149]

The Durood of Abul Fadl Qoomasaani رَحِمَهُٱللَّه

Hazrat Abul Fadl Qoomasaani رَحِمَهُٱللَّه says:

A man from Khurasaan once came to me and said, "While I was in Madinah Munawwarah, I saw Rasulullah صَلَّىٱللَّهُعَلَيْهِوَسَلَّمَ in a dream and he said to me, 'When you go to Hamdaan, convey my salaams to Abul Fadl Zeeruk.' I then asked Rasulullah صَلَّىٱللَّهُعَلَيْهِوَسَلَّمَ, 'O Rasulullah صَلَّىٱللَّهُعَلَيْهِوَسَلَّمَ, what is the reason for this?' Rasulullah صَلَّىٱللَّهُعَلَيْهِوَسَلَّمَ replied, 'It is because of the fact that he recites these words of Durood upon me one hundred times or more daily.'"

اَللَّهُمَّ صَلِّ عَلَى مُحَمَّدٍ النَّبِيِّ الْأُمِّيِّ وَعَلَى آلِ مُحَمَّدٍ جَزَى اللهُ مُحَمَّدًا صَلَّى اللهُ عَلَيْهِ وَسَلَّمَ عَنَّا مَا هُوَ أَهْلُهُ

O Allah تَبَارَكَوَتَعَالَى, shower Salaat upon Muhammad صَلَّىٱللَّهُعَلَيْهِوَسَلَّمَ, the unlettered Nabi, and upon the family of Muhammad صَلَّىٱللَّهُعَلَيْهِوَسَلَّمَ. May Allah تَبَارَكَوَتَعَالَى reward Muhammad صَلَّىٱللَّهُعَلَيْهِوَسَلَّمَ on our behalf such a reward of which he is worthy and deserving.

Hazrat Abul Fadl رَحِمَهُٱللَّه further states, "The man swore by Allah تَبَارَكَوَتَعَالَى that he never knew me before the time that Rasulullah صَلَّىٱللَّهُعَلَيْهِوَسَلَّمَ gave him the message. I then wanted to give him some grain, but he refused to accept it saying, 'It is not my intention to

---

[149] الفجر المنير للفاكهاني ص ٢٢ ، الجملة الأخيرة: "إنك على كل شيئٍ قدير" مذكورة في فضائل درود ص ١٥١

sell the message that Rasulullah ﷺ gave me.' The man then departed and I never saw him again." [150]

Durood taught by Hazrat Rasulullah ﷺ in a dream

Kamaal Ad-Dameeri رحمه الله has narrated in Sharhul-Minhaaj that Shaikh Abu Abdillah bin Nu'maan رحمه الله was blessed to see Hazrat Rasulullah ﷺ in his dream one hundred times. During the last dream in which he saw Hazrat Rasulullah ﷺ, he asked, "O Rasul of Allah ﷺ! Which Durood is virtuous for me to recite upon you?"

Hazrat Rasulullah ﷺ replied by instructing him to recite the following Durood:

اَللّٰهُمَّ صَلِّ عَلٰى سَيِّدِنَا مُحَمَّدِ الَّذِيْ مَلَأْتَ قَلْبَهُ مِنْ جَلَالِكَ وَعَيْنَهُ مِنْ جَمَالِكَ فَأَصْبَحَ فَرِحًا مَسْرُوْرًا مُؤَيَّدًا مَنْصُوْرًا

O Allah تبارك وتعالى! Send salutations upon our master, Muhammad ﷺ, the one whose heart You filled with Your grandeur, and whose eye You filled with Your beauty, he thus became happy and delighted, helped and assisted. [151]

---

[150] الدر المنضود ١٨٤/١، القول البديع صـ ٣٣٩

[151] النجم الوهاج في شرح المنهاج ٤٨٧/٨، القول البديع صـ ١٤٧

The Words of Praise which Pleased Hazrat Rasulullah ﷺ

Imaam Tabraani رَحِمَهُ الله has mentioned in his kitaab of dua that he was once blessed to see Rasulullah ﷺ in a dream. In the dream, the blessed appearance of Rasulullah ﷺ was exactly as described to us (in the numerous narrations discussing the blessed appearance of Rasulullah ﷺ). Imaam Tabraani رَحِمَهُ الله (in the dream) greeted Rasulullah ﷺ with Salaam and then said, "O Rasul of Allah ﷺ! Allah تَبَارَكَ وَتَعَالَى has inspired me to recite a few words." Rasulullah ﷺ asked, "What are these words?"

Imaam Tabraani رَحِمَهُ الله replied by reciting the following:

اَللّٰهُمَّ لَكَ الْحَمْدُ بِعَدَدِ مَنْ حَمِدَكَ وَلَكَ الْحَمْدُ بِعَدَدِ مَنْ لَمْ يَحْمَدْكَ وَلَكَ الْحَمْدُ كَمَا تُحِبُّ أَنْ تُحْمَدَ اَللّٰهُمَّ صَلِّ عَلٰى مُحَمَّدٍ بِعَدَدِ مَنْ صَلّٰى عَلَيْهِ وَصَلِّ عَلٰى مُحَمَّدٍ بِعَدَدِ مَنْ لَمْ يُصَلِّ عَلَيْهِ وَصَلِّ عَلٰى مُحَمَّدٍ كَمَا تُحِبُّ أَنْ يُصَلّٰى عَلَيْهِ

O Allah تَبَارَكَ وَتَعَالَى! All praise is due to You alone, equal to the number of all those who praise You, and all praise is due to You alone, equal to the number of all those who do not praise You, and all praise is due to You alone, as You like to be praised. O Allah! Send salutations upon Muhammad ﷺ equal to the number of all those who send salutations upon him, and send salutations upon him equal to all those who do not send salutations upon him, and send salutations upon him as You like salutations to be sent upon him.

On hearing the unique praise of Allah تَبَارَكَوَتَعَالَى and Durood that Imaam Tabraani رَحِمَهُ ٱللَّهُ had recited, Rasulullah صَلَّى ٱللَّهُ عَلَيْهِ وَسَلَّمَ smiled, until his blessed front teeth could be seen and the noor (divine radiance) that would emit from the gap between his blessed front teeth was apparent. [152]

---

[152] القول البديع ص١٣٠

CHAPTER TEN

Beautiful Incidents regarding the Blessings of Durood and Salaam

Incident One - The Mahr of Hazrat Aadam عَلَيْهِ ٱلسَّلَام

Shaikh Abdul Haq Dehlawi رَحْمَةُ ٱللَّٰه writes in "Madaarijun Nubuwwwah" that when Hazrat Hawwaa رَضِيَ ٱللَّٰهُ عَنْهَا was created, Hazrat Aadam عَلَيْهِ ٱلسَّلَام wanted to stretch forth his hands towards her. The angels then said, "Be patient until the nikaah is performed and you give her the mahr." Hazrat Aadam عَلَيْهِ ٱلسَّلَام then inquired, "What is the mahr?" The angels replied, "The recitation of Durood upon Rasulullah صَلَّى ٱللَّٰهُ عَلَيْهِ وَسَلَّم." (According to another report, the mahr was twenty Durood upon Hazrat Rasulullah صَلَّى ٱللَّٰهُ عَلَيْهِ وَسَلَّم.) [153]

---

[153] فضائل درود ص ١٥٥، القول البديع ص ١٣٢، شرح الزرقاني على المواهب ١٠١/١

Incident Two - Glad Tidings from the Side of Hazrat Rasulullah ﷺ

Hazrat Muhammad Utbi رحمه الله relates:

I entered Madinah Munawwarah, and presented myself before the mubaarak grave of Hazrat Nabi ﷺ. Subsequently, I had seen a villager arrive. He seated his camel at the door of the Musjid and presented himself before the mubaarak grave of Rasulullah ﷺ. He offered his Salaam with utmost humility and love, and supplicated to Allah تبارك وتعالى in dua in a beautiful way.

He then said, "O Rasulullah ﷺ, may my parents be sacrificed for you! Indeed, Allah تبارك وتعالى had divinely selected you as his Final Messenger and revealed wahi (revelation of the Quraan Majeed) to you. He revealed to you such a unique book (the Quraan Majeed), that encompasses the knowledge of the former and the latter Ambiyaa and Rasuls عليهم السلام. Allah تبارك وتعالى has stated in the Quraan Majeed, and His word is the truth:

وَلَوْ أَنَّهُمْ إِذ ظَّلَمُوا أَنفُسَهُمْ جَاءُوكَ فَاسْتَغْفَرُوا اللَّهَ وَاسْتَغْفَرَ لَهُمُ الرَّسُولُ لَوَجَدُوا اللَّهَ تَوَّابًا رَّحِيمًا ۝

And if, they (the servants of Allah تبارك وتعالى) after wronging themselves (through committing sins), had come to you, [O Muhammad ﷺ], and begged Allah's تبارك وتعالى forgiveness, and the Messenger had sought forgiveness on their behalf, they would have surely found Allah تبارك وتعالى Most Forgiving, Most Merciful.[154]

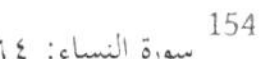

The villager then said, "O Nabi of Allah ﷺ, I have come to your grave in compliance with the verse of Allah تَبَارَكَ وَتَعَالَى. I admit that I have wronged myself by committing excessive sins and I beg you to intercede on my behalf before Allah تَبَارَكَ وَتَعَالَى." He then turned to the mubaarak grave and poured out his heart reciting the following couplets:

يَا خَيْرَ مَنْ دُفِنَتْ بِالْقَاعِ أَعْظُمُهُ ** فَطَابَ مِنْ طِيبِهِنَّ الْقَاعُ وَالْأَكَمُ

O the greatest from all those who are buried beneath the earth! From the splendid fragrance emitting from your mubaarak limbs, the mountains and plains become fragranced.

نَفْسِيْ الْفِدَاءُ لِقَبْرٍ أَنْتَ سَاكِنُهُ ** فِيْهِ الْعَفَافُ وَفِيْهِ الْجُوْدُ وَالْكَرَمُ

May my life be sacrificed for that grave wherein you are residing, in it is buried the embodiment of purity, nobility and generosity.

After reciting these beautiful words in praise and honour of Rasulullah ﷺ, the villager mounted his conveyance and began to leave. Muhammad Utbi (the narrator of the incident) says, "I was overcome by sleep, and in a vision, I was blessed with the vision of Rasulullah ﷺ. Rasulullah ﷺ addressed me saying, 'O Utbi! Hasten towards the villager and give him the glad tidings from my side that Allah تَبَارَكَ وَتَعَالَى has forgiven his sins.'" [155]

---

[155] الأذكار للنووي ص ٣٠٤، القول البديع ص ٣٤٢

Incident Three - Reciting One Thousand Durood Daily

Hazrat Abul Hasan Baghdaadi Ad-Daarimi رَحِمَهُ ٱللّٰه says:

I had often seen Abu Abdillah Haamid رَحِمَهُ ٱللّٰه in a dream after his death. I asked him what had transpired with him and he said, "Allah تَبَارَكَ وَتَعَالَى forgave me and had mercy on me." I then asked him, "Please inform me of one such deed, which will admit me directly into Paradise." He replied, "Perform one thousand nafl rakaats, and in each rakaat, recite Surah Ikhlaas one thousand times." I replied, "But this is indeed an extremely difficult deed to fulfil." He said, "In that case, recite Durood upon Rasulullah صَلَّى ٱللّٰهُ عَلَيْهِ وَسَلَّمَ one thousand times every night." Abul Hasan further says, "This has been my routine since then." [156]

Incident Four - Salvation through the Abundant Recitation of Durood

A person once saw Abu Hafs Al-Kaaghazi رَحِمَهُ ٱللّٰه, who was a very pious person, in a dream after his demise. On seeing Abu Hafs رَحِمَهُ ٱللّٰه, he asked him, "How did Allah تَبَارَكَ وَتَعَالَى deal with you?" Abu Hafs رَحِمَهُ ٱللّٰه replied, "Allah تَبَارَكَ وَتَعَالَى had mercy on me, forgave me and admitted me into Jannah." When Abu Hafs رَحِمَهُ ٱللّٰه was asked the reason for him being honoured and blessed in this manner, he said, "When I stood before Allah تَبَارَكَ وَتَعَالَى, He commanded the angels to commence counting my deeds. They thus counted my sins and counted my Durood upon Rasulullah صَلَّى ٱللّٰهُ عَلَيْهِ وَسَلَّمَ, and

---

156 القربة لابن بشكوال صـ ١٣٠، القول البديع صـ ٢٥٩

found that my Durood upon Rasulullah صَلَّى ٱللَّهُ عَلَيْهِ وَسَلَّمَ outnumbered my sins. Allah تَبَارَكَ وَتَعَالَى then said to the angels, 'O My angels! This is sufficient! Do not take him to account for his sins and enter him into my Jannah!'" [157]

Incident Five - Abundant Durood Brings the Forgiveness of Allah تَبَارَكَ وَتَعَالَى

Shaikh Ibnu Hajar Makki رَحِمَهُ ٱللَّهُ reports that a saintly person was once seen in a dream after his demise. He was questioned regarding his condition in the Hereafter. The saintly person replied, "Allah تَبَارَكَ وَتَعَالَى had mercy upon me, pardoned my sins and admitted me into Paradise." When asked the reason for this he replied, "The angels were commanded to count my sins and the number of Durood I had recited upon Nabi صَلَّى ٱللَّهُ عَلَيْهِ وَسَلَّمَ. When it was seen that the number of my Durood exceeded the number of my sins, Allah تَبَارَكَ وَتَعَالَى addressed the angels and said, 'This is sufficient (for his forgiveness). Let no further reckoning take place. Usher him into Paradise.'" [158]

Incident Six - An Incident of a Face Changing Colour

In Ihyaa Uloomiddeen, Imaam Ghazaali رَحِمَهُ ٱللَّهُ relates this incident as narrated by Abdul Waahid bin Zaid Basri رَحِمَهُ ٱللَّهُ who says:

I once went on a journey to perform hajj. With me, a certain person travelled as my companion. All the time, whether walking,

---

[157] ابن بشكوال كما في القول البديع صُ ٢٥٩

[158] الدر المنضود صُ ١٨٣

sitting or standing, he continued to recite Durood upon Nabi صَلَّى ٱللَّهُ عَلَيْهِ وَسَلَّمَ. I therefore asked him the reason for his abundant recitation of Durood. He replied:

When I performed my first hajj, my father accompanied me. On our return, we reached one of the resting places and slept there. While we were there, I had seen a dream in which someone was telling me, "Wake up, your father has passed away and his face has turned black." I awoke in great distress, and when I removed the cloth from the face of my father, I discovered that he had indeed passed away and that his face was turning black. This filled me with great sorrow and I was overcome with fear.

I fell asleep and again dreamt that four dark skinned men with iron rods, about to torment him, were sitting by his head. At that point, a handsome man dressed in two green sheets passed by and chased these four men away. He then stroked the face of my father with his hands and said to me, "Rise up (and rejoice), for Allah تَبَارَكَ وَتَعَالَى has changed the colour of your father's face. It is now white." I said to him in great joy and happiness, "May my father and mother be sacrificed for you, who are you?" He replied, "My name is Muhammad صَلَّى ٱللَّهُ عَلَيْهِ وَسَلَّمَ." Since then, I never stopped reciting Durood upon Nabi صَلَّى ٱللَّهُ عَلَيْهِ وَسَلَّمَ. [159]

Incident Seven - Face Transformed to a Swine

In Nuzhatul Majaalis, the following incident is recorded:

---

[159] إحياء علوم الدين ٤/٥٠٧

A man and his son were on a journey. On the way, the father passed away and his face was transformed to that of a swine. The son, seeing this, cried bitterly and made dua to Allah تَبَارَكَوَتَعَالَى for the welfare of his father.

The son soon fell asleep and saw a man telling him, "Your father used to consume interest, and it is for this reason that you now see his face in this condition. But rejoice, for Rasulullah صَلَّىٱللَّهُعَلَيْهِوَسَلَّمَ has interceded on his behalf, for whenever he heard the blessed name of Rasulullah صَلَّىٱللَّهُعَلَيْهِوَسَلَّمَ, he recited Durood upon him. Through the intercession of Rasulullah صَلَّىٱللَّهُعَلَيْهِوَسَلَّمَ, his face has now been restored to its original form." [160]

Incident Eight - Safe from the Discomfort of Death due to Abundant Durood

In "Nuzhatul Majaalis", the following incident is related:

Once, a man went to visit a seriously ill person at the time when he was in the throes of death. He asked the sick man, "How do you find the bitter pangs of death at this moment of departure?" He replied, "I do not feel any discomfort at all. I heard the Ulama mention that the one who recites abundant Durood upon Rasulullah صَلَّىٱللَّهُعَلَيْهِوَسَلَّمَ will find himself safe from the discomfort of death at the moment of passing away." [161]

---

[160] مفيد العلوم ومبيد الهموم ص ١٨٤، نزهة المجالس ٨٢/٢

[161] فضائل درود ص ١٨١

Incident Nine - The Incident of Hazrat Ebrahim bin Khawaas رَحِمَهُ ٱللَّهُ

It is reported from "Nuzhatul Basaateen" that Hazrat Ebrahim bin Khawaas رَحِمَهُ ٱللَّهُ says:

Once, while on a journey, I felt such extreme thirst that I fell down unconscious. While I lay there, I felt someone sprinkling water on my face. When I opened my eyes, I saw a handsome young man on horseback near me. He gave me water to drink and begged me to accompany him. After having travelled for a little while, he asked me, "What do you see?" I replied, "This is Madinah Tayyibah." He then said, "You may descend here. Go to the mubaarak grave of Rasulullah صَلَّى ٱللَّهُ عَلَيْهِ وَسَلَّمَ and convey to him my salaams. Tell him that his brother, Khidar, has conveyed salaams to him." [162]

Incident Ten - The Experience of Shaikh Abul Khair Aqtaa رَحِمَهُ ٱللَّهُ

Shaikh Abul Khair Aqta' رَحِمَهُ ٱللَّهُ says:

When I came to Madinah Tayyibah and had spent five days there, I experienced poverty and difficulty. I therefore went to the mubaarak grave of Rasulullah صَلَّى ٱللَّهُ عَلَيْهِ وَسَلَّمَ and greeted him, and also to the graves of Abu Bakr and Umar رَضِيَ ٱللَّهُ عَنْهُمَا. I then said to Rasulullah صَلَّى ٱللَّهُ عَلَيْهِ وَسَلَّمَ, "O Rasulullah صَلَّى ٱللَّهُ عَلَيْهِ وَسَلَّمَ, today I want to be your guest."

---

[162] فضائل درود ص ١٨٧

Thereafter, I left that spot and went to sleep behind the mimbar. In a dream, I had seen Rasulullah ﷺ with Abu Bakr رضي الله عنه on his right, and Umar رضي الله عنه on his left, and Ali رضي الله عنه in front of him. Ali رضي الله عنه came to me and said, "Rise up, Rasulullah ﷺ is coming." I hastily rose from my resting place and kissed Rasulullah ﷺ between his eyes. He gave me some bread, from which I ate one half and kept the other half. When I awoke from the dream, the other half of the bread was still in my hand.[163]

Incident Eleven - Durood Coming to One's Aid after Demise

The following incident is recorded in Al-Raudhul Faa'iq. Hazrat Sufyaan Thauri رحمه الله mentioned:

Once, while performing tawaaf, I saw a man also engaged in tawaaf. Throughout his entire tawaaf, he was only reciting Durood upon Rasulullah ﷺ, at every step, and did not recite any tasbeeh, tahleel etc.

When I asked him the reason, he replied, "And who are you?" I replied, "I am Sufyaan Thauri." He then said:

"Had you not been the only scholar of your calibre, I would not have revealed something which is my secret. My father and I went for hajj. Enroute, my father fell ill. While I was doing my utmost to treat him, he suddenly passed away, and his entire face turned

---

[163] طبقات الصوفية ص ٢٨١، القول البديع ص ٣٣٨

black. This distressed me greatly and (recognizing this to be a bad sign,) I said, 'Innaa lillah.'

"I then covered his face with a cloth. Soon thereafter, my eyes closed and I fell off to sleep in this sorrow. In a vision, I saw a man approaching. I had never seen a man as handsome as he, clothes as clean as his, and a fragrance as sweet as his. He approached in haste, removed the cloth from my father's face, and put his hand over his face. Immediately, the face of my father turned white.

"As he was about to depart, I held onto him and asked, 'May Allah تَبَارَكَوَتَعَالَى have mercy upon you. Please tell me who are you, for Allah تَبَارَكَوَتَعَالَى has shown mercy to my father in his great need because of you.' He replied, 'Do you not recognize me? I am Muhammad صَلَّىٰاللهُعَلَيْهِوَسَلَّمَ, the son of Abdullah, the person of the Quraan Majeed. Your father was a very great sinner, but he always recited Durood upon me abundantly. Hence, when through his sins, evils descended on him, I saw his great need and hastened to assist him, as I do for all those who recite Durood upon me.'" [164]

Incident Twelve - Forgiven through the Blessing of Durood

A certain pious person narrated the following incident:

I once saw the person who was known by the title 'Mistah' in a dream after he passed away. He was a sinful person during his lifetime. On seeing him in the dream, I asked him, "How did Allah

---

[164] الروض الفائق ص ٢٤١

تَبَارَكَوَتَعَالَى deal with you?" He replied, "Allah تَبَارَكَوَتَعَالَى forgave me". I asked him, "On account of which action?" He answered, "On one occasion, I asked a certain Muhaddith to recite a Hadith to me with its chain to Rasulullah صَلَّىَاللهُعَلَيْهِوَسَلَّم. On taking the blessed name of Rasulullah صَلَّىَاللهُعَلَيْهِوَسَلَّم, the Muhaddith recited Durood upon him. I also recited Durood upon Rasulullah صَلَّىَاللهُعَلَيْهِوَسَلَّم in a loud tone. Hearing me recite Durood aloud, all the people who were present in the gathering also recited Durood upon Rasulullah صَلَّىَاللهُعَلَيْهِوَسَلَّم. At that moment, Allah تَبَارَكَوَتَعَالَى forgave the sins of each and every one of us." [165]

Incident Thirteen - Honoured by Allah تَبَارَكَوَتَعَالَى due to Reciting Abundant Durood

It is reported regarding Abul Abbaas, Ahmed bin Mansoor رَحِمَهُٱللَّه, that after he passed away, a man from the inhabitants of Sheeraaz saw him in a dream. In the dream, Ahmed bin Mansoor was standing in the mihraab of the Jaami' Musjid of Sheeraaz. He was adorned in a set of (beautiful) clothing and had a crown on his head which was decorated with precious stones.

The man asked him, "How did Allah تَبَارَكَوَتَعَالَى deal with you?" He replied, "Allah تَبَارَكَوَتَعَالَى forgave my sins, granted me honour, crowned me with the crown of Paradise and blessed me with entry into Jannah." The man then asked, "On account of which action did Allah تَبَارَكَوَتَعَالَى honour you with this lofty position?" He

---

[165] القربة لابن بشكوال صـ ١٢٦، القول البديع صـ ٢٥٩

replied, "On account of the abundant Durood that I would recite on Rasulullah ﷺ." [166]

Incident Fourteen - Durood Coming to One's Assistance at the Time of Need

Shaikh Shibli رَحِمَهُ ٱللّٰهُ reports the following incident:

On one occasion, one of my neighbors passed away. Sometime later, I saw him in a dream. I asked him, "How did Allah تَبَارَكَ وَتَعَالَى deal with you?" He replied:

"O Shibli! I underwent great distress and difficulty, as I was unable to reply to the questions of the angels in the grave! When I found that I was unable to speak and reply, I thought to myself, 'Why am I undergoing such hardship? Did I not pass away with imaan?' As soon as this thought crossed my mind, a voice called out to me, 'This is the punishment for you being negligent regarding the use of your tongue in the dunya.'

"Thereafter, when the two angels wished to punish me, a man who was most handsome and had an extremely exquisite fragrance emitting from him intervened between me and the angels and assisted me to give the correct answer. After giving the correct answer to the angels and being saved from the punishment, I asked the man, 'Who are you? May Allah تَبَارَكَ وَتَعَالَى have mercy on you!' The man answered, 'I am a man who has been created by Allah تَبَارَكَ وَتَعَالَى through the abundant Durood that you recited on

<hr>

166 القربة لابن بشكوال صـ ١٢٢، القول البديع صـ ٢٥٩

Rasulullah ﷺ. I have been sent and commanded to assist you at the time of your difficulty.'" [167]

Incident Fifteen – Saved from Punishment through Reciting Abundant Durood

A man once saw a person in his dream in the most horrific and dreadful form. Upon enquiry from the person as to who he was, the man replied, "I am your evil deeds." The man then asked, "And how can I be saved from you?" He replied, "By continuously reciting abundant Durood upon Muhammad ﷺ." [168]

Incident Sixteen - Reciting a Fixed Amount of Durood before Retiring to Sleep

Shaikh Ibnu Hajar Makki رحمه الله relates an incident about a saintly person who committed himself to reciting a fixed number of Durood upon Nabi ﷺ before retiring to bed. One night, he had seen Nabi ﷺ in a dream. Nabi ﷺ entered his home and the entire home became illuminated with the noor of Rasulullah ﷺ. Rasulullah ﷺ said to him, "Bring forth towards me that mouth that recites Durood upon me and allow me to kiss it." Out of shyness, he offered his cheek and Rasulullah ﷺ kissed it. Upon awakening, he found that his entire home was fragrant with the smell of musk. [169]

---

[167] ابن بشكوال كما في لقول البديع صـ ٢٦٥

[168] الدر المنضود صـ ١٨٣، القول البديع صـ ٢٦٠

[169] الدر المنضود صـ ١٨٧

Incident Seventeen - Reciting Durood before Sleeping

Hazrat Muhammad bin Sa'eed bin Mutarrif رَحِمَهُ اللّٰه was a righteous and pious person. He narrated the following incident:

I had made it my ma'mool (fixed daily ibaadah) to recite a certain amount of Durood upon Rasulullah صَلَّى اللّٰهُ عَلَيْهِ وَسَلَّم every night on retiring to bed.

One night, when I was in my room, I completed reciting the Durood and fell asleep. As I fell asleep, I had a dream in which I saw that Rasulullah صَلَّى اللّٰهُ عَلَيْهِ وَسَلَّم entered my room through the door. As he entered, the entire room was illuminated with his mubaarak noor.

Rasulullah صَلَّى اللّٰهُ عَلَيْهِ وَسَلَّم then turned towards me and said, "Present to me this mouth with which you recite abundant Durood upon me so that I can kiss it." I felt shy to present my mouth to Rasulullah صَلَّى اللّٰهُ عَلَيْهِ وَسَلَّم, so I presented my cheek to him. Rasulullah صَلَّى اللّٰهُ عَلَيْهِ وَسَلَّم then placed his mubaarak mouth on my cheek and kissed it.

Immediately thereafter, I awoke from the dream in a state of great excitement and also awoke my wife who was asleep at my side. On awakening, we found that the entire room was filled with the smell of musk on account of the fragrance emanating from the mubaarak body of Rasulullah صَلَّى اللّٰهُ عَلَيْهِ وَسَلَّم. The fragrance of musk from the mubaarak kiss of Rasulullah صَلَّى اللّٰهُ عَلَيْهِ وَسَلَّم remained on my cheek for eight days. For every day of the eight days, my wife would smell this fragrance on my cheek. [170]

Incident Eighteen - Incident of Hazrat Shaikh Moulana Muhammad Zakariyya رَحِمَهُ ٱللَّهُ

In Pakistan, a certain Aalim had once seen Rasulullah صَلَّى ٱللَّهُ عَلَيْهِ وَسَلَّمَ in a dream. He asked Rasulullah صَلَّى ٱللَّهُ عَلَيْهِ وَسَلَّمَ as to who was the most beloved to Rasulullah صَلَّى ٱللَّهُ عَلَيْهِ وَسَلَّمَ from the entire Ummah at that time. Rasulullah صَلَّى ٱللَّهُ عَلَيْهِ وَسَلَّمَ replied, "Hazrat Shaikhul Hadith Moulana Muhammad Zakariyya Kandhelwi رَحِمَهُ ٱللَّهُ is the most beloved to me."

The Aalim then enquired, "On account of which special action did Hazrat Shaikh رَحِمَهُ ٱللَّهُ receive this position?" Rasulullah صَلَّى ٱللَّهُ عَلَيْهِ وَسَلَّمَ explained, "It is on account of a particular Durood that he is punctual on reciting for the last fifty years." The Aalim then asked Rasulullah صَلَّى ٱللَّهُ عَلَيْهِ وَسَلَّمَ in the dream regarding the Durood. Rasulullah صَلَّى ٱللَّهُ عَلَيْهِ وَسَلَّمَ recited the Durood. When the Aalim awoke from the dream, he wrote the Durood he heard from Rasulullah صَلَّى ٱللَّهُ عَلَيْهِ وَسَلَّمَ and placed it in his pocket.

After performing hajj, the Aalim visited Madinah Tayyibah and subsequently met Hazrat Shaikh رَحِمَهُ ٱللَّهُ. Upon meeting Hazrat Shaikh رَحِمَهُ ٱللَّهُ, he asked Hazrat Shaikh رَحِمَهُ ٱللَّهُ as to which Durood he was punctual in reciting for the last fifty years. Hazrat Shaikh رَحِمَهُ ٱللَّهُ initially became disturbed by this person wishing to know

---

[170] الدر المنضود ص ١٨٧، القول البديع ص ٢٨٨

Hazrat's personal ma'moolaat. Hence Hazrat Shaikh رَحِمَهُ ٱللَّهُ asked him, "What is the reason that you wish to know, and how does this concern you?" The Aalim then removed the piece of paper from his pocket and showed it to Hazrat Shaikh رَحِمَهُ ٱللَّهُ. Contained in it was the Durood which he heard from Rasulullah صَلَّى ٱللَّهُ عَلَيْهِ وَسَلَّمَ.

The Aalim addressed Hazrat Shaikh رَحِمَهُ ٱللَّهُ saying, "Perhaps this is the Durood you have been reciting for the last fifty years." Hazrat Shaikh رَحِمَهُ ٱللَّهُ was surprised and asked the Aalim how he had come to know of this. The Aalim thereafter related the dream to Hazrat Shaikh رَحِمَهُ ٱللَّهُ.

When Hazrat Shaikh رَحِمَهُ ٱللَّهُ heard the dream, his facial expression changed and he began to weep uncontrollably out of humility and happiness. After weeping for some while, Hazrat Shaikh رَحِمَهُ ٱللَّهُ mentioned, "Who am I, and what worth does my Durood have? This is nothing but the kindness of Rasulullah صَلَّى ٱللَّهُ عَلَيْهِ وَسَلَّمَ and his affection upon me." [171]

Incident Nineteen - Durood is a Source of Mercy for Both the Living and the Dead

In Raudhul Faa'iq, the following story is related:

There was once a woman who had a very evil son. In spite of the fact that she admonished him on numerous occasions, he paid no attention to her advice and never heeded her warnings. In this state, without repenting for his evil, he passed away. His mother

---

[171] درود شریف کے فضائل اور ثمرات

felt great sorrow and suffered much grief that he had died without having repented. She therefore had a great wish to be able to see him in a dream. However, when she did see him in a dream, she was even more distressed as she saw him suffering great punishment.

After some time, it so happened that she saw him in a dream again. However, on this occasion, she saw him in great ease and comfort and extremely happy. When she asked him the reason for the change in his condition, he replied:

"A great sinner passed our graveyard. When he saw our graves, he was greatly affected and took heed that he should change his life and become obedient to Allah تَبَارَكَ وَتَعَالَى before it is too late. He began to cry bitterly over his past sins, and with a sincere heart, he repented for his sins. He then recited some verses of the Quraan Majeed and recited Durood on Rasulullah صَلَّى ٱللَّهُ عَلَيْهِ وَسَلَّمَ twenty times, and conveyed the rewards thereof to the inmates of the graves. I was one of the recipients, and the portion that came to me had such an effect that it lifted me from my previous condition to what you now see.

"O mother, Durood on Rasulullah صَلَّى ٱللَّهُ عَلَيْهِ وَسَلَّمَ is the light of the hearts, a means of forgiveness of sins, and a source of mercy for both the living and the dead." [172]

---

[172] الروض الفائق ص ٤

Incident Twenty - Reciting Durood while in Pain

Hazrat Abdur Raheem bin Abdur Rahmaan رَحِمَهُ ٱللَّهُ says:

Once, my arm was injured because of a fall in the bathroom, and it was badly swollen. That night, the pain caused me great discomfort. At last, my eyes closed and I slumbered a little. In a vision, I saw Rasulullah صَلَّى ٱللَّهُ عَلَيْهِ وَسَلَّمَ and all I could say was, "Ya Rasulullah صَلَّى ٱللَّهُ عَلَيْهِ وَسَلَّمَ."

Rasulullah صَلَّى ٱللَّهُ عَلَيْهِ وَسَلَّمَ replied, "The numerous recitations of Durood by you because of the pain in your hand have greatly concerned and worried me." When I awoke, I found that the pain had subsided completely and the swelling had disappeared.[173]

Incident Twenty One - Glad Tidings for Durood Recited

Hazrat Muhammad bin Maalik رَحِمَهُ ٱللَّهُ says:

I travelled to Baghdaad in order to study under Qaari Abu Bakr bin Mujaahid رَحِمَهُ ٱللَّهُ. While we were seated in a circle around him and reciting, an old man entered with a very old turban on his head, wearing an old tattered shirt and a very old shawl over his shoulders. When Qaari Abu Bakr رَحِمَهُ ٱللَّهُ saw him enter, he stood up in honour and respect. He rose from his seat, seated the old man in his place and enquired about his health and the welfare of his family.

---

173 القول البديع ص ٣٤١

The old man replied, "Last night, a son was born to me, and my wife asked me for butter and honey." After hearing what hard times the old man was passing through in poverty, the Shaikh became very sad, and in this state, his eyes closed and he saw Rasulullah ﷺ in a dream.

Rasulullah ﷺ said, "O Abu Bakr! Why this sadness and sorrow? Go to the wazeer, Ali bin Isa, and convey to him my salaams, and say to him, 'You are a man who never sleeps on Friday nights until you have recited one thousand Durood, but this Friday, you only recited seven hundred Durood because the messenger of the king interrupted your recitation as he came to call you to the king's presence. You went there, and upon returning, you completed the rest of your Durood. Having told him that, tell him to give a hundred dinaars (gold coins) to the father of the newly born child for his necessities.'"

Qaari Abu Bakr bin Mujaahid رَحِمَهُ ٱللَّهُ rose immediately and took the old man with him to the wazeer. Arriving there, he said, "Rasulullah ﷺ has sent this old man to you." When the wazeer heard this, he rose from his seat and made the old man sit there. Qaari Abu Bakr bin Mujaahid رَحِمَهُ ٱللَّهُ then related to him the entire incident.

The wazeer became extremely happy and full of joy. He commanded his slave to bring the money bag, and from the bag, he handed over one hundred dinaars to the old man. He took another hundred dinaars to give Qaari Abu Bakr bin Mujaahid رَحِمَهُ ٱللَّهُ, but he refused to accept it. The wazeer insisted saying, "Do take it because of the glad tidings that you have brought me. This

was a practice between Allah ﺗَﺒَﺎﺭَﻙَﻭَﺗَﻌَﺎﻟَﻰ and myself about which you have brought me good news. No one else knew about it. Here, take another hundred. This is for the good news you have brought me. You have made me happy to know that Rasulullah ﺻَﻠَّﻰﺍﻟﻠﻪُﻋَﻠَﻴْﻪِﻭَﺳَﻠَّﻢَ is aware of my Durood recited upon him. Take another hundred for the trouble you underwent to come here."

In this manner, he took out one hundred after another, till an entire thousand had been given. However, Qaari Abu Bakr Mujaahid ﺭَﺣِﻤَﻪُﺍﻟﻠﻪُ refused to take any of it saying, "Rasulullah ﺻَﻠَّﻰﺍﻟﻠﻪُﻋَﻠَﻴْﻪِﻭَﺳَﻠَّﻢَ commanded us to take only one hundred dinaars, thus we shall not take anything more than that." [174]

Incident Twenty Two - Durood Recited as Esaal-e-Thawaab

Once, a woman came to Hasan Basri ﺭَﺣِﻤَﻪُﺍﻟﻠﻪُ and said to him, "O Imaam, my daughter has passed away and I desire to see her in a dream. (Is there any way for me to see her?)"

Hasan Basri ﺭَﺣِﻤَﻪُﺍﻟﻠﻪُ told her, "After completing your Esha Salaah, perform four rakaats of nafl salaah. In each of the rakaats, recite Surah Faatihah and Surah Takaathur. Thereafter, as you lie down, continue reciting Durood on Rasulullah ﺻَﻠَّﻰﺍﻟﻠﻪُﻋَﻠَﻴْﻪِﻭَﺳَﻠَّﻢَ until sleep overtakes you."

The woman did as she was advised, and that very night, she saw her daughter in a dream. She saw her undergoing torture on

174 القول البديع صـ ٣٤٠

account of the sins she committed. She was covered in tar, her hands were bound, and her feet were tied in hot, burning chains of fire. The woman was greatly distressed and saddened to see her daughter in this condition. When she awoke the next morning, she hastened to Hasan Basri رَحِمَهُ ٱللَّه, and in great distress, told him what she had seen. He told her, "Give charity on her behalf. Perhaps Allah تَبَارَكَ وَتَعَالَى will pardon her through your sadaqah."

The following day, Hasan Basri رَحِمَهُ ٱللَّه saw the girl in a dream. He saw her in a beautiful garden while she was seated on a throne with a crown of honour on her head. He asked her, "Who are you?" She replied saying, "O Hasan, do you not recognize me?" He replied in the negative. She then said, "I am the daughter of the woman who spoke to you." Hasan Basri رَحِمَهُ ٱللَّه replied, "How is it that I see you in ease and comfort, whereas your mother told me of your pitiful condition?"

The girl replied, "All that my mother had told you was true. Certainly, that was my previous condition, and like me, there were seventy thousand people undergoing the same torment. However, we all were forgiven by Allah تَبَارَكَ وَتَعَالَى on account of the Durood of a saintly man. The saintly man, while passing by our graveyard, recited Durood upon Rasulullah صَلَّى ٱللَّهُ عَلَيْهِ وَسَلَّم once and conveyed the reward of the Durood to the inmates of the graves. That Durood was so beloved and appreciated by Allah تَبَارَكَ وَتَعَالَى that He emancipated us all from the torment and punishment of the

grave. It is through the blessings of that saintly man's Durood that you find me in this condition." [175]

Incident Twenty Three - A Means of Gaining Closeness to Allah تَبَارَكَ وَتَعَالَى

Ka'b Ahbaar رَحِمَهُ ٱللَّهُ (a Taab'iee who was among the learned Jewish scholars prior to accepting Islam) reports:

Allah تَبَارَكَ وَتَعَالَى addressed Moosa عَلَيْهِ ٱلسَّلَامُ saying, "O Moosa, do you desire to be close to Me, even closer than your speech is to your tongue, or your inner feelings are to your heart, or closer than your soul is to your body, or your eyesight is to your eyes?" Moosa عَلَيْهِ ٱلسَّلَامُ replied in the affirmative. Allah تَبَارَكَ وَتَعَالَى then said, "Then recite Salaat in abundance upon Muhammad صَلَّى ٱللَّهُ عَلَيْهِ وَسَلَّمَ." [176]

Incident Twenty Four - The Light of the Durood upon Hazrat Nabi صَلَّى ٱللَّهُ عَلَيْهِ وَسَلَّمَ

Hazrat Abul Qaasim Marwazi رَحِمَهُ ٱللَّهُ relates:

My father and I used to study Ahaadith at night. It was seen in a dream that on the spot where we sat, a brilliant light had appeared which stretched right to the heavens. Someone then enquired as to what this beam of light was. It was explained that this was the

175 الدر المنضود ص ١٨٥، القول البديع ص ٢٨١

176 الترغيب والترهيب لقوام السنة ٣٣٢/٢، القول البديع ص ٢٧٠

light of the Durood upon Nabi ﷺ which these two scholars had recited while they were studying Ahaadith.[177]

Incident Twenty Five - Fragrant Smell Due to Abundant Durood

The son-in-law of Moulana Faizul Hasan Sahaaranpuri رحمه الله once mentioned to Hazrat Shaikhul Hadith Moulana Muhammad Zakariyya رحمه الله that upon the demise of Moulana Faizul Hasan رحمه الله, a fragrant, sweet smell used to spread forth from his room. This continued for an entire month after his demise.

When this condition was related to Moulana Qaasim Naanotwi رحمه الله, he remarked, "This is the blessing of the Durood he used to recite upon Nabi ﷺ." During his lifetime, Moulana Faizul Hasan Saheb رحمه الله had accustomed himself to recite abundant Durood upon Nabi ﷺ, particularly on a Friday night (i.e. the night preceding Friday).[178]

Incident Twenty Six – Gaining the Special Proximity of Hazrat Rasulullah ﷺ

Qaadhi Iyaadh رحمه الله was a leading Muhaddith of his time. He had prepared a kitaab on the rights of Rasulullah ﷺ and sending durood upon him called Al-Shifaa.

<hr>

[177] القربة لابن بشكوال صـ ١٢٢، القول البديع صـ ٤٩١

[178] فضائل درود صـ ١٥٣

It is reported that the nephew of Qaadhi Iyaadh رَحِمَهُ ٱللَّهُ had once seen in a dream that his uncle, Qaadhi Iyaadh رَحِمَهُ ٱللَّهُ, was seated with Rasulullah صَلَّى ٱللَّهُ عَلَيْهِ وَسَلَّمَ on a throne of gold. On seeing the great position of honour and proximity that his uncle enjoyed with Rasulullah صَلَّى ٱللَّهُ عَلَيْهِ وَسَلَّمَ, he was deeply affected and surprised.

When Qaadhi Iyaadh رَحِمَهُ ٱللَّهُ came to know of his nephew's dream as well as his surprise, he addressed him saying, "O my nephew! Hold firmly to my kitaab, Al-Shifaa, and use it as a means to gain acceptance by Allah تَبَارَكَ وَتَعَالَى!"

In this manner, Qaadhi Iyaadh رَحِمَهُ ٱللَّهُ explained to his nephew that the cause for him being blessed with the special proximity of Rasulullah صَلَّى ٱللَّهُ عَلَيْهِ وَسَلَّمَ was his kitaab, Al-Shifaa, which was filled with Durood upon Rasulullah صَلَّى ٱللَّهُ عَلَيْهِ وَسَلَّمَ and incidents of the love of Rasulullah صَلَّى ٱللَّهُ عَلَيْهِ وَسَلَّمَ.[179]

Incident Twenty Seven - Remaining in the Company of Those who Recite Durood

Hazrat Sa'd Zanjaani رَحِمَهُ ٱللَّهُ once mentioned the following:

There was an ascetic man who lived among us in Egypt. His name was Abu Sa'eed Al-Khayyaat رَحِمَهُ ٱللَّهُ. He would neither mix and socialize with people, nor would he participate in any of the gatherings and majaalis that would be held. However, after some time, he began to punctually attend the majlis (gathering) of Ibnu Rasheeq رَحِمَهُ ٱللَّهُ.

---

[179] بستان المحدثين ص ٣٤٤

When the people noticed this, they were surprised and asked him why he was attending the majlis of Ibnu Rasheeq رَحِمَهُ ٱللَّهُ. Abu Sa'eed Al-Khayyaat رَحِمَهُ ٱللَّهُ replied, "I saw Rasulullah صَلَّى ٱللَّهُ عَلَيْهِ وَسَلَّمَ in a dream and he said to me, 'Attend the majlis of Ibnu Rasheeq, as he sends abundant salutations upon me.'" [180]

Incident Twenty Eight - The Name of Hazrat Nabi صَلَّى ٱللَّهُ عَلَيْهِ وَسَلَّمَ in the Taurah

Allaamah Sakhaawi رَحِمَهُ ٱللَّهُ relates:

There was once an evil person from amongst the Bani Israa'eel. When he passed away, the people did not afford him any respect and merely left his body on the ground. Allah تَبَارَكَ وَتَعَالَى then revealed to Moosa عَلَيْهِ ٱلسَّلَامُ, "O Moosa, wash him and perform his janaazah, for I have forgiven his sins and pardoned him."

Moosa عَلَيْهِ ٱلسَّلَامُ asked, "O Allah تَبَارَكَ وَتَعَالَى, what is the reason for this?" Allah تَبَارَكَ وَتَعَالَى replied, "Once, his sight fell on the name of Muhammad صَلَّى ٱللَّهُ عَلَيْهِ وَسَلَّمَ in the Taurah and he recited Durood upon Nabi صَلَّى ٱللَّهُ عَلَيْهِ وَسَلَّمَ. On account of this action, I have forgiven him." [181]

Incident Twenty Nine - Adding 'wasallam' in the Durood

Hazrat Ebrahim Nasafi رَحِمَهُ ٱللَّهُ relates:

On one occasion, I had seen Rasulullah صَلَّى ٱللَّهُ عَلَيْهِ وَسَلَّمَ in a dream. In the dream, I was unsure as to whether he was displeased with me.

---

[180] الترغيب للتيمي كما في القول البديع صـ ١٣١

[181] القول البديع صـ ٢٦٠.

I stretched forth my hand, took hold of the hands of Rasulullah ﷺ and kissed them.

I asked in great anxiety, "O Rasulullah ﷺ, I am indeed one of the servants of Hadith. I belong to the Ahlus Sunnah (those who follow your way) and I am a traveller from afar. Have compassion on me. Have I displeased you?" Rasulullah ﷺ smiled and said, "Whenever you recite Salaat, why do you not recite Salaam?" Thereafter, it became a fixed habit of mine to recite 'wasallam' as well.[182]

Incident Thirty - The Love of Rasulullah ﷺ for his Ummah

It has been recorded in "Mawaahib Ladunniyah" from "Tafseer Qushairy" that on the day of Judgement, a believer shall appear for reckoning with a small measure of righteous deeds. Rasulullah ﷺ shall appear, and place on the side of the righteous deeds, a small piece of paper that will be the size of the tip of one's finger. The result will be that the scale of good deeds will far outweigh the evil deeds.

Seeing this, the believer will exclaim, "May my mother and father be sacrificed for your sake, who are you? How beautiful is your physical appearance, and how sublime is your conduct!" Rasulullah ﷺ shall answer, "Verily I am your Nabi ﷺ. This which I have placed on your scale is the Salaat and Salaam that you

---

182 القول البديع ص ٤٨٨

used to recite upon me during your lifetime. Now I have come to your aid and assistance at your time of need." [183]

Incident Thirty One - The Stone that Would Make Salaam to Hazrat Rasulullah ﷺ

Hazrat Jaabir bin Samurah ﵁ reports that Rasulullah ﷺ said, "Indeed, I recognize a stone in Makkah Mukarramah that would make Salaam to me before I received nubuwwah. Indeed, I recognize that stone even now." [184]

Incident Thirty Two - The Tree that made Salaam to Hazrat Rasulullah ﷺ

Hazrat Ya'laa bin Murrah Thaqafee ﵁ reports:

We were once travelling with Rasulullah ﷺ when we halted at a certain place. After halting, Rasulullah ﷺ went to sleep. Thereafter, a tree came, forging its way through the earth, until it covered Rasulullah ﷺ, after which it left and returned to its place.

When Rasulullah ﷺ awoke, I mentioned to him what had transpired. Rasulullah ﷺ said, "It is a tree that asked its Rabb for permission to (come to me and) make Salaam to me. Allah ﵎ granted permission to this tree." [185]

---

[183] شرح الزرقاني على المواهب ٣٥٩/١٢

[184] صحيح مسلم، الرقم: ٢٢٧٧

[185] مسند أحمد، الرقم: ١٧٥٦٥، القول البديع ص: ١٦٢

Incident Thirty Three - Saved from Wild Animals through Reciting Durood

It has been reported regarding Shaikh Abul Hasan Shaazili رَحِمَهُ ٱللَّهُ that on one occasion, he was in the wilderness when wild animals began to approach him. Fearing that these animals would harm him, he immediately resorted to reciting Durood and Salaat upon Rasulullah صَلَّى ٱللَّهُ عَلَيْهِ وَسَلَّمَ.

The reason for him doing this is that it is reported in the authentic Ahaadith that when a person sends one Salaat upon Rasulullah صَلَّى ٱللَّهُ عَلَيْهِ وَسَلَّمَ, Allah تَبَارَكَ وَتَعَالَى sends ten Salaat (i.e. mercies) upon him, and the one upon whom Allah تَبَارَكَ وَتَعَالَى showers His mercy, Allah تَبَارَكَ وَتَعَالَى suffices him for all the worries and difficulties that he faces. Hence, through reciting Durood upon Rasulullah صَلَّى ٱللَّهُ عَلَيْهِ وَسَلَّمَ, Shaikh Shaazili رَحِمَهُ ٱللَّهُ was saved from the wild animals.[186]

Incident Thirty Four - A Means of Earning the Intercession of Hazrat Rasulullah صَلَّى ٱللَّهُ عَلَيْهِ وَسَلَّمَ

Hazrat Qutb Al-Halabi رَحِمَهُ ٱللَّهُ mentions:

I once met Abu Ishaaq, Ebrahim bin Ali bin Atiyyah At-Taleedami رَحِمَهُ ٱللَّهُ. He said to me, "I was blessed with the mubaarak vision of Rasulullah صَلَّى ٱللَّهُ عَلَيْهِ وَسَلَّمَ in a dream. On seeing him, I said to him, 'O Rasul of Allah صَلَّى ٱللَّهُ عَلَيْهِ وَسَلَّمَ! I request you to intercede for me on the

---

[186] الدر المنضود ص ١٨٤، القول البديع ص ٢٦٥

day of Qiyaamah!' Rasulullah صَلَّ ٱللَّهُ عَلَيْهِ وَسَلَّمَ replied, 'Recite abundant Durood upon me.'" [187]

Incident Thirty Five - The Blessing of the Mubaarak Ahaadith of Hazrat Rasulullah صَلَّ ٱللَّهُ عَلَيْهِ وَسَلَّمَ

Hazrat Abu Ahmad, Abdullah bin Bakr bin Muhammad رَحِمَهُ ٱللَّهُ, once mentioned, "The knowledge which has the most blessing, which is the greatest knowledge, and is most beneficial in this world and the next, after the knowledge of the kitaab of Allah تَبَارَكَ وَتَعَالَى, is the knowledge of the Mubaarak Ahaadith of Rasulullah صَلَّ ٱللَّهُ عَلَيْهِ وَسَلَّمَ. One will acquire the most blessings through the Mubaarak Ahaadith on account of the abundant Durood that he will recite on Rasulullah صَلَّ ٱللَّهُ عَلَيْهِ وَسَلَّمَ when reading the Mubaarak Ahaadith. The Mubaarak Ahaadith of Rasulullah صَلَّ ٱللَّهُ عَلَيْهِ وَسَلَّمَ are like orchards and gardens in which you will find every form of goodness, righteousness, virtue and zikr." [188]

Incident Thirty Six - Engaging in Durood at the Time of an Epidemic

Hazrat Moulana Hakeem Muhammad Akhtar Saheb رَحِمَهُ ٱللَّهُ mentioned the following:

---

[187] القول البديع ص ٢٦٧

[188] الترغيب والترهيب لقوام السنة ٢/ ٣٣٤، القول البديع ص ٢٨٧

Hazrat Moulana Ashraf Ali Thaanwi رَحْمَةُ اللهِ had prepared a kitaab named "Nashrut-Teeb" in regard to the love of Rasulullah صَلَّى اللهُ عَلَيْهِ وَسَلَّم. The entire kitaab revolves around love for Rasulullah صَلَّى اللهُ عَلَيْهِ وَسَلَّم, and through reading this kitaab, one can gauge the deep love within the heart of the author for Rasulullah صَلَّى اللهُ عَلَيْهِ وَسَلَّم.

During the time when Hazrat Moulana Ashraf Ali Thaanwi رَحْمَةُ اللهِ was engaged in the compilation of Nashrut-Teeb, Thanabowan (the town in which Hazrat Thaanwi رَحْمَةُ اللهِ resided) was afflicted by a plague. It was noticed that on the day when Hazrat Thaanwi رَحْمَةُ اللهِ wrote any portion of this kitaab, there would be no reports of people passing away due to the plague. However, on the day when Hazrat Thaanwi رَحْمَةُ اللهِ did not write any portion of the kitaab, reports of many people passing away would be heard.

When this observation reached Hazrat Thaanwi رَحْمَةُ اللهِ via many people, he would not leave out writing this kitaab on any day. It was through the barakah (blessings) of writing about the great virtues and esteemed position of Hazrat Rasulullah صَلَّى اللهُ عَلَيْهِ وَسَلَّم during that time that Allah تَبَارَكَ وَتَعَالَى caused the plague to come to an end.

After mentioning the above incident, Hazrat Moulana Hakeem Muhammad Akhtar Saheb رَحْمَةُ اللهِ concluded:
The recitation of abundant Durood upon Rasulullah صَلَّى اللهُ عَلَيْهِ وَسَلَّم is extremely beneficial in repelling calamities and disasters. Through reciting a single Durood, one's rank is elevated by ten stages, ten good deeds are recorded in one's account, and ten sins

are forgiven. Additionally, through reciting abundant Durood, one is trying to fulfill the right of love which he owes to Rasulullah صَلَّى ٱللَّهُ عَلَيْهِ وَسَلَّمَ.[189]

Incident Thirty Seven - Benefit of Reciting One Thousand Durood on Friday

Hazrat Abu Abdir Rahmaan Al-Muqri رَحِمَهُ ٱللَّهُ relates that Khallaad bin Katheer رَحِمَهُ ٱللَّهُ was in the throes of death. Under his pillow, a piece of paper was found wherein it was written:

هٰذِهِ بَرَاءَةٌ مِنَ النَّارِ لِخَلَّادِ بْنِ كَثِيْرٍ

This is a certificate of freedom from the fire of Jahannum for Khallaad bin Katheer

The people then enquired from his wife as to the reason for him receiving this good fortune. She replied that it was his practice to recite the following Durood one thousand times every Friday:

اَللّٰهُمَّ صَلِّ عَلٰى مُحَمَّدٍ النَّبِيِّ الْأُمِّيِّ

O Allah, shower your choicest Durood on Muhammad صَلَّى ٱللَّهُ عَلَيْهِ وَسَلَّمَ the unlettered Nabi.[190]

---

[189] آداب عشق الرسول صلى الله عليه وسلم ص ١١

[190] طبقات المحدثين بأصبهان لابن حيان ٢/ ٣٤٥

Incident Thirty Eight - The Author of Dalaa'ilul Khairaat

It is mentioned regarding the author of Dalaa'ilul Khairaat that he once set out on a journey. During the journey, he required water to perform wudhu. Subsequently, he came across a well, but due to not having a bucket and rope, he could not draw out the water from the well. Out of concern for his salaah, he became extremely worried.

While in this state, a young girl (who was not yet baaligh) saw him and came to him. She asked him what the matter was, and he explained to her the problem. She immediately spat into the well whereupon the water rose to the top of the well by itself.

Witnessing this miracle performed by the young girl, he was overcome by surprise and thus asked the girl, "How did you perform this miracle?" The girl replied, "This was through the blessings of the Durood which I have recited upon Nabi ﷺ." It was this miracle that motivated him to write the book Dalaa'ilul Khairaat.[191]

Allaamah Zardaq رَحِمَهُ ٱللَّه reports that upon the demise of the author of Dalaa'ilul Khairaat, the fragrant smell of musk and amber used to spread forth from the grave. This was due to the blessings of the Durood.[192]

---

[191] مقدمة دلائل الخيرات ص ١٤

[192] فضائل درود ص ١٥٢

Incident Thirty Nine - Al-Qawlul Badee'

Allaamah Sakhaawi رَحِمَهُٱللَّهُ says:

A very reliable student from among the students of Shaikh Raslaan رَحِمَهُٱللَّهُ told me that Rasulullah صَلَّىٱللَّهُعَلَيْهِوَسَلَّمَ appeared in his dream and the kitaab 'Al-Qawlul Badee' (a detailed kitaab concerning Durood written by Allaamah Sakhaawi رَحِمَهُٱللَّهُ) was presented to him, and Rasulullah صَلَّىٱللَّهُعَلَيْهِوَسَلَّمَ accepted it.

This pleased me very much, and I therefore hope that Allah تَبَارَكَوَتَعَالَى and Rasulullah صَلَّىٱللَّهُعَلَيْهِوَسَلَّمَ accept it, and that I will be greatly rewarded in both the worlds. I therefore urge you all to continue reciting Salaat on Rasulullah صَلَّىٱللَّهُعَلَيْهِوَسَلَّمَ in all sincerity, for indeed your Salaat reaches Rasulullah صَلَّىٱللَّهُعَلَيْهِوَسَلَّمَ in his mubaarak grave, and your name is mentioned in his presence.[193]

Incident Forty - Qaseedah Burdah

Allaamah Busairi رَحِمَهُٱللَّهُ was a scholar of Deen and a saintly personality. During his life, he was afflicted with a stroke. He prepared his poetry (the Qaseedah Burdah) with the hope that these poems of the praise and love of Rasulullah صَلَّىٱللَّهُعَلَيْهِوَسَلَّمَ would become a means for him seeking the mercy of Allah تَبَارَكَوَتَعَالَى and curing him from his affliction.

---

[193] القول البديع ص ٣٤٧

One night, he saw Rasulullah ﷺ in a dream and presented before Rasulullah ﷺ the poetry he composed out of the love of Rasulullah ﷺ. Rasulullah ﷺ placed his mubaarak hand on him, and when he awoke in the morning, he was cured and was able to walk.[194]

Incident Forty One – The Incident of Sayyid Ahmed Rifaa'ee ﷦

Sayyid Ahmed Rifaa'ee ﷦ is very well known as one of the foremost saints of Islam. In the year 555 A.H., he proceeded for hajj. Thereafter, he visited Madinah Munawwarah, and while standing before the blessed grave of Rasulullah ﷺ, he recited the following couplets:

في حالة البعد روحي كنت أرسلها   تقبل الأرض عني فهي نائبتي

وهذه نوبة الأشباح قد حضرت   فامدد يمينك كي تحظى بها شفتي

From far off to thee did I send my soul

On my behalf to greet you in your resting place

Here now, O Rasulullah ﷺ is my body to greet you

Stretch forth your hand that my lips can kiss you

On reciting these couplets, the blessed hand of Rasulullah صَلَّى ٱللَّهُ عَلَيۡهِ وَسَلَّمَ extended from the grave, and in the presence of an estimated 90 000 visitors, Sayyid Ahmed Rifaa'ee رَحمَهُ ٱللَّه kissed it. They all had the good fortune of seeing the blessed hand of Rasulullah صَلَّى ٱللَّهُ عَلَيۡهِ وَسَلَّمَ, and among those present was Shaikh Abdul Qaadir Jeelaani رَحمَهُ ٱللَّه.[195]

Incident Forty Two - Reward of Writing 'Sallallahu Alaihi Wasallam'

Hasan bin Muhammad رَحمَهُ ٱللَّه says:

I once saw Imaam Ahmad bin Hambal رَحمَهُ ٱللَّه in a dream. He said to me, "If only you could witness with your eyes the great rewards and blessings that shines before us in store for those who write Durood upon Rasulullah صَلَّى ٱللَّهُ عَلَيۡهِ وَسَلَّمَ in their books."[196]

Note: When writing the name of Hazrat Rasulullah صَلَّى ٱللَّهُ عَلَيۡهِ وَسَلَّمَ, then one should write the complete صَلَّى ٱللَّهُ عَلَيۡهِ وَسَلَّمَ in Arabic or 'sallallahu 'alaihi wasallam' in English. One should not suffice upon the abbreviations such as 'SAW' or PBUH etc. as this is not in keeping with the demands of respect that should be shown to Rasulullah صَلَّى ٱللَّهُ عَلَيۡهِ وَسَلَّمَ.

---

[195] الحاوي للفتاوي ٢/٣١٤

[196] الدر المنضود ص ٢٥٦، القول البديع ص ٤٨٦

Incident Forty Three - Writing ﷺ when Copying Down Ahaadith

Hazrat Abul Hasan Maimooni رَحِمَهُ ٱللَّٰه says:

I once saw my ustaaz, Abu Ali رَحِمَهُ ٱللَّٰه, in a dream. I noticed that something was written on his fingers in gold or saffron. I asked him, "O Abu Ali, what is this?" He replied, "Whenever I came across the name of Rasulullah ﷺ while copying down Ahaadith, I used to write ﷺ (and this is the reward for writing the Durood)." [197]

Incident Forty Four - Writing 'ﷺ' in Full

Hazrat Ubaidullaah bin Umar Qawaareeri رَحِمَهُ ٱللَّٰه said:

I had a close companion who was a scribe by profession. After his demise, I once saw him in a dream and enquired from him as to how Allah تَبَارَكَ وَتَعَالَى had dealt with him. He replied that Allah تَبَارَكَ وَتَعَالَى had forgiven him.

When I asked him the reason, he said, "It was my habit during my lifetime that whenever I wrote the blessed name of Nabi ﷺ, I always wrote 'ﷺ' after the mubaarak name. Allah تَبَارَكَ وَتَعَالَى loved this action so much that He has granted me bounties which no eye has ever seen, nor has any ear ever heard, and neither did the thought of such boons and bounties ever cross the mind of any person." [198]

---

[197] الترغيب والترهيب لقوام السنة ٢/٣٣٣، القول البديع صـ ٤٨٧

[198] الصلة في تاريخ أئمة الأندلس لابن بشكوال ١/٣٠٨، القول البديع صـ ٤٨٩

Incident Forty Five - Taking Precaution in Writing Durood

Hazrat Abu Sulaimaan, Muhammad bin Husain رَحِمَهُ ٱللَّهُ, says:

Amongst my neighbours, there was a man by the name of Fadhl who would engross himself in performing nafl salaah and observing nafl fasts.

He once mentioned to me, "I used to copy the Ahaadith of Rasulullah صَلَّى ٱللَّهُ عَلَيْهِ وَسَلَّمَ, but was never in the habit of writing the Durood after the name of Rasulullah صَلَّى ٱللَّهُ عَلَيْهِ وَسَلَّمَ. Rasulullah صَلَّى ٱللَّهُ عَلَيْهِ وَسَلَّمَ then appeared in a dream and told me, 'Why is it that you fail to recite Durood upon me whenever my name is spoken or written?'"

Fadhl then took great precaution in reciting Durood upon Rasulullah صَلَّى ٱللَّهُ عَلَيْهِ وَسَلَّمَ whenever the name of Rasulullah صَلَّى ٱللَّهُ عَلَيْهِ وَسَلَّمَ was mentioned. A few days later, he saw Rasulullah صَلَّى ٱللَّهُ عَلَيْهِ وَسَلَّمَ again in a vision and Rasulullah صَلَّى ٱللَّهُ عَلَيْهِ وَسَلَّمَ told him, "Continue reciting Durood upon me whenever my name is mentioned for verily your Durood reaches me." [199]

Incident Forty Six - Failing to Write Durood upon Hazrat Rasulullah صَلَّى ٱللَّهُ عَلَيْهِ وَسَلَّمَ

Hazrat Hasan bin Moosa Al-Hadrami رَحِمَهُ ٱللَّهُ, who is well known as Ibnu Ujainah رَحِمَهُ ٱللَّهُ, relates:

---

[199] الترغيب والترهيب لقوام السنة ٣٢٨/٢، القول البديع صـ ٤٨٧

I used to write Ahaadith, and in my haste, I used to forget to write Salaat on Rasulullah ﷺ at the places where the name of Rasulullah ﷺ appeared. Thereafter, I saw Rasulullah ﷺ in a dream. He said to me, "How is it that you fail to write Salaat with my name in the manner that Abu Amr Tabari رحمه الله does?"

When I awoke, I felt greatly distressed and filled with anguish, and there and then I made a resolution that in future, whenever I write down any Hadith, I shall certainly write "ﷺ". [200]

Incident Forty Seven - Reaching Lofty Positions through Writing Abundant Durood

Hazrat Ja'far bin Abdullah رحمه الله relates:

On one occasion, I saw Imaam Abu Zur'ah رحمه الله (a famous scholar of Hadith) in a dream. I saw him in the heavens leading the angels in salaah.

I asked him, "O Abu Zur'ah, how did you reach this high position of honour?" He replied, "With this hand of mine, I have written one million Ahaadith, and whenever I wrote the blessed name of Rasulullah ﷺ, I also wrote Salaat and Salaam, and Rasulullah ﷺ said, 'Whoever recites Salaat on me once, Allah تبارك وتعالى bestows ten mercies upon him.'"

[200] القربة لابن بشكوال ص ١٢٤، القول البديع ص ٤٩٢

According to this calculation, it would mean that (through him writing the Durood one million times), the mercies from Allah تَبَارَكَ وَتَعَالَى would amount to ten million upon him. One can well imagine that when only one mercy from the side of Allah تَبَارَكَ وَتَعَالَى is more valuable than everything on earth, then how fortunate will be the person upon whom ten million mercies of Allah تَبَارَكَ وَتَعَالَى rain upon! [201]

Incident Forty Eight - Writing Durood in a Unique Form

Hazrat Abu Ali, Hasan bin Ali At-Taar رَحِمَهُ ٱللَّهُ, says:

Abu Taahir رَحِمَهُ ٱللَّهُ once gave me a few scripts of Ahaadith. I saw therein that whenever the name of Rasulullah صَلَّى ٱللَّهُ عَلَيْهِ وَسَلَّمَ was mentioned, Salaat was written in these words:

$$صَلَّى اللهُ عَلَيْهِ وَسَلَّمَ تَسْلِيْمًا كَثِيْرًا كَثِيْرًا$$

I then asked Abu Taahir, "Why do you write Durood upon Rasulullah صَلَّى ٱللَّهُ عَلَيْهِ وَسَلَّمَ in this manner?"

He replied:

In my youth, I used to write Ahaadith and I did not write Salaat with the name of Rasulullah صَلَّى ٱللَّهُ عَلَيْهِ وَسَلَّمَ. I then saw Rasulullah صَلَّى ٱللَّهُ عَلَيْهِ وَسَلَّمَ in a dream and greeted him, but Rasulullah صَلَّى ٱللَّهُ عَلَيْهِ وَسَلَّمَ turned his blessed face away from me. I then came to him from

201 الدر المنضود ص ٢٥٧، القول البديع ص ٤٨٩

the other side and again greeted him, but once again he turned his blessed face away from me. Once again, for the third time, I approached him from the front and enquired, "O Rasulullah ﷺ, why do you turn your blessed face away from me?" Rasulullah ﷺ replied, "The reason is that whenever you write my name in your kitaab, you do not offer Salaat upon me." Since that time, it has become my habit that whenever I write the name of Rasulullah ﷺ, I also write:

$$ صَلَّى اللهُ عَلَيْهِ وَسَلَّمَ تَسْلِيْمًا كَثِيْرًا كَثِيْرًا كَثِيْرًا ٢٠٢ $$

Incident Forty Nine - Adding 'Tasleema' in the Durood

Hazrat Abu Ishaaq, Nahshal رَحِمَهُ اللهُ, says:

I used to write books on Ahaadith, and whenever I wrote the name of Rasulullah ﷺ then I used to write it in this manner:

$$ قَالَ النَّبِيُّ صَلَّى اللهُ عَلَيْهِ وَسَلَّمَ تَسْلِيْمًا $$

Thereafter, I had a dream in which I saw Rasulullah ﷺ with this book in his hands, looking through it. After looking through the book, Rasulullah ﷺ said, "This is excellent." [203]

---

٢٠٢ القربة لابن بشكوال ص ١٢٣، القول البديع ص ٤٩٣

203 تاريخ بغداد ٦٩/٦، القول البديع ص ٤٩٢

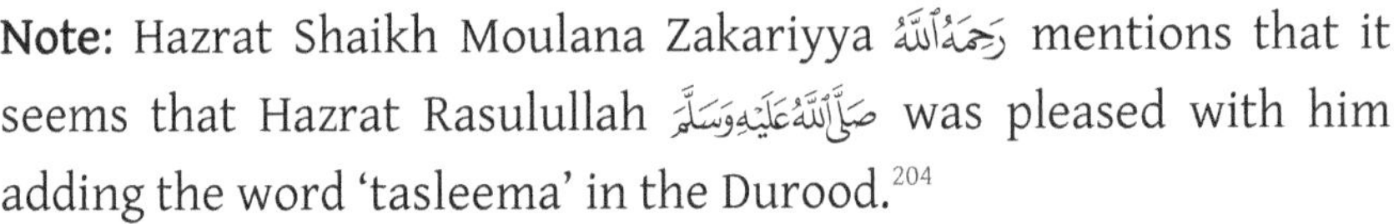

Note: Hazrat Shaikh Moulana Zakariyya رَحْمَهُٱللَّه mentions that it seems that Hazrat Rasulullah صَلَّىٱللَّهُعَلَيْهِوَسَلَّم was pleased with him adding the word 'tasleema' in the Durood.[204]

Incident Fifty - Adding 'Salaam' in the Durood

Hazrat Abu Sulaimaan Harraani رَحْمَهُٱللَّه says:

I once saw Rasulullah صَلَّىٱللَّهُعَلَيْهِوَسَلَّم in a dream and he said to me, "O Abu Sulaimaan, when you copy Ahaadith and my name is mentioned, I notice that you suffice on 'Salaat' and you do not send 'Salaam' upon me. Salaam (i.e. Wasallam) is a four-letter word, and for every letter, one will receive a tenfold reward (amounting to forty additional rewards). Why then do you throw away forty rewards?"[205]

Incident Fifty One – The Incident of Mulla Jaami رَحْمَهُٱللَّه

It is related that Mulla Jaami رَحْمَهُٱللَّه, having composed a qaseedah on the love of Rasulullah صَلَّىٱللَّهُعَلَيْهِوَسَلَّم, decided to proceed for hajj. His further intention was to stand before the Raudhah Mubaarak and recite his poem before Rasulullah صَلَّىٱللَّهُعَلَيْهِوَسَلَّم.

After performing hajj, when he intended to leave for Madinah Munawwarah, Rasulullah صَلَّىٱللَّهُعَلَيْهِوَسَلَّم appeared in the dream of the governor of Makkah Mukarramah and told him that he should not allow Mulla Jaami to enter Madinah Munawwarah. The governor

---

204 فضائل درود ص ١٦٧

205 القول البديع ص ٤٨٨

prohibited him from leaving for Madinah Munawwarah, however his love and longing for Rasulullah ﷺ was such that inspite of the order, he secretly set off for Madinah Munawwarah.

Once again, the governor saw a dream in which Rasulullah ﷺ was telling him that Mulla Jaami had left Makkah, and he should not allow him to come to Madinah Munawwarah.

This time, the governor sent a few men after him to bring him back. They caught up with him and treated him most harshly as they arrested him, and thereafter cast him into jail.

For a third time, Rasulullah ﷺ appeared in the dream of the governor, scolding him and reprimanding him. Rasulullah ﷺ said to him that Mulla Jaami was not a criminal (hence, he should not be treated harshly). However, all that he had done was that out of his love for Rasulullah ﷺ, he had composed poetry which he intended to recite in the presence of Rasulullah ﷺ. Rasulullah ﷺ said to the governor that if he recited the poetry, then Rasulullah ﷺ would have to extend his hand to shake the hand of Mulla Jaami, and this would cause great confusion among the people.

Thereafter, the governor set him free and treated him with the greatest honour and respect.[206]

---

[206] Hazrat Shaikh Moulana Muhammad Zakariyya رَحِمَهُ ٱللّٰه mentioned this incident in Fazaail-e-Durood (pg. 195) and thereafter said that he had heard this incident during his

Incident Fifty Two – The Scribe of Durood

Hazrat Shaikhul Hadith, Moulana Muhammad Zakariyya رَحمَهُٱللَّه mentioned:

A reliable friend of mine informed me regarding a scribe of Lucknow. He would commence his daily work after writing durood on a sheet of paper which he had reserved for this very purpose.

At the time of his death, he was overcome with fear of the Hereafter saying, "What will become of me after I depart this world?" On saying this, a majzoob (saint constantly engaged in the remembrance of Allah تَبَارَكَوَتَعَالَ) appeared and said, "Why are you so worried? The sheet of paper (upon which you would write Durood) is with Rasulullah صَلَّىٱللَّهُعَلَيْهِوَسَلَّم and is being adorned."[207]

Incident Fifty Three – Reciting Durood in a Gathering

The author of Nuzhatul Majaalis narrates the following incident from a certain saint:

I had a neighbour who was very sinful. I always urged him to repent, but he would not listen. After he passed away, I saw him in Jannah. When I enquired as to how he had reached Jannah, he said, "I was once present in the gathering of a Muhaddith (Hadith scholar) who said, 'The one who recites Durood upon Rasulullah

---

childhood. However, due to old age and ill health, he was unable to search for the source of the incident at the time he prepared the kitaab Fazaail-e-Durood.

[207] فضائل درود ص ١٥٣

صَلَّى ٱللّٰهُ عَلَيْهِ وَسَلَّمَ aloud will be guaranteed Jannah.' I thus recited Durood aloud, and others did so as well. Hence, we were all pardoned by Allah تَبَارَكَ وَتَعَالَى."[208]

Incident Fifty Four – Being Blessed with the Clothes of Jannah

Hazrat Sufyaan bin Uyainah رَحِمَهُ ٱللّٰهُ narrates that Khalaf رَحِمَهُ ٱللّٰهُ said:

I had a friend with whom I used to study Hadith. After he passed away, I saw in a dream that he was wandering freely, wearing a new pair of green clothes. I asked him, "We used to study Hadith together, so how then did you reach this high station of honour and dignity?" He replied, "Yes, we did write Hadith together, but whenever I came across the blessed name of Rasulullah صَلَّى ٱللّٰهُ عَلَيْهِ وَسَلَّمَ, I would write صَلَّى ٱللّٰهُ عَلَيْهِ وَسَلَّمَ underneath. In return for this deed, Allah تَبَارَكَ وَتَعَالَى granted me this honour that you see."[209]

Incident Fifty Five – Acquiring Forgiveness through Writing Durood

Hazrat Ibnu Abi Sulaimaan رَحِمَهُ ٱللّٰهُ mentions:

I saw my father in a dream after his demise. I asked, "How did Allah تَبَارَكَ وَتَعَالَى deal with you?" He replied, "Allah تَبَارَكَ وَتَعَالَى forgave

208 نزهة المجالس ٢/٨٧

209 القربة لابن بشكوال صـ ١٢١، القول البديع صـ ٤٨٦

me." I asked, "Due to which deed did He forgive you?" He answered, "I used to write Durood after the name of Rasulullah صَلَّى ٱللَّهُ عَلَيْهِ وَسَلَّمَ in every Hadith."[210]

Incident Fifty Six – Reciting Durood in Abundance

Haafiz Abu Nu'aim رَحِمَهُ ٱللَّهُ relates that Hazrat Sufyaan Thauri رَحِمَهُ ٱللَّهُ mentioned:

I was once leaving my house when my gaze fell upon a youth who was reading اَللّٰهُمَّ صَلِّ عَلَى مُحَمَّدٍ وَّعَلَى آلِ مُحَمَّدٍ with every step he took. I asked him, "Is there any proof for your practice (or is it based on your own opinion)?" He asked, "Who are you?" I replied, "Sufyaan Thauri." He asked me, "Sufyaan of Iraq?" I replied in the affirmative.

He then asked, "Do you have the cognisance (recognition) of Allah تَبَارَكَ وَتَعَالَى?" I replied in the affirmative. He asked, "How did you attain it?" I said, "He takes the night out of the day and the day out of the night, and He fashions the child in the mother's womb." He said, "You have not truly recognized Him."

I thus asked him, "So how have you come to recognize Him?" He replied, "I firmly decide on doing something, but I end up having to cancel it. I resolve to do something, but find that I am unable to

---

210 الأخلاق الزكية ص ٢٠١

fulfill it. Through this, I have realised that there is another being who is governing my affairs."

I then asked him regarding his recitation of Durood with every step. He said, "I was traveling for hajj with my mother, but she passed away during the journey. After passing away, her face turned black and her stomach bloated, through which I realised that she had committed a grave sin.

"As I lifted my hands towards the sky to make dua to Allah تَبَارَكَ وَتَعَالَى, I saw a cloud coming from Tihaamah (Hijaaz) from which a man appeared. He passed his hand over my mother's face making it luminous, and over her stomach causing the swelling to disappear.

"I asked him, 'Who are you? You have allieviated this great tragedy from my mother and I.' He replied, 'I am your prophet, Muhammad صَلَّى اللهُ عَلَيْهِ وَسَلَّمَ.'

"I then asked him for some advice, to which Rasulullah صَلَّى اللهُ عَلَيْهِ وَسَلَّمَ instructed, 'Whenever you take a step, read,

$$\text{اَللّٰهُمَّ صَلِّ عَلٰى مُحَمَّدٍ وَّعَلٰى آلِ مُحَمَّدٍ}^{٢١١}$$

٢١١ الدر المنضود صـ ٢٤٦

Incident Fifty Seven – Hazrat Umar رَضِىَ اللّٰهُ عَنْهُ Praising Hazrat Rasulullah صَلَّى اللّٰهُ عَلَيْهِ وَسَلَّمَ

The author of Ihyaa has written that after the demise of Hazrat Rasulullah صَلَّى اللّٰهُ عَلَيْهِ وَسَلَّمَ, Hazrat Umar رَضِىَ اللّٰهُ عَنْهُ was weeping and saying the following:

O Messenger of Allah صَلَّى اللّٰهُ عَلَيْهِ وَسَلَّمَ, may my parents be sacrificed for you! The trunk of the date tree on which you would lean and deliver the khutbah before the erection of the mimbar cried after you ascended the mimbar, saddened by your separation. You then passed your hand over it and comforted it. O Messenger of Allah صَلَّى اللّٰهُ عَلَيْهِ وَسَلَّمَ! Your followers have more reason to cry over your separation than this date tree (i.e. they are more in need of your consoling and comforting upon your separation).

O Messenger of Allah صَلَّى اللّٰهُ عَلَيْهِ وَسَلَّمَ, may my parents be sacrificed for you! Your status with Allah تَبَارَكَ وَتَعَالَى is so exalted that your obedience has been declared obedience to Him. Allah تَبَارَكَ وَتَعَالَى says in the Quraan Majeed, "He who obeys the Messenger has indeed obeyed Allah."

O Messenger of Allah صَلَّى اللّٰهُ عَلَيْهِ وَسَلَّمَ, may my parents be sacrificed for you! You are so great in the sight of Allah تَبَارَكَ وَتَعَالَى that your mistakes were excused before you even requested forgiveness. Hence, Allah تَبَارَكَ وَتَعَالَى says in the Quraan Majeed, "Allah pardon you! Why did you give them leave?"

O Messenger of Allah ﷺ, may my parents be sacrificed for you! Your lofty rank with Allah تَبَارَكَ وَتَعَالَى is such that you have been mentioned foremost in the covenant taken from the Ambiyaa عَلَيْهِمُ السَّلَامُ, even though you are the last Nabi to be sent. Allah تَبَارَكَ وَتَعَالَى says in the Quraan Majeed, "And recall when we took a pledge from the Ambiyaa and from you, and from Nooh, and Ebrahim, and Moosa, and Isa عَلَيْهِمُ السَّلَامُ, the son of Maryam رَضِيَ اللهُ عَنْهَا. And we took from them a solemn bond."

O Messenger of Allah ﷺ, may my parents be sacrificed for you! You are so great in the sight of Allah تَبَارَكَ وَتَعَالَى that the disbelievers in Jahannum will be regretful for not obeying you and will say, "Ah! If only we had obeyed Allah and the Messenger."

O Messenger of Allah ﷺ, may my parents be sacrificed for you! Indeed, Allah تَبَارَكَ وَتَعَالَى granted Moosa عَلَيْهِ السَّلَامُ the miracle of making rivers flow from stone, but it is not as extraordinary as Allah تَبَارَكَ وَتَعَالَى making water gush forth from your fingers.

O Messenger of Allah تَبَارَكَ وَتَعَالَى, may my parents be sacrificed for you! If the wind was subservient to Sulaimaan عَلَيْهِ السَّلَامُ and would transport him in the morning over a distance covered in one month and likewise in the evening, it is not more amazing than your transcending the seven heavens on the Buraaq and returning to Makkah Mukaramah by morning. May Allah تَبَارَكَ وَتَعَالَى confer blessings upon you!

O Messenger of Allah ﷺ, may my parents be sacrificed for you! If Isa عَلَيْهِ السَّلَام was granted the miracle of bringing the dead back to life, it is not more amazing than a goat being cut into many pieces and being roasted, and then speaking to you and telling you not to eat it because it had been poisoned.

O Messenger of Allah ﷺ, may my parents be sacrificed for you! Nooh عَلَيْهِ السَّلَام made dua against his people saying, "My Lord! Leave not of the infidels any inhabitant upon the earth." Had you made dua against us, none from among us would have survived. The disbelievers placed the intestines of a camel on your back while you were in sajdah. In the Battle of Uhud, they caused your face to be covered in blood and broke your tooth. Despite this, you did not curse them. Instead, you supplicated, "O Allah, forgive my people for they know not."

O Messenger of Allah ﷺ, may my parents be sacrificed for you! Within a short period of your life (twenty three years as a Rasul), more people accepted Islam than those who accepted during the lengthy lifetime (approximately one thousand years) of Nooh عَلَيْهِ السَّلَام (at the time of the Farewell Hajj, one hundred and twenty four thousand Sahaabah were present, and only Allah تَبَارَكَ وَتَعَالَى knows how many had entered the fold of Islam but were unable to attend). The number of people who brought imaan upon you is great (in the Hadith narrated in Saheeh Bukhaari, Hazrat Rasulullah ﷺ said that he saw his followers in such a great number that they had covered the horizon). Very few people

brought imaan upon Nooh عَلَيْهِ ٱلسَّلَامُ. Allah تَبَارَكَ وَتَعَالَى says in the Quraan Majeed, "And these had not believed with him save a few."

O Messenger of Allah صَلَّى ٱللَّهُ عَلَيْهِ وَسَلَّمَ, may my parents be sacrificed for you! If you were only to entertain and meet those of the same standing as you, you would never have sat with us. If you were not to marry except a woman of the same status as yourself, never would you have married any of our women. If you were to feed only those who were as exalted as you, never would you have fed anyone amongst us. Indeed, you sat with us, married our women, allowed us sit and eat with you, wore clothes made of hair, mounted a donkey and sat on the floor and ate. You would lick your fingers after eating and all this was out of humility. May Allah تَبَارَكَ وَتَعَالَى confer blessings upon you.[212]

Incident Fifty Eight – Receiving Special Food

Shah Waliyullah رَحِمَهُ ٱللَّهُ writes in Al-Hirzuth Thameen (under number nineteen) that his father related the following:

I was once travelling in the blessed month of Ramaadhaan. It was extremely hot at the time and I was undergoing great difficulty. In that state, I fell asleep and saw Rasulullah صَلَّى ٱللَّهُ عَلَيْهِ وَسَلَّمَ. Rasulullah صَلَّى ٱللَّهُ عَلَيْهِ وَسَلَّمَ gave me a most delicious sweet dish containing rice, saffron, sugar and ghee, and I ate to my fill. Thereafter, Rasulullah صَلَّى ٱللَّهُ عَلَيْهِ وَسَلَّمَ gave me some water. Thus, my thirst and hunger were

---

[212] إحياء علوم الدين ١/ ٣١٠

totally satiated, and when I awoke, I could smell the fragrance of saffron on my fingers.[213]

Note: The father of Shah Waliyullah رَحِمَهُ ٱللَّهُ and his family were ardent lovers of Hazrat Rasulullah صَلَّى ٱللَّهُ عَلَيْهِ وَسَلَّمَ and would recite abundant durood.

Incident Fifty Nine – The Superiority of the Night over the Day

In Nuzhatul Majaalis, an amazing story has been narrated regarding a debate that took place between night and day, each one of them trying to prove its virtue over the other.

Day said to night, "I am greater than you. Three obligatory prayers are performed in me while only two take place in you. I contain the moment of acceptance on a Friday wherein no person asks Allah تَبَارَكَ وَتَعَالَى for anything except that it is granted to him. The fasts of Ramadhaan are observed in me too. You are just a time for sleep and a time wherein people are absentminded. I am accompanied by wakefulness and activity, and there are great blessings in being active. The sun also rises in me and brings light to the whole world."

Night replied by saying, "If you pride yourself over the sun, then I consider the hearts of those who stand in prayer at night and the

---

hearts of those who ponder over the wisdom behind Allah's تَبَارَكَوَتَعَالَى creation much greater than the sun. How can you ever reach the pinnacle of ecstasy which the lovers experience when they are in solitude with me? How can you compare yourself to the Night of Mi'raaj? What reply do you have to the order of Allah تَبَارَكَوَتَعَالَى to His Messenger صَلَّىٰاللَّهُعَلَيْهِوَسَلَّمَ when He said, 'And from (part of) the night, perform salaah therein as an additional act of worship for you.' Allah تَبَارَكَوَتَعَالَى created me before you. I contain the Night of Decree in which Allah تَبَارَكَوَتَعَالَى bestows countless favours. Allah تَبَارَكَوَتَعَالَى calls out in the latter portion of the night, 'Is there anyone who asks of Me that I may bestow upon him? Is there anyone seeking forgiveness so that I may forgive him?' Are you not aware that Allah تَبَارَكَوَتَعَالَى has said 'O the one who wraps himself (in a shawl)! Stand (to perform salaah) throughout the night, except for a little!' Have you not heard Allah تَبَارَكَوَتَعَالَى say, 'Glorified be He who took His servant by night from Musjid Al-Haraam to the Musjid Al-Aqsa.'?"[214]

---

214 نزهة المجالس ٢/ ٩٠

CHAPTER ELEVEN

Inspirational Incidents regarding Love and Sacrifice for Rasulullah صَلَّى ٱللَّهُ عَلَيْهِ وَسَلَّمَ

THE LOVE AND SACRIFICE OF THE SAHAABAH FOR RASULULLAH صَلَّى ٱللَّهُ عَلَيْهِ وَسَلَّمَ

Incident One - The Love of Hazrat Abu Bakr Siddeeq رَضِيَ ٱللَّهُ عَنْهُ for Hazrat Rasulullah صَلَّى ٱللَّهُ عَلَيْهِ وَسَلَّمَ

Rasulullah صَلَّى ٱللَّهُ عَلَيْهِ وَسَلَّمَ and Hazrat Abu Bakr Siddeeq رَضِيَ ٱللَّهُ عَنْهُ set out for the hijrah early at night. During the journey, at times Hazrat Abu Bakr Siddeeq رَضِيَ ٱللَّهُ عَنْهُ walked ahead of Hazrat Rasulullah صَلَّى ٱللَّهُ عَلَيْهِ وَسَلَّمَ, and at times behind. At times, he walked on the right of Hazrat Rasulullah صَلَّى ٱللَّهُ عَلَيْهِ وَسَلَّمَ and at times, on the left.

When Hazrat Rasulullah صَلَّى ٱللَّهُ عَلَيْهِ وَسَلَّمَ noticed this peculiar behaviour, he asked, "O Abu Bakr! I see you moving in front of me or behind me at times and beside me at times. What prompts you to behave in this way?" Hazrat Abu Bakr Siddeeq رَضِىَٱللَّهُعَنْهُ replied, "Whenever the thought of the enemy pursuing you from the back occurs to me, I move swiftly towards the back, and whenever the fear overcomes me of the enemy waiting ahead in ambush, then I rush ahead of you. Likewise, when the thought crosses my mind of the enemy attacking from the right or left, then I move in that direction."

Hazrat Rasulullah صَلَّىٱللَّهُعَلَيْهِوَسَلَّمَ then said, "O Abu Bakr! Do you prefer that your life be sacrificed for me?" Hazrat Abu Bakr Siddeeq رَضِىَٱللَّهُعَنْهُ replied, "Most definitely O Messenger of Allah, I swear by the Being who has sent you with the truth of Islam!" [215]

Incident Two - Hazrat Abu Bakr رَضِىَٱللَّهُعَنْهُ Giving Milk to Hazrat Rasulullah صَلَّىٱللَّهُعَلَيْهِوَسَلَّمَ

Hazrat Abu Bakr Siddeeq رَضِىَٱللَّهُعَنْهُ relates regarding the journey of hijrah with Hazrat Rasulullah صَلَّىٱللَّهُعَلَيْهِوَسَلَّمَ:

We travelled hastily the entire day and night until the afternoon heat became intense. I then found the road to be empty and no one was walking on it, I looked ahead to see whether I could find any shade so that we could take shelter in it. I then spotted a cave in which we could take refuge and seek shelter from the heat. I then said, "O Rasulullah صَلَّىٱللَّهُعَلَيْهِوَسَلَّمَ, remain outside the cave and allow me to enter so that if there is any harmful creature in the cave, it will harm me and not you."

[215] المستدرك على الصحيحين للحاكم، الرقم: ٤٢٦٨، وقال: هذا حديث صحيح الإسناد على شرط الشيخين لولا إرسال فيه ولم يخرجاه وقال الذهبي: صحيح مرسل

After entering the cave, I began cleaning it and spread out a cloth upon which Rasulullah ﷺ could lie down. I then requested him to enter and take a rest and he acceded to my request.

Once Rasulullah ﷺ lay down to rest, I went to see whether I could spot anyone who was searching for us. I then spotted a slave shepherd nearby and asked him who his owner was. He named a man from Makkah whom I knew. (As it was a prevalent custom at that time that people would allow travellers and wayfarers to benefit from the milk from their flock, Hazrat Abu Bakr Siddeeq رضي الله عنه requested for some milk and the following dialogue ensued):

Hazrat Abu Bakr Siddeeq رضي الله عنه: "Do any of the goats have milk?"

The shepherd: "Yes."

Hazrat Abu Bakr Siddeeq رضي الله عنه: "Will you milk some for me?"

He agreed, and milked one of the goats for me and poured it into my container. I added some water to the milk to cool the hot milk. I then took the milk to present it to Rasulullah ﷺ. As I approached Rasulullah ﷺ, I found him awake. I said, "Partake of this, O Rasulullah ﷺ." The sight of Rasulullah ﷺ relishing the milk brought extreme joy and happiness to my heart." [216]

---

[216] صحيح البخاري، الرقم: ٣٦١٥، صحيح مسلم، الرقم: ٢٠١٤

Incident Three - Hazrat Abu Bakr Siddeeq رَضِىَ اللّٰهُ عَنْهُ in the cave of Thaur

While in the cave on the journey of hijrah, it is reported that Hazrat Abu Bakr Siddeeq رَضِىَ اللّٰهُ عَنْهُ was concerned that no creature should come out from any hole in the cave and harm Hazrat Rasulullah صَلَّى اللّٰهُ عَلَيْهِ وَسَلَّمَ. Thus, he began closing all the holes inside the cave with pieces of his lower garment. However, there were still two holes which he was unable to close (due to insufficient clothing), so Hazrat Abu Bakr Siddeeq رَضِىَ اللّٰهُ عَنْهُ placed both his feet in those holes. Thereafter, Hazrat Rasulullah صَلَّى اللّٰهُ عَلَيْهِ وَسَلَّمَ placed his mubaarak head on the lap of Hazrat Abu Bakr Siddeeq رَضِىَ اللّٰهُ عَنْهُ and fell asleep.

While Hazrat Rasulullah صَلَّى اللّٰهُ عَلَيْهِ وَسَلَّمَ was asleep, Hazrat Abu Bakr Siddeeq رَضِىَ اللّٰهُ عَنْهُ perceived a bite under his foot by a snake in the hole. Not wishing to inconvenience and disturb the sleep of Hazrat Rasulullah صَلَّى اللّٰهُ عَلَيْهِ وَسَلَّمَ in the least, Hazrat Abu Bakr Siddeeq رَضِىَ اللّٰهُ عَنْهُ bore the pain and did not move an inch. However, being in excruciating pain and not being able to withstand the effects, tears began to uncontrollably roll down the face of Hazrat Abu Bakr Siddeeq رَضِىَ اللّٰهُ عَنْهُ and fell on the mubaarak countenance of Hazrat Rasulullah صَلَّى اللّٰهُ عَلَيْهِ وَسَلَّمَ.

Hazrat Rasulullah صَلَّى اللّٰهُ عَلَيْهِ وَسَلَّمَ suddenly awoke and asked, "What has happened, O Abu Bakr?" Hazrat Abu Bakr Siddeeq رَضِىَ اللّٰهُ عَنْهُ replied, "I have been bitten, may my parents be sacrificed for you, O Rasulullah صَلَّى اللّٰهُ عَلَيْهِ وَسَلَّمَ." Rasulullah صَلَّى اللّٰهُ عَلَيْهِ وَسَلَّمَ placed his mubaarak saliva on the affected area, and the pain immediately subsided.[217]

Incident Four – The Love of Hazrat Abu Bakr رضي الله عنه Conforming to the Love of Hazrat Rasulullah ﷺ

Hazrat Abu Bakr رضي الله عنه once addressed Hazrat Rasulullah ﷺ saying, "Though I am happy that my father embraced Islam, the happiness I would have experienced with the Islam of your uncle, Abu Taalib, would have been far greater. The reason is that if your uncle, Abu Taalib, embraced Islam, it would have brought great happiness to you." [218]

Incident Five - The Life and Wealth of Hazrat Abu Bakr رضي الله عنه being Sacrificed for Hazrat Rasulullah ﷺ

Hazrat Abu Hurairah رضي الله عنه reports that once Hazrat Rasulullah ﷺ said, "No person's wealth benefitted me as much as the wealth of Abu Bakr Siddeeq رضي الله عنه." Upon hearing this, Hazrat Abu Bakr Siddeeq رضي الله عنه wept profusely and said, "O Rasulullah ﷺ, certainly my entire life and wealth belongs to you." [219]

---

[217] مشكوة المصابيح عن رزين الرقم: ٦٠٣٤، شرح البخاري للسفيري ١٣٩/١

[218] مسند البزار، الرقم: ٦١٣١

[219] سنن ابن ماجة، الرقم: ٩٤، وهذا إسناد رجاله ثقات كما في مصباح الزجاجة ١٦/١

Incident Six - Hazrat Abu Bakr ﷺ being Prepared to Sacrifice Everything for Hazrat Rasulullah ﷺ

During the battle of Badr, Hazrat Abu Bakr Siddeeq's ﷺ son, Hazrat Abdur Rahmaan ﷺ, fought on the side of the disbelievers as he had not yet accepted Islam.

Later, after embracing Islam, whilst seated with his father, Hazrat Abu Bakr Siddeeq ﷺ, he exclaimed, "O my beloved father, during the battle of Badr, you came under my sword a few times. However, considering you being my father, I spared you."

Hazrat Abu Bakr Siddeeq ﷺ spontaneously retorted, "Had you come under my sword during the battle, I would have never spared you, as you were fighting against Rasulullah ﷺ."[220]

Incident Seven - The love of Sahaabah ﷺ for Hazrat Rasulullah ﷺ

Somebody once asked Hazrat Ali ﷺ, "How much love did the Sahaabah ﷺ really possess for Rasulullah ﷺ?"

Hazrat Ali ﷺ replied, "I take a qasm on Allah ﷺ, Rasulullah ﷺ was more beloved and dearer to us than our riches, our children and our mothers, and his company was more cherished than a drink of cold water at the time of severest thirst."[221]

---

[220] تاريخ الخلفاء ٣٣/١

[221] الشفاء بتعريف حقوق المصطفى ٥٢/٢

Incident Eight - The Love of Hazrat Zaid bin Dathinah رضي الله عنه for Hazrat Rasulullah ﷺ

When the disbelievers were about to execute the great Sahaabi, Hazrat Zaid bin Dathinah رضي الله عنه, they asked him, "Would you be happier if Muhammad ﷺ was in your place and you were left free to be with your family?"

His spontaneous response was, "By Allah تبارك وتعالى, I cannot even bear that I be sitting comfortably with my family while even a thorn is pricking Rasulullah ﷺ." On hearing this, Abu Sufyaan remarked, "There is no parallel anywhere in the world to the love which the companions of Muhammad ﷺ have for him." [222]

Incident Nine - Love of Hazrat Uthmaan رضي الله عنه for Hazrat Rasulullah ﷺ

On the occasion of Hudaybiyah, Hazrat Uthmaan رضي الله عنه was commissioned by Hazrat Rasulullah ﷺ to negotiate with the Quraish in Makkah Mukarramah. When Hazrat Uthmaan رضي الله عنه had left for Makkah Mukarramah, some of the Sahaabah رضي الله عنهم envied Hazrat Uthmaan رضي الله عنه for being able to perform tawaaf of the House of Allah تبارك وتعالى. On the other hand, Hazrat Rasulullah ﷺ remarked, "I do not think he will ever desire to perform tawaaf without me." [223]

[222] سيرة ابن هشام ٢/١٧٢

[223] كنز العمال، الرقم: ٣٠١٥٢

When Hazrat Uthmaan رَضِىَ اللهُ عَنْهُ entered Makkah Mukarramah, Abaan bin Sa'eed took him into his protection and said to him, "You may move around freely wherever you wish. Nobody here can touch you."

Hazrat Uthmaan رَضِىَ اللهُ عَنْهُ carried out his negotiations with Abu Sufyaan and the other chiefs of Makkah Mukarramah on behalf of Hazrat Rasulullah صَلَّى اللهُ عَلَيْهِ وَسَلَّمَ, and when he was about to return, the Quraish themselves said to him, "Now when you are here in Makkah Mukarramah, you can perform tawaaf before you return." Hazrat Uthmaan رَضِىَ اللهُ عَنْهُ replied, "How can it ever be possible for me to perform tawaaf (without Hazrat Rasulullah صَلَّى اللهُ عَلَيْهِ وَسَلَّمَ)?"

This reply was most unpalatable for the Quraish and they decided to detain Hazrat Uthmaan رَضِىَ اللهُ عَنْهُ in Makkah Mukarramah. News had reached the Muslims that Hazrat Uthmaan رَضِىَ اللهُ عَنْهُ had been martyred. On this news reaching Hazrat Rasulullah صَلَّى اللهُ عَلَيْهِ وَسَلَّمَ, he took the oath of allegiance from all the Sahaabah رَضِىَ اللهُ عَنْهُمْ to fight till the last drop of their blood. When the Quraish learnt of this, fear overcame them and they immediately released Hazrat Uthmaan رَضِىَ اللهُ عَنْهُ.[224]

Incident Ten – The Love of a Sahaabi for Hazrat Rasulullah صَلَّى اللهُ عَلَيْهِ وَسَلَّمَ

A Sahaabi once came to Hazrat Rasulullah صَلَّى اللهُ عَلَيْهِ وَسَلَّمَ and asked, "O Rasulullah صَلَّى اللهُ عَلَيْهِ وَسَلَّمَ, when is the day of Qiyaamah?" Hazrat

[224] مسند أحمد، الرقم: ١٨٩١٠

Rasulullah ﷺ replied, "What preparations have you made for that day?" The Sahaabi said, "O Rasulullah ﷺ, I do not claim to have much salaah, fasts and sadaqah to my credit, but I do have the love of Allah تَبَارَكَوَتَعَالَ and His Messenger ﷺ in my heart." Hazrat Rasulullah ﷺ then said, "Surely on the day of Qiyaamah, you will be with those whom you love." [225]

Hazrat Anas رَضِىَٱللَّهُعَنْهُ says, "Nothing made the Sahaabah رَضِىَٱللَّهُعَنْهُمْ happier than these words of Rasulullah ﷺ." [226]

Incident Eleven - Hazrat Ummu Sulaym رَضِىَٱللَّهُعَنْهَا and the Mubaarak Perspiration of Hazrat Rasulullah ﷺ

Hazrat Ummu Sulaym رَضِىَٱللَّهُعَنْهَا (who was a mahram of Hazrat Rasulullah ﷺ) narrates that once, Hazrat Rasulullah ﷺ visited her, and took his afternoon rest (qayloolah) at her home. Whilst sleeping, Hazrat Rasulullah ﷺ began perspiring.

She narrates that she took a small bottle and began collecting his blessed perspiration. When Rasulullah ﷺ awoke and asked her what she was doing, she informed Rasulullah ﷺ that she was collecting his blessed perspiration, as there was no fragrance sweeter than it. Rasulullah ﷺ permitted her to do so and did not disapprove of this action. [227]

[225] صحيح البخاري، الرقم: ٦١٦٧

[226] سنن الترمذي، الرقم: ٢٣٨٥، وقال: هذا حديث حسن صحيح

[227] صحيح مسلم الرقم: ٢٣٣٢

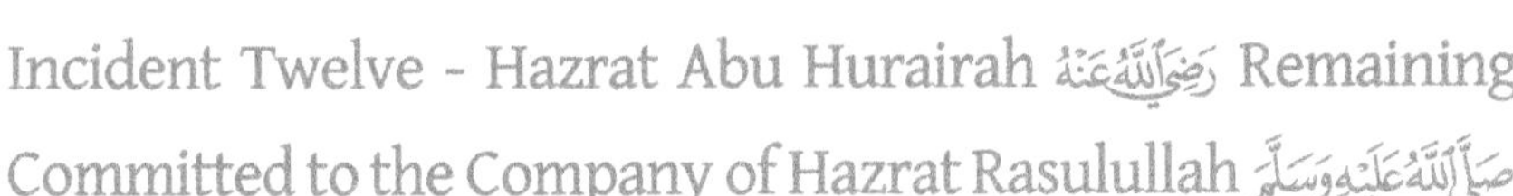

Incident Twelve - Hazrat Abu Hurairah رَضِىَٱللَّهُعَنْهُ Remaining Committed to the Company of Hazrat Rasulullah صَلَّىٱللَّهُعَلَيْهِوَسَلَّمَ

Hazrat Abu Hurairah رَضِىَٱللَّهُعَنْهُ is a famous Sahaabi of Hazrat Rasulullah صَلَّىٱللَّهُعَلَيْهِوَسَلَّمَ. No other Sahaabi has narrated as many Ahaadith as he has done. He embraced Islam in 7 A.H. and since Hazrat Rasulullah صَلَّىٱللَّهُعَلَيْهِوَسَلَّمَ passed away in 11 A.H., he had been with him for only four years. People used to marvel at how he could remember so many Ahaadith in such a short period.

He explains this himself saying:

People wonder how I narrate so many Ahaadith. The fact is that my Muhaajir brothers remained busy in trade and my Ansaar brothers did their farming, while I was always with Rasulullah صَلَّىٱللَّهُعَلَيْهِوَسَلَّمَ. I was among the people of Suffah. I was not concerned with earning a livelihood, and constantly remained with Rasulullah صَلَّىٱللَّهُعَلَيْهِوَسَلَّمَ, being content with whatever little food I received. I would be with Rasulullah صَلَّىٱللَّهُعَلَيْهِوَسَلَّمَ at times when no one else was there.

I once complained to Rasulullah صَلَّىٱللَّهُعَلَيْهِوَسَلَّمَ about my poor memory. He said to me, "Spread out your shawl." I immediately did so. He thereafter made some signs with his mubaarak hands on my shawl and said, "Now wrap this shawl around you." I wrapped it around my chest. Since then, I have not forgotten anything that I have wished to remember. [228]

---

[228] صحيح البخاري، الرقم: ٢٠٤٧

Incident Thirteen - Hazrat Abu Ubaidah رَضِىَ اللهُ عَنْهُ loses His Teeth.

During the battle of Uhud, Rasulullah ﷺ was severely attacked by the enemy and two links of his helmet penetrated his mubaarak face.

Hazrat Abu Bakr Siddeeq رَضِىَ اللهُ عَنْهُ and Hazrat Abu Ubaidah رَضِىَ اللهُ عَنْهُ immediately ran to assist Rasulullah ﷺ. Hazrat Abu Ubaidah رَضِىَ اللهُ عَنْهُ began pulling out the links with his teeth. By the time one of the links was removed, he had lost one of his teeth. Not regretting the loss of his tooth, he again used his teeth to pull out the other link as well. He succeeded in removing the other link, however in the process, he lost another tooth.

When the links were drawn out, the blood began to ooze out from the body of Rasulullah ﷺ. Hazrat Malik bin Sinaan رَضِىَ اللهُ عَنْهُ, the father of Hazrat Abu Sa'eed Khudri رَضِىَ اللهُ عَنْهُ, licked the blood with his lips. At this, Rasulullah ﷺ remarked, "The fire of Hell cannot touch the person who has my blood mixed with his."[229]

[229] مسند أبي داود الطيالسي، الرقم: ٦، فتح الباري ٣٦٦/٧، الآحاد والمثاني لابن أبي عاصم، الرقم: ٢٠٩٧

Incident Fourteen - Hazrat Talhah رَضِيَ ٱللَّهُ عَنْهُ in the Battle of Uhud

Hazrat Zubair bin Awwaam رَضِيَ ٱللَّهُ عَنْهُ reports that Hazrat Rasulullah صَلَّى ٱللَّهُ عَلَيْهِ وَسَلَّمَ wore two suits of armour on his mubaarak body in the battle of Uhud.

During the battle, Hazrat Rasulullah صَلَّى ٱللَّهُ عَلَيْهِ وَسَلَّمَ intended climbing a rock, but was unable to do so. He therefore requested Hazrat Talhah رَضِيَ ٱللَّهُ عَنْهُ to sit, and with his assistance, he climbed the rock. Hazrat Zubair رَضِيَ ٱللَّهُ عَنْهُ says that he heard Hazrat Rasulullah صَلَّى ٱللَّهُ عَلَيْهِ وَسَلَّمَ say, "It has become waajib for Talhah (i.e. Jannah or the intercession of Hazrat Rasulullah صَلَّى ٱللَّهُ عَلَيْهِ وَسَلَّمَ is waajib for Talhah)."[230]

In the battle of Uhud, Hazrat Talhah رَضِيَ ٱللَّهُ عَنْهُ very bravely accompanied and protected Hazrat Rasulullah صَلَّى ٱللَّهُ عَلَيْهِ وَسَلَّمَ. Whenever the Sahaabah رَضِيَ ٱللَّهُ عَنْهُمْ discussed the battle of Uhud, they would say that this day belonged to Hazrat Talhah رَضِيَ ٱللَّهُ عَنْهُ. Hazrat Talhah رَضِيَ ٱللَّهُ عَنْهُ shielded Hazrat Rasulullah صَلَّى ٱللَّهُ عَلَيْهِ وَسَلَّمَ with his body. He received more than eighty wounds on his body, yet he did not leave the side of Hazrat Rasulullah صَلَّى ٱللَّهُ عَلَيْهِ وَسَلَّمَ, even though his hand had become paralyzed.[231]

---

[230] سنن الترمذي، الرقم: ١٦٩٢، و قال هذا حديث حسن غريب لا نعرفه إلا من حديث محمد بن اسحاق

[231] مسند أبي داود الطيالسي، الرقم: ٦، وقال الحافظ: الحديث بهذا الاسناد ضعيف كما في المطالب العلمية ٣٨٢/١٧، صحيح البخاري، الرقم: ٣٧٢٤

Incident Fifteen – Hazrat Anas bin Nadhr's رضى الله عنه Love for Hazrat Rasulullah ﷺ and his Martyrdom in Uhud

When the Muslims were facing defeat in Uhud, the rumour began spreading that Hazrat Rasulullah ﷺ had been killed. This news caused many of the Sahaabah رضى الله عنهم to despair and lose heart.

Hazrat Anas bin Nadhr رضى الله عنه happened to see Hazrat Umar and Hazrat Talhah رضى الله عنهما with a group of Sahaabah رضى الله عنهم in a state of utter grief and despondency. He said to them, "Why am I seeing you all so despondent and grieved?" They replied, "Rasulullah ﷺ has been slain."

Hazrat Anas رضى الله عنه exclaimed, "Then who would like to live after him? Come, let us go forward with our swords and join our beloved, the Messenger ﷺ!" No sooner did he utter these words than he plunged into the enemy lines and fought bravely till he was martyred.

Hazrat Anas رضى الله عنه had such extreme love for Hazrat Rasulullah ﷺ that he did not consider this life worth living without him. [232]

---

232 دلائل النبوة ٣/٢٤٥

Incident Sixteen – The Message of Hazrat Sa'd رَضِىَٱللَّهُعَنْهُ for The Muslims.

During the battle of Uhud, Hazrat Rasulullah صَلَّىٱللَّهُعَلَيْهِوَسَلَّمَ inquired, "Where is Sa'd bin Rabee? I do not know of his condition." Thereafter, one of the Sahaabah رَضِىَٱللَّهُعَنْهُمْ was sent to search for him. He went to the spot where the bodies of the martyrs were laying.

He shouted Hazrat Sa'd's رَضِىَٱللَّهُعَنْهُ name to see if he was alive. At one place, while he was announcing that he was deputed by Hazrat Rasulullah صَلَّىٱللَّهُعَلَيْهِوَسَلَّمَ to enquire about Hazrat Sa'd bin Rabee رَضِىَٱللَّهُعَنْهُ, he heard a feeble voice coming from one direction. He turned to that direction and found that Hazrat Sa'd رَضِىَٱللَّهُعَنْهُ was lying among the martyrs and was about to breathe his last.

Hazrat Sa'd رَضِىَٱللَّهُعَنْهُ was heard saying, "Convey my salaam to Rasulullah صَلَّىٱللَّهُعَلَيْهِوَسَلَّمَ with the following message, 'O Rasulullah صَلَّىٱللَّهُعَلَيْهِوَسَلَّمَ, may Allah تَبَارَكَوَتَعَالَ grant you, on my behalf, a reward more exalted and more handsome than any reward that Allah تَبَارَكَوَتَعَالَ has ever granted a Messenger on behalf of any of his followers.'"

Thereafter, he said to the one who was sent to search for him, "Inform my Muslim brothers that nothing will absolve them from blame on the day of Qiyaamah if the enemy succeeds in reaching Rasulullah صَلَّىٱللَّهُعَلَيْهِوَسَلَّمَ and killing him before all of them die." With these words, Hazrat Sa'd رَضِىَٱللَّهُعَنْهُ breathed his last and departed from the world.[233]

---

[233] موطأ الإمام مالك، الرقم: ١٦٩١، تاريخ الطبري ٢/٥٢٨

The Sahaabah رضى الله عنهم have given a true proof of their devotion to Hazrat Rasulullah ﷺ. While they suffered wound after wound and were on their last breath, they had no complaint nor wish on their lips and could not think of anything else except the safety and welfare of Hazrat Rasulullah ﷺ. May we be blessed with an atom of the true love that the Sahaabah رضى الله عنهم bore for Hazrat Rasulullah ﷺ.[234]

Incident Seventeen – Sahaabah رضى الله عنهم Emulating the Mubaarak Sunnah of Rasulullah ﷺ in Everything

Once, a person said to Hazrat Ibnu Umar رضى الله عنهما, "Allah تبارك وتعالى has made mention in the Quraan regarding salaah in peace and salaah in fear, but He has not made mention regarding salaah during a journey."

Hazrat Ibnu Umar رضى الله عنهما replied, "O my nephew! Allah تبارك وتعالى sent Muhammad ﷺ as His Messenger to us when we were ignorant and knew nothing. We should follow him in everything he did."[235]

Note: Hazrat Shaikh Moulana Muhammad Zakariyya Kandhelwi رحمه الله mentioned, "This shows that it is not necessary that each and every law be explicitly found in the Quraan Majeed. The life of Hazrat Rasulullah ﷺ and his actions are a guide for us to follow. Hazrat Rasulullah ﷺ said, "I have been given the

<hr>

234 فضائل اعمال ص ١٧٠

235 صحيح ابن حبان، الرقم: ٢٧٣٥

Quraan Majeed and also other commandments. Beware of the time which is coming shortly when carefree people sitting on their couches will say, 'Stick to the Quraan Majeed only. Carry out only the commandments contained therein.'" [236]

Incident Eighteen - An Ansaari Woman's Anxiety about Hazrat Rasulullah ﷺ

In the battle of Uhud, the Muslims suffered heavy losses and quite a large number of them were killed. When the news of their heavy casualties reached Madinah Munawwarah, the women came out of their homes eager to know the details of the war.

On seeing the large crowd of people gathered at a certain place, a woman of the Ansaar anxiously inquired, "How is Rasulullah ﷺ?" When she was told that her father was killed in the battle, she uttered 'Inna lillahi wa inna ilaihi raaji'oon' and impatiently repeated the same question about Hazrat Rasulullah ﷺ.

This time, she was told that her husband was no more, her brother was dead and that her son too was slain. With ever-growing anxiety, she repeated the same question about the welfare of Hazrat Rasulullah ﷺ.

She was told that he was safe and sound, but she would not rest contented, and insisted on seeing him herself. When at last she had satisfied her eyes with his sight, she said:

كُلُّ مُصِيْبَةٍ بَعْدَكَ جَلَلٌ

"O Rasulullah ﷺ, with the blessing of seeing you, every affliction is eased and every worry is removed." [237]

Incident Nineteen - Hazrat Abdullah bin Amr رضي الله عنه Burns His Sheet

Hazrat Abdullah bin Amr bin Aas رضي الله عنهما says:

Once, we were accompanying Rasulullah ﷺ on a journey. I went to see him and I was wearing a saffron coloured sheet. He asked me, "What is this that you are wearing?" I felt that he did not like my wearing a cloth of that colour. Hence, when I reached home and found a fire burning, I threw my garment into the fire.

The next day, when I went to Hazrat Rasulullah ﷺ, he inquired, "Where is that sheet?" On informing him of what I had done with it, he remarked, "You could have given it to one of the ladies in your house. Women are permitted to wear clothes of that colour." [238]

Hazrat Abdullah bin Amr bin Aas رضي الله عنهما was so perturbed at Hazrat Rasulullah's ﷺ displeasure that he did not hesitate to avail of the first opportunity of doing away with the sheet that caused the displeasure. He did not even think of finding any other use for that garment. If we had been in his place, we would have

---

[237] الكامل في التاريخ ٢/٥٢

[238] سنن أبي داود، الرقم: ٤٠٦٦

thought of some excuse or the other for keeping it, or at least finding some other use for it.

Incident Twenty - An Ansaari razes a building to the ground

Hazrat Rasulullah ﷺ was once passing through a street of Madinah Munawwarah when he saw a building with a dome. He inquired from the Sahaabah رضي الله عنهم, "What is this?" They informed him that it was a new building built by one of the Ansaar. Hazrat Rasulullah ﷺ remained silent.

At another time, the Ansaari who had built that house came to Hazrat Rasulullah ﷺ and greeted him with salaam. However, Hazrat Rasulullah ﷺ turned his face away from him. He repeated the Salaam, but Hazrat Rasulullah ﷺ again did not respond. This Sahaabi رضي الله عنه was extremely concerned on account of Hazrat Rasulullah ﷺ not responding to his salaam.

When he enquired from the Sahaabah رضي الله عنه, he was informed that Hazrat Rasulullah ﷺ passed by the new building that he had constructed and inquired about it. He immediately went and razed the new building to the ground, and did not even inform Hazrat Rasulullah ﷺ about his action.

Sometime later, Hazrat Rasulullah ﷺ happened to pass that way again. He inquired, "Where is that building with a dome that I remember seeing the last time we passed by this spot?" The Sahaabah رضي الله عنهم informed him of the Ansaari razing it to the ground, as he felt that it was the cause of Rasulullah's ﷺ displeasure. At that juncture, Hazrat Rasulullah ﷺ remarked, "Every structure (which is constructed without a real need) will be a burden for one, except that structure which is absolutely essential."

The conduct of the Sahaabi exhibited true love and devotion. The Sahaabah رضى الله عنهم could not bear the displeasure of Hazrat Rasulullah ﷺ, and no sooner did they sense the displeasure of Hazrat Rasulullah ﷺ through any action, they immediately abandoned that action at all costs. [239]

Incident Twenty One - Sahaabah's رضى الله عنهم Deep Love for Hazrat Rasulullah ﷺ

When the treaty of Hudaybiyah was being negotiated, Urwah bin Mas'ood رضى الله عنه, an envoy of the Quraish (who at the time of the treaty of Hudaybiyyah had not yet embraced Islam), had an opportunity of witnessing the conduct of the Sahaabah رضى الله عنهم with Hazrat Rasulullah ﷺ. When he returned to his people, he said to them:

I have been to the courts of great kings and monarchs as an envoy. I have met the Emperors of Persia, Rome and Abyssinia. Nowhere have I seen people around a sovereign so respectful to him as I saw the companions of Muhammad ﷺ.

---

[239] سنن أبي داود، الرقم: ٥٢٣٧، وإسناده جيد كما قال العراقي في المغني عن حمل الأسفار في الأسفار ٢/١١١٥

When he spits, his mubaarak saliva is not allowed to fall on the ground. It is taken by somebody in his hands to anoint his face and body therewith (in order to acquire blessings). When he issues some order, every person hastens to carry it out. When he makes wudhu, his companions race with one another to snatch the water trickling down from his limbs, in such a way that an observer would think they are going to fight over that water. When he speaks, everybody is silent (out of respect). Nobody raises his eyes to look at him, out of respect for him. [240]

Incident Twenty Two - Hazrat Waa'il رَضِيَ ٱللَّهُ عَنْهُ Has His Hair Cut

Hazrat Waa'il bin Hujar رَضِيَ ٱللَّهُ عَنْهُ says:

I once visited Rasulullah صَلَّى ٱللَّهُ عَلَيْهِ وَسَلَّمَ when the hair on my head was extremely long. While I was sitting with him, he uttered the words, "Zubaab, Zubaab" (meaning something evil). I thought that he was referring to my hair. I returned home and immediately had my hair cut.

The next day, when I went to visit him again, he said, "I was not referring to your hair when I uttered those words yesterday. Anyway, it is good that you had your hair cut." [241]

---

[240] صحيح البخاري، الرقم: ٢٧٣١

[241] سنن أبي داود، الرقم: ٤١٩٠، وفي إسناده عاصم بن كليب الجرمي وقد احتج به مسلم في صحيحه كما في مختصر سنن أبي داود للمنذري، الرقم: ٤١٩٠)

This action of this Sahaabi رضي الله عنه reflects the true love he possessed for Hazrat Rasulullah ﷺ within his heart. No sooner did he doubt that Hazrat Rasulullah ﷺ was displeased with him on account of his long hair, he immediately had his hair cut. One can well imagine that if this was the level of the love they possessed, where just a mere doubt of Hazrat Rasulullah's ﷺ displeasure would make them uneasy, then could it have been possible for them to disobey the command of Hazrat Rasulullah ﷺ or go against his mubaarak sunnah?

Incident Twenty Three - Wearing the Pants above the Ankles

Suhail bin Hanzalah رضي الله عنه once mentioned:

On one occasion, Rasulullah ﷺ made mention of Khuraim Asadi رضي الله عنه and said, "He is a good man except for two habits viz. he keeps the hair of his head too long and he allows his izaar (lower garment) to go below his ankles."

When Khuraim رضي الله عنه learnt of this, he immediately cut his hair up to his ears and began to keep his izaar up to the middle of the calf of his leg. [242]

[242] سنن أبي داود، الرقم: ٤٠٨٩، وإسناده حسن كما في رياض الصالحين ص ٢٦٠

Incident Twenty Four - Hazrat Hakeem bin Hizaam رَضِيَٱللَّهُعَنْهُ Gives up Begging

Hazrat Hakeem bin Hizaam رَضِيَٱللَّهُعَنْهُ once came to Hazrat Rasulullah صَلَّىٱللَّهُعَلَيْهِوَسَلَّمَ and begged him for some assistance. Hazrat Rasulullah صَلَّىٱللَّهُعَلَيْهِوَسَلَّمَ gave him something. Thereafter, he again came and asked for something from Hazrat Rasulullah صَلَّىٱللَّهُعَلَيْهِوَسَلَّمَ, and Hazrat Rasulullah صَلَّىٱللَّهُعَلَيْهِوَسَلَّمَ gave him something on this occasion as well.

When he came to beg for the third time, Hazrat Rasulullah صَلَّىٱللَّهُعَلَيْهِوَسَلَّمَ gave him something and then said, "O Hakeem! Money has a deceptive appearance. It appears to be very sweet (but it is really not so). It is a blessing when earned with contentment of heart, but there is no satisfaction in it when it is acquired with greed (begging etc)." Hazrat Hakeem رَضِيَٱللَّهُعَنْهُ said, "O Rasulullah صَلَّىٱللَّهُعَلَيْهِوَسَلَّمَ, I will not beg again from anyone after this." [243]

Incident Twenty Five - Hazrat Bilaal رَضِيَٱللَّهُعَنْهُ returns to Madinah Tayyibah

After Hazrat Rasulullah صَلَّىٱللَّهُعَلَيْهِوَسَلَّمَ passed away, it became extremely difficult for Hazrat Bilaal رَضِيَٱللَّهُعَنْهُ to remain in Madinah Tayyibah. This was on account of the deep love that he possessed for Hazrat Rasulullah صَلَّىٱللَّهُعَلَيْهِوَسَلَّمَ. Remaining in Madinah Munawwara caused him to remember Hazrat Rasulullah صَلَّىٱللَّهُعَلَيْهِوَسَلَّمَ at every step and every corner. He therefore left

---

243 
صحيح البخاري، الرقم: ١٤٧٢

Madinah Tayyibah and decided to pass the rest of his life striving in the path of Allah تَبَارَكَ وَتَعَالَى.

Once he saw Hazrat Rasulullah ﷺ in his dream saying to him, "O Bilaal, why is it that you have become estranged from me (i.e. you do not visit me)?" He immediately set out for Madinah Tayyibah.

On reaching there, Hazrat Hasan and Hazrat Husain رَضِيَ اللّٰهُ عَنْهُمَا, the grandchildren of Hazrat Rasulullah ﷺ, requested him to call out the azaan. He could not refuse them, for they were very dear and beloved to him.

As soon as the azaan was called, the people of Madinah Tayyibah cried openly in remembrance of the time of Hazrat Rasulullah ﷺ. Hazrat Bilaal رَضِيَ اللّٰهُ عَنْهُ left Madinah Tayyibah again after a few days and passed away in Damascus in the year 20 A.H. [244]

---

[244] عن أبي الدرداء قال: لما دخل عمر بن الخطاب من فتح بيت المقدس فصار إلى الجابية سأل بلالٌ أن يقرّئه بالشام ففعل ذلك قال: وأخى أبو رويحة الذي آخا بيني وبينه رسول الله ﷺ فنزل داربا في خولان فأقبل هو وأخوه إلى قوم من خولان فقال لهم قد أتيناكم خاطبين وقد كنا كافرين فهدانا الله ومملوكين لله فأعتقنا الله وفقيرين فأغنانا الله فإن تزوجونا فالحمد لله وإن تردُّونا فلا حول ولا قوة إلا بالله فزَوَّجوهما ثم إن بلالا رأى في منامه رسولَ الله ﷺ وهو يقول له: ما هذه الجفوة يا بلال أما آنَ لك أن تزورني يا بلال؟ فانتَبَه حزيناً وجلاً خائفا فكب راحلته وقصد المدينة فأتى قبر النبي ﷺ فجعل يبكي عنده ويمرغ وجهه عليه فأقبل الحسن والحسين رضي الله عنهما فجعل يضمّهما ويقبّلهما فقالا له : نشتهي نسمع أذانك الذي كنت تؤذن به لرسول الله ﷺ في المسجد ففعل فعلا سطح المسجد فوقف موقفه الذي كان يقف فيه فلما أن قال: الله أكبر الله أكبر ارتَجّت المدينة فلما أن قال: أشهد أن لا إله إلا الله ازداد رجتها فلما أن قال: أشهد أن محمدا رسول الله خرجت العوالي من خدورهن وقالوا: أبُعِث رسول الله فما رأي يوما أكبر باكيا ولا ناكهة بالمدينة بعد رسول الله من ذلك اليوم . رواه ابن عساكر وقال التقي السبكي في شفاء السقام: إسناده جيد. قال الشيخ المحدث حبيب أحمد الكيرانوي رحمه الله: وهذا الحديث مما تعارَضَ فيه رأيا الحافظَين: الحافظ تقي الدين السبكي ، فجوّد إسناده واحتج به في شفاء السقام ، والحافظ ابن حجر ، وهو من تلامذة أصحاب السبكي ، فإنه قد حكم على هذه القصة بالوضع ، حيث قال في اللسان ١ / ١٠٨ في ترجمة (إبراهيم بن محمد بن سليمان بن بلال بن أبي الدرداء) : ترجم له ابن عساكر ، ثم ساق من روايته عن أبيه عن جده عن أم الدرداء عن أبي الدرداء في قصة رحيل بلال إلى الشام ، وفي قصة مجيئه إلى المدينة ، وأذانه بها وارتحاج بالبكاء لذلك ، وهي قصة بيّنة الوضع . وتبعه السيوطي في ذيل اللآلى ص ١٠٤ ، وتبعه علي القاري في موضوعاته ص ٨٨ .

تأييد السبكي :

Incident Twenty Six - The Sacrifice of the Sahaabah صَلَّى ٱللَّهُ عَلَيْهِ وَسَلَّمَ for Hazrat Rasulullah رَضِيَ ٱللَّهُ عَنْهُم

Hazrat Faatimah's رَضِيَ ٱللَّهُ عَنْهَا house was a distance away from the house of Hazrat Rasulullah صَلَّى ٱللَّهُ عَلَيْهِ وَسَلَّمَ. Hazrat Rasulullah صَلَّى ٱللَّهُ عَلَيْهِ وَسَلَّمَ once said to her, "It is my desire that you live near me." Hazrat Faatimah رَضِيَ ٱللَّهُ عَنْهَا replied, "Haarithah's house is close to your house. If you ask him to exchange his house with mine, he will happily accept." Hazrat Rasulullah صَلَّى ٱللَّهُ عَلَيْهِ وَسَلَّمَ replied, "He has already exchanged once on my request. I feel shy to request him a second time."

However, Hazrat Haarithah رَضِيَ ٱللَّهُ عَنْهُ somehow came to know that Hazrat Rasulullah صَلَّى ٱللَّهُ عَلَيْهِ وَسَلَّمَ was desirous that Hazrat Faatimah رَضِيَ ٱللَّهُ عَنْهَا live close to him. He at once came to Hazrat Rasulullah صَلَّى ٱللَّهُ عَلَيْهِ وَسَلَّمَ and said, "O Rasulullah صَلَّى ٱللَّهُ عَلَيْهِ وَسَلَّمَ, I have come to know that you wish for Faatimah رَضِيَ ٱللَّهُ عَنْهَا to live near you. Here are my houses at your disposal. No other house is closer to yours than

---

ويؤيّد السبكيَّ قولُ الحافظ أبي محمد عبد الغني المقدسي رحمه الله في الكمال في ترجمة بلال : ولم يُؤذِّن لأحد بعد رسول الله ﷺ فيما رُوي إلا مرة واحدة في قدمة قدمها المدينة لزيارة قبر النبي ﷺ ، طلب إليه الصحابة ذلك ، فأذّن ولم يتم الأذان .

وذكره أيضا الحافظ أبو الحجاج المزي في شفاء السقام ص ٣٩ . وذكره الحافظ ابن الأثير في أسد الغابة جازما به ، فقال : (وروى أبو الدرداء أن عمر بن الخطاب لما رحل من فتح بيت المقدس) ، ولم يتعقبه بشيء ١ / ٢٠٨ . وجوّد إسناده القاضي الشوكاني في نيل أيضا ٤ / ٣٢٧ . وقدّمنا أن له معرفة بالموضوعات جيدة .

ولم يحكم عليها الذهبي بالوضع مع تعنّته وتقشّفه ؛ بل اكتفى بقوله في (إبراهيم بن محمد بن سليمان) : فيه جهالة ، روى عنه محمد بن فيض الغساني . من الميزان ١ / ٣٠ . والمراد بها جهالة الحال ، لا جهالة العين ، فإن جهالة العين قد ارتفعت بتحديث محمد بن فيض الغساني عنه ، وهو من أجلّة المحدثين في زمانه ، روى عنه أحمد ابن عدي وأبو أحمد الحاكم وأبو بكر بن المقرئ ، وهو كناه لهم بـ (أبي إسحاق) ، وأرّخَ وفاته سنة اثنين وثلاثين ومئتين . والراوي إذا عُرف باسمه وكنيته واسم أبيه وجده وتاريخ وفاته ، لا يبقى مجهول العين قطعا ، وإنما هو مستور ، إذا وثقه أحد من أهل الفن ولو مبهما ، كأن صحّح الإسناد الذي هو فيه ، أو جوّده أو حسّنه ، فهو ثقة عند المحدثين ، كما ذكرناه في المقدمة من قول الحافظ نفسه . ولم يجود السبكي إسناد الحديث إلا بعد البحث عن رجاله واحد بعد واحد ، كما في شفاء السقام ص ٤٠ .

وأما الحافظ ابن حجر فالظاهر من صنيعه أنه إنما حكم عليه بالوضع بمجرّد ذوقه ؛ لأنه لم يعين مَن وضعه ، ولم يتّهم أحدا من رواته ، ومثله لا يكون حجة إلا على من شهد ما شهد ذوقُه بمثل ما شهد به . (الإنصاف ص ٥١٤-٥١٦)

these houses of mine. Faatimah رضى الله عنها can have her house exchanged with any of my houses. O Rasulullah ﷺ, what you accept from me is dearer to me than what you leave for me."

Hazrat Rasulullah ﷺ accepted the offer saying, "I know that you are sincere in what you say", and Hazrat Rasulullah ﷺ made dua for him. [245]

Incident Twenty Seven - The Overwhelming love of the Sahaabah رضى الله عنهم for Hazrat Rasulullah ﷺ

Once, a person came to Hazrat Rasulullah ﷺ and said, "O Rasulullah ﷺ, my love for you is such that when I think of you, I am overwhelmed by your love, to the extent that I do not find any satisfaction until I see you. O Rasulullah ﷺ, the thought crosses my heart that if Allah تبارك وتعالى has to bless me with Paradise, it will be very difficult for me to see you, for you will be in a lofty position where I will not be able to reach."

Hazrat Rasulullah ﷺ consoled him by reciting the foregoing verses in his reply.

$$\text{وَمَنْ يُّطِعِ اللهَ وَالرَّسُوْلَ فَأُولٰٓئِكَ مَعَ الَّذِيْنَ اَنْعَمَ اللهُ عَلَيْهِمْ مِّنَ النَّبِيّٖنَ وَالصِّدِّيْقِيْنَ وَالشُّهَدَآءِ}$$

$$\text{وَالصّٰلِحِيْنَ ۚ وَحَسُنَ أُولٰٓئِكَ رَفِيْقًا ۝}$$

245 الطبقات الكبرى ٨/١٩

All those who obey Allah تَبَارَكَ وَتَعَالَى and the Messenger are in the company of those on whom is the Grace of Allah عَلَيْهِمُ ٱلسَّلَامُ; تَبَارَكَ وَتَعَالَى the Ambiyaa , *the Siddeeqeen, the martyrs, and the righteous.* [246]

Incident Twenty Eight - Longing for the Companionship of Hazrat Rasulullah صَلَّى ٱللَّهُ عَلَيْهِ وَسَلَّمَ

Once, a Sahaabi رَضِيَ ٱللَّهُ عَنْهُ came to Hazrat Rasulullah صَلَّى ٱللَّهُ عَلَيْهِ وَسَلَّمَ and said, "O Rasulullah صَلَّى ٱللَّهُ عَلَيْهِ وَسَلَّمَ, you are dearer to me than my life, my wealth and my family. While I am within the confines of my home, I begin to think of you and become restless. My restlessness does not end until my sight falls upon you. O Rasulullah صَلَّى ٱللَّهُ عَلَيْهِ وَسَلَّمَ, death is inevitable. After death, you will be in a high, exalted position as you are a Nabi and Rasul of Allah تَبَارَكَ وَتَعَالَى, whilst I will be distant from you. O Rasulullah صَلَّى ٱللَّهُ عَلَيْهِ وَسَلَّمَ, perhaps I may not be blessed with the honour of seeing you. Whenever I think of this separation between us which will be caused through death, I become extremely saddened and grieved."

Hazrat Rasulullah صَلَّى ٱللَّهُ عَلَيْهِ وَسَلَّمَ observed silence over this until Hazrat Jibreel عَلَيْهِ ٱلسَّلَامُ descended with the following verse of the Quraan Majeed:

وَمَنْ يُّطِعِ اللّٰهَ وَالرَّسُوْلَ فَاُولٰٓئِكَ مَعَ الَّذِيْنَ اَنْعَمَ اللّٰهُ عَلَيْهِمْ مِّنَ النَّبِيّٖنَ وَالصِّدِّيْقِيْنَ وَالشُّهَدَآءِ وَالصّٰلِحِيْنَ ۚ وَحَسُنَ اُولٰٓئِكَ رَفِيْقًا ۝

---

[246] المعجم الكبير للطبراني، الرقم: ١٢٥٥٩، وفيه عطاء بن السائب وقد اختلط كما في مجمع الزوائد، الرقم: ١٠٩٣٦

All those who obey Allah تَبَارَكَوَتَعَالَى and the Messenger are in the company of those on whom is the Grace of Allah تَبَارَكَوَتَعَالَى; the Ambiyaa عَلَيْهِمُالسَّلَامُ, the Siddeeqeen, the martyrs, and the righteous. [247]

Incident Twenty Nine - Hazrat Bilaal رَضِيَاللّٰهُعَنْهُ on his Deathbed

When Hazrat Bilaal رَضِيَاللّٰهُعَنْهُ was about to pass away, his wife began to say, "Ah, how sad! You are departing from this world."

Hazrat Bilaal رَضِيَاللّٰهُعَنْهُ replied, "How pleasant and joyful it is that tomorrow, we will meet our friends, we will meet Muhammad صَلَّىاللّٰهُعَلَيْهِوَسَلَّمَ and his companions." [248]

Incident Thirty - Happiness of Hazrat Umar رَضِيَاللّٰهُعَنْهُ

Hazrat Umar رَضِيَاللّٰهُعَنْهُ once said to Hazrat Abbaas رَضِيَاللّٰهُعَنْهُ (the uncle of Hazrat Rasulullah صَلَّىاللّٰهُعَلَيْهِوَسَلَّمَ), "I was more pleased with your Islam than the Islam of my father, for your Islam gave pleasure to Rasulullah صَلَّىاللّٰهُعَلَيْهِوَسَلَّمَ." [249]

Incident Thirty One - Hazrat Umar's رَضِيَاللّٰهُعَنْهُ Deep Love and Memories of Hazrat Rasulullah صَلَّىاللّٰهُعَلَيْهِوَسَلَّمَ

One night, Hazrat Umar رَضِيَاللّٰهُعَنْهُ was on his security patrol when he saw a light and heard a sound coming from a house. He found an

---

[247] المعجم الأوسط للطبراني، الرقم: ٤٧٧، ورجاله رجال الصحيح غير عبد الله بن عمران العابدي وهو ثقة كما في مجمع الزوائد، الرقم: ١٠٩٣٧

[248] سير أعلام النبلاء ٢١٨/٣

[249] شرح معاني الآثار ٣٢١/٣

old lady in it spinning wool and singing a few couplets with the following meaning:

"May Allah تَبَارَكَوَتَعَالَى accept the prayers of the pious and the elect, seeking blessings for Muhammad صَلَّىٱللَّهُعَلَيْهِوَسَلَّمَ.

"O messenger of Allah صَلَّىٱللَّهُعَلَيْهِوَسَلَّمَ, you worshipped each night, and you wept before the dawning of each day.

"I wish to know if I could be together with my beloved صَلَّىٱللَّهُعَلَيْهِوَسَلَّمَ, for death comes in different states (of mind) And I do not know how I shall die."

On hearing these couplets, Hazrat Umar رَضِيَٱللَّهُعَنْهُ sat down, weeping in love and memory of Hazrat Rasulullah صَلَّىٱللَّهُعَلَيْهِوَسَلَّمَ.[250]

---

[250] كتاب الزهد والرقائق لابن المبارك، الرقم: ١٠٢٤

THE LOVE AND OBEDIENCE DISPLAYED BY THE PIOUS FOR RASULULLAH ﷺ

Incident One - The Respect of Imaam Maalik رَحِمَهُ ٱللَّهُ

Imaam Maalik رَحِمَهُ ٱللَّهُ possessed great love for the land of Madinah Munawwarah. This love was on account of the love he had for Hazrat Rasulullah ﷺ.

Allaamah Ibnu Khallikaan رَحِمَهُ ٱللَّهُ writes:

Imaam Maalik رَحِمَهُ ٱللَّهُ never rode a conveyance in the blessed city of Madinah Munawwarah. Even at the time when he grew old and became extremely weak, he preferred to walk rather than being transported by a conveyance. When Imaam Maalik رَحِمَهُ ٱللَّهُ was asked the reason, he mentioned, "I feel extremely difficult to ride on a conveyance in the mubaarak city of Madinah Munawwarah, whereas Rasulullah ﷺ is buried beneath the ground." [251]

Incident Two - Giving Preference to the neighbours of Hazrat Rasulullah ﷺ

Imaam Maalik رَحِمَهُ ٱللَّهُ used to commence teaching the students of Hadith and those residing in Madinah Munawwarah before teaching others. When he was asked the reason for showing preference to the students of Hadith and the people of Madinah,

---

[251] وفيات الأعيان ٤/١٣٦

he exclaimed: "These are the neighbours of Rasulullah ﷺ."[252]

Incident Three - Travelling for a Single Hadith

Hazrat Kathir bin Qais رحمه الله narrates:

I was once sitting with Hazrat Abu Dardaa رضي الله عنه in a musjid in Damascus, when a person came to him and said, "O Abu Dardaa رضي الله عنه, I have travelled all the way from Madinah Tayyibah to acquire one Hadith from you, as I have learnt that you have heard it directly from Rasulullah ﷺ."

Hazrat Abu Dardaa رضي الله عنه asked, "Do you have any other work in Damascus?" The person replied, "No (i.e. I have only come to Damascus to acquire the Hadith)." Hazrat Abu Dardaa رضي الله عنه asked again, "Are you sure that you have no other work in Damascus?" The person again replied, "I have come to this place with the sole purpose of learning this Hadith."

Hazrat Abu Dardaa رضي الله عنه then said, "Listen, I have heard Rasulullah ﷺ saying, 'Allah تبارك وتعالى eases the way to Paradise for the one who traverses some distance to seek knowledge. The angels spread their wings under his feet, and everything in the heavens and the earth (even the fish in the water) make dua to Allah تبارك وتعالى for his forgiveness. The superiority and high rank of a person possessing Deeni knowledge over a person engaged in worship (without having Deeni

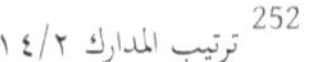

252 ترتيب المدارك ٢/١٤

knowledge) is like the superiority of the moon over the stars. The Ulama are the inheritors of Rasulullah ﷺ. The legacy of Ambiyaa عَلَيْهِمُالسَّلَام is neither gold nor silver. Rather, their legacy is the knowledge of Deen. A person who acquires Deeni knowledge has certainly acquired great wealth.'" [253]

Incident Four - Giving up Sins through the Dua of Hazrat Rasulullah ﷺ

Hazrat Ja'far As-Saa'igh رَحِمَهُاللَّه relates:

In the neighbourhood of Imaam Ahmad bin Hambal رَحِمَهُاللَّه, there was a person who was leading a life of sin and vice. One day, he attended the discourse of Imaam Ahmad رَحِمَهُاللَّه. Upon entering the majlis of Imaam Ahmad رَحِمَهُاللَّه, he greeted the Imaam with salaam. Though Imaam Ahmad رَحِمَهُاللَّه answered his salaam, the man perceived that the Imaam had shown some disinclination towards him.

He addressed Imaam Ahmad رَحِمَهُاللَّه saying, "O Abu Abdillah, I notice that you are feeling uncomfortable with my presence. (Perceiving that the Imaam's natural aversion towards him was on account of the sins and transgression he was involved in, he said,) I wish to inform you that I have given up my life of sin and have resolved to lead a life of obedience and submission."

He further explained to Imaam Ahmad bin Hambal رَحِمَهُاللَّه, "Last night, I had a dream of Rasulullah ﷺ. Rasulullah ﷺ

---

[253] سنن أبي داود، الرقم: ٣٦٤١

came to me and asked, 'Why do you not request me to make dua for you?' I replied, 'O Rasulullah ﷺ, due to my excessive sinning and leading a life of transgression, I feel extremely ashamed to come in your presence.' Rasulullah ﷺ said, 'Do not worry, even though you feel ashamed, stand up and I will make dua to Allah تَبَارَكَوَتَعَالَى on your behalf.'"

He then says, "I stood up and Rasulullah ﷺ made dua for me. Once I awoke, I found that Allah تَبَارَكَوَتَعَالَى had placed natural aversion and resentment within my heart for all the sins I was involved in." [254]

Incident Five - Ayyoob Sakhtiyaani رَحِمَهُٱللَّه in Madinah Tayyibah

Hazrat Abdullah bin Mubaarak رَحِمَهُٱللَّه says:

I heard Imaam Abu Hanifah رَحِمَهُٱللَّه say, "When Ayyoob Sakhtiyaani رَحِمَهُٱللَّه was in Madinah Tayyibah, I was also present and I watched to see how he was going to present his Salaam to Rasulullah ﷺ. I saw him facing the grave with his back towards the qiblah. He was standing there without saying a word. Rather, he just cried and cried." [255]

---

[254] كتاب التوابين ص ٢٦٤

[255] خلاصة الوفا ١/ ٤٢٨

Incident Six - A Bedouin by the Grave of Hazrat Rasulullah ﷺ

Once, a bedouin visited the grave of Hazrat Rasulullah ﷺ and said, "O Allah تَبَارَكَوَتَعَالَى, You have commanded that slaves be set free. Here lies Your most beloved Messenger and here stands Your slave at the final resting place of Your Messenger. I beseech You, set free this humble slave from the fire of Hell." From the unseen, a voice was heard saying, "For yourself alone did you ask freedom, why not on behalf of all mankind? We have set you free from the fire of Jahannum." [256]

Hazrat Isma'ee رَحِمَهُٱللَّهُ narrates:

Once, a bedouin stood in front of the grave of Hazrat Rasulullah ﷺ saying, "O Allah تَبَارَكَوَتَعَالَى, here lies Your beloved. I am Your slave and Shaitaan is Your enemy. If You forgive me, Your beloved here shall be pleased, Your slave shall be successful and the heart of Your enemy will be displeased. O my Sustainer, if You do not forgive me, the heart of Your beloved will grieve, Your enemy will be overjoyed and this slave of Yours will be defeated. O Allah تَبَارَكَوَتَعَالَى, it is a custom among the Arabs that whenever a great ruler among them passes away, they used to set free slaves besides his grave. O Allah تَبَارَكَوَتَعَالَى, here lies the master among all the leaders and rulers, and here I stand as Your slave. O Allah تَبَارَكَوَتَعَالَى, set me free from the fire of Jahannum."

---

[256] المواهب اللدنية ٣ / ٥٩٧

Hazrat Isma'ee رَحِمَهُ اللَّه says further, "Hearing the supplication of this bedouin, I said to him, 'O Arab, for that most appropriate supplication and manner of asking, Allah تَبَارَكَ وَتَعَالَى will definitely forgive your sins.'" [257]

Incident Seven - The Cure of Allaamah Qastallani رَحِمَهُ اللَّه

Allaamah Qastallani رَحِمَهُ اللَّه, the famous scholar of Hadith, writes in his kitaab 'Mawaahib Ladunni':

Once, I became so ill that the doctors despaired for my health, and I remained in this condition for many years. Then, one day, on the 28th of Jumaadul Ulaa 893 A.H. while in Makkah Mukarramah, I made dua to Allah تَبَارَكَ وَتَعَالَى through the waseelah of Rasulullah صَلَّى اللَّهُ عَلَيْهِ وَسَلَّم, that Allah تَبَارَكَ وَتَعَالَى heals me of my affliction.

While I was asleep, I saw a vision in which I saw a man with a piece of paper in his hand on which was written, "Rasulullah صَلَّى اللَّهُ عَلَيْهِ وَسَلَّم has commanded that this medicine be given to Ahmad bin Qastallani." When I awoke, I found that no sign of my illness had remained. [258]

Incident Eight - The incident of Abu Imraan Waasity رَحِمَهُ اللَّه

Hazrat Abu Imraan Waasity رَحِمَهُ اللَّه narrates:

---

[257] خلاصة الوفا ٤٥١/١

[258] المواهب اللدنية ٣/٦.٦

Once, I was on a journey towards Madinah Tayyibah, when along the way, I felt such extreme thirst that I feared for my life. Fearing that death was about to overtake me, I sat down under a thorn tree.

Suddenly a rider appeared before me on a green horse, with green reins and a green saddle. In his hand was a green glass with a greenish drink. I drank three times from that glass and not a drop decreased from it. He then asked me where I was going, to which I replied that I was proceeding to Madinah Munawwarah to convey my Salaam to Nabi ﷺ and his two companions.

He then replied, "When you have reached Madinah Munawwarah and you have greeted them, then convey my Salaam as well to Nabi ﷺ and his two companions. Tell them that Ridwaan has conveyed his Salaams. (Ridwaan is the angel who is the gatekeeper of Paradise)." [259]

Incident Nine - Honour and Respect for the Blessed Hair of Hazrat Rasulullah ﷺ

Hazrat Abu Hafs, Umar bin Hasan Samarqandi رَحِمَهُ ٱللَّهُ, narrates the following incident in his kitaab, Rownaqul Majaalis:

There was once a wealthy businessman who resided in the city of Balkh and had two sons. After his demise, his two sons divided his estate between them equally.

---

[259] فضائل مدينه ص ۱۳۰

Included in the estate were three strands of the blessed hair of Rasulullah ﷺ. In winding up the estate, each son took one strand, leaving the third strand belonging to both of them. Hence, the elder brother suggested, "Let us cut the third strand into half so that we can each take our share from the strand." However, the younger brother did not agree to this saying, "No! By Allah تَبَارَكَ وَتَعَالَى, the respect and honour that we are supposed to show to Rasulullah ﷺ is such that it is inappropriate for us to cut the strand of his blessed hair."

When the elder brother witnessed the love and respect that his younger brother had for the blessed hair of Rasulullah ﷺ, he proposed, "Why don't you take all three strands of hair in exchange of your share of the inheritance?" Out of love for Rasulullah ﷺ, the younger brother agreed. Accordingly, the elder brother took all the wealth of the estate while the younger brother took the three strands of hair.

The younger brother placed them in his pocket with utmost respect. Thereafter, he would continuously take them out of his pocket, gaze at them with love and recite Durood upon Rasulullah ﷺ. He would then return them to his pocket.

After some period of time had passed, all the wealth of the elder brother had depleted, whereas the younger brother was granted abundant wealth by Allah تَبَارَكَ وَتَعَالَى. After some time, however, the younger brother passed away.

After he left this world, a pious person had a dream in which he saw the younger brother together with Rasulullah ﷺ.

Rasulullah ﷺ addressed the pious person and said, "Tell the people that if anyone has a need from Allah تَبَارَكَ وَتَعَالَى, he should go to the grave of this person (referring to the younger brother) and make dua to Allah تَبَارَكَ وَتَعَالَى to fulfill his need. His needs will be fulfilled."

People would thereafter come to the grave of this brother in order to make dua, until even those who would be passing by on their conveyances would dismount and walk on foot out of respect before reaching the grave.[260]

Incident Ten - Conveying Durood on behalf of Someone at the Grave of Hazrat Rasulullah ﷺ

Hazrat Yazeed bin Abi Sa'eed Al-Madani رَحِمَهُ ٱللَّٰه mentions:

On one occasion (when intending to travel to Madinah Munawwarah), I bid farewell to Umar bin Abdil Azeez رَحِمَهُ ٱللَّٰه. Umar رَحِمَهُ ٱللَّٰه said to me, "I have a wish which I need you to fulfill for me." I replied, "O Ameerul Mu'mineen! What wish do you need me to fulfill?"

He answered, "When you reach Madinah Munawwarah and you see the blessed grave of Rasulullah ﷺ, then convey my Salaams to Rasulullah ﷺ."[261]

---

[260] رونق المجالس كما في القول البديع صـ ٢٧٦

[261] شعب الإيمان، الرقم: ٣٨٧٠، القول البديع صـ ٤٢١

CHAPTER TWELVE

Virtues of Visiting the Raudhah Mubaarak of Hazrat Rasulullah صَلَّى ٱللَّهُ عَلَيْهِ وَسَلَّمَ

The famous muhaddith of the Hanafi mazhab, Mulla Ali Qaari رَحمَهُ ٱللَّه, has written that there is consensus that to visit the grave of Rasulullah صَلَّى ٱللَّهُ عَلَيْهِ وَسَلَّمَ is an important act of virtue and piety, and a very desirable form of ibaadah. It is also a successful way to attain spiritual elevation and a cause for gaining the intercession of Rasulullah صَلَّى ٱللَّهُ عَلَيْهِ وَسَلَّمَ.

Some Ulamaa have mentioned that it is waajib (obligatory) upon the person who has the means to reach Madinah Munawwarah. The renowned jurist, Allaamah Shaami رَحمَهُ ٱللَّه, has quoted this view from Haafiz Ibnu Hajar رَحمَهُ ٱللَّه, that to avoid going to Madinah Munawwarah is an act of sheer negligence and disregard.

In view of the countless favours of Rasulullah صَلَّى ٱللَّهُ عَلَيْهِ وَسَلَّمَ on the ummah, it is the right that we owe Rasulullah صَلَّى ٱللَّهُ عَلَيْهِ وَسَلَّمَ that we visit his mubaarak raudhah if we have the means to do so. It is indeed unfortunate if one travels for haj or umrah, and despite having the means, he does not visit the raudah mubaarak.

There is consensus among the four mazhabs that it is mustahab to visit the grave of Rasulullah ﷺ.[262]

Gaining the Intercession of Hazrat Rasulullah ﷺ

Hazrat Ibnu Umar رضي الله عنهما reports that Hazrat Rasulullah ﷺ said, "Whoever visits my grave, my intercession becomes necessary for him (i.e. I will definitely intercede with Allah تبارك وتعالى on the day of Qiyaamah to forgive that person)."[263]

Blessed to Visit Hazrat Rasulullah ﷺ

Hazrat Ibnu Umar رضي الله عنهما reports that Hazrat Rasulullah ﷺ said, "The one who visits me after my death is like the one who visited me during my life."[264]

---

[262] فضائل حج صص ١٧٩–١٨٠

[263] عن ابن عمر قال قال رسول الله صلى الله عليه وسلم من زار قبري وجبت له شفاعتي (سنن الدارقطني، الرقم: ٢٦٩٥) رواه البزار والدارقطني قاله النووي وقال ابن حجر في شرح المناسك: رواه ابن خزيمة في صحيحه وصححه جماعة كعبد الحق والتقي السبكي وقال القاري في شرح الشفا: صححه جماعة من أئمة الحديث. (فضائلِ حج صص ١٨٢)

[264] عن ابن عمر عن النبي صلى الله عليه وسلم قال من زار قبري بعد موتي كمن زارني في حياتي (المعجم الأوسط، الرقم: ٢٨٧) رواه الطبراني والدارقطني والبيهقي وضعفه كذا في الإتحاف وفي المشكوة برواية البيهقي في الشعب بلفظ : من حج فزار قبري بعد موتي كان كمن زارني في حياتي واستدل به الموفق في المغني على استحباب الزيارة (فضائلِ حج صص ١٨٤)

Being the Neighbour of Hazrat Rasulullah ﷺ on the Day of Qiyaamah

Hazrat Rasulullah ﷺ said, "The one who undertakes a journey specifically to visit my grave will be my neighbour on the day of Qiyaamah, and the one who lives in Madinah Munawwarah and patiently bears its hardships and difficulties, for him I will be a witness and intercessor on the day of Qiyaamah, and the one who passes away in either of the Haramain (Makkah Mukarramah or Madinah Munawwarah) will be raised on the day of Qiyaamah with those who have been granted safety." [265]

Needs Being Fulfilled

Hazrat Abu Hurairah رَضِىَ اللَّهُ عَنْهُ reports that Hazrat Rasulullah ﷺ said, "When a person stands at my grave reciting Durood upon me, I hear it, and whoever sends Salaam upon me in any other place, his every need in this world and in the Hereafter

---

[265] عن رجل من آل الخطاب عن النبي صلى الله عليه وسلم قال من زارني متعمدا كان في جواري يوم القيامة ومن سكن المدينة وصبر على بلائها كنت له شهيدا وشفيعا يوم القيامة ومن مات في أحد الحرمين بعثه الله من الآمنين يوم القيامة (شعب الإيمان، الرقم: ٣٨٥٦) رواه البيهقي في الشعب كذا في المشكوة وفي الإتحاف برواية الطيالسي بسنده إلى ابن عمر ثم قال : وعن رجل من آل خطاب رفعه من زارني متعمدا كان في جواري يوم القيامة ... الحديث أخرجه البيهقي وهو مرسل والرجل المذكور مجهول وبسط الكلام على طرقه السبكي وقال : هو مرسل جيد (فضائل حج ص ١٨٥)

gets fulfilled, and on the day of Qiyaamah, I shall be his witness and intercessor." [266]

Hazrat Rasulullah ﷺ Replying to the Salaam

Hazrat Abu Hurairah رضى الله عنه reports that Hazrat Rasulullah ﷺ said, "Whenever anyone makes Salaam to me at my grave, Allah تبارك وتعالى returns my soul to my body so that I reply to his greetings." [267]

In Sharh-e-Manaasik, Haafiz Ibnu Hajar رحمه الله writes that the meaning of the return of the soul is that Allah تبارك وتعالى grants Rasulullah ﷺ the ability to speak. Hazrat Qaadhi Iyaaz رحمه الله writes that the soul of Rasulullah ﷺ remains absorbed in the presence of Allah تبارك وتعالى, and on being greeted with Salaam, inclines towards the greeting.

The majority of Ulama (such as Haafiz Ibnu Hajar رحمه الله and Allaamah Zurqaani رحمه الله) are of the opinion that the meaning of the return of the soul is not that the body of Hazrat Rasulullah ﷺ was without a soul, but has now been given a soul. The

---

[266] وعن أبي هريرة رضي الله عنه قال قال رسول الله صلى الله عليه وسلم من صلى علي عند قبري سمعته ومن صلى علي نائياً كفى أمر دنياه وآخرته وكنت له شهيداً وشفيعاً يوم القيامة رواه البيهقي في الشعب والخطيب وابن عساكر كذا في الدر وبسط طرقه السبكي في شفاء الأسقام وفي المواهب وشرحه عزاه إلى ابن أبي شيبة وعبد الرزاق (فضائل حج صـ ١٩٢)

[267] عن أبي هريرة أن رسول الله صلى الله عليه وسلم قال: ما من أحد يسلم علي إلا رد الله علي روحي حتى أرد عليه السلام (سنن أبي داود، الرقم: ٢٠٤١، وسنده جيد كما قال العراقي في المغني عن حمل الأسفار في الأسفار صـ ٣٦٧) رواه أحمد في رواية عبد الله للموفق كذا في المغني وأخرجه أبو داود بدون لفظ عند قبري لكن رواه في باب زيارة القبور بعد أبواب المدينة من كتاب الحج (فضائل حج صـ ١٨٩)

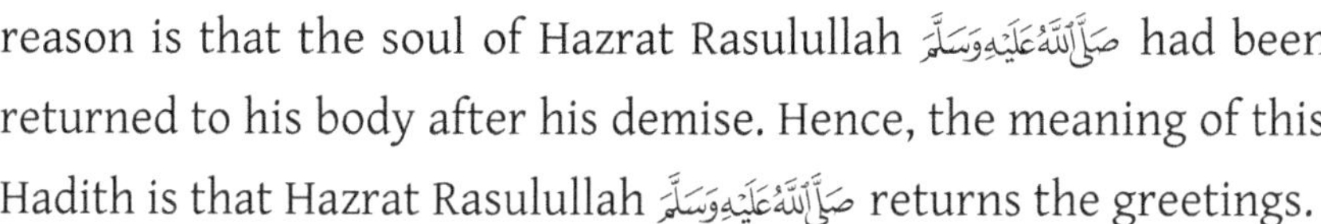

reason is that the soul of Hazrat Rasulullah ﷺ had been returned to his body after his demise. Hence, the meaning of this Hadith is that Hazrat Rasulullah ﷺ returns the greetings.

The Dua of the Angels

It is reported that when a person stands at the grave of Hazrat Rasulullah ﷺ and recites the following aayah:

اِنَّ اللّٰهَ وَمَلٰٓئِكَتَهٗ يُصَلُّوْنَ عَلَى النَّبِيِّ ۚ يٰٓاَيُّهَا الَّذِيْنَ اٰمَنُوْا صَلُّوْا عَلَيْهِ وَسَلِّمُوْا تَسْلِيْمًا ۝

and he thereafter recites the following durood seventy times:

صَلَّى اللهُ عَلَيْكَ يَا مُحَمَّدْ

an angel says, "May Allah's تَبَارَكَوَتَعَالَى blessings be on you too", and then Allah تَبَارَكَوَتَعَالَى fulfils his every need.[268]

Mullah Ali Qaari رَحِمَهُٱللَّٰه is of the view that if in place of 'Ya Muhammad', one says 'Ya Rasulallah' it will be better. Allaamah Qastallaani رَحِمَهُٱللَّٰه has reported a similar view from Hazrat Shaikh Zainud-deen Maraaghi رَحِمَهُٱللَّٰه and others as well.

The reason for this is that we have been prohibited from calling Rasulullah ﷺ by his name. However, if in the Hadith

٢٦٨ قال ابن أبي فديك : سمعت بعض من أدركت يقول : بلغنا أنه من وقف عند قبر النبي صلى الله عليه وسلم فتلا هذه الآية : اِنَّ اللّٰهَ وَ مَلٰٓئِكَتَهٗ يُصَلُّوْنَ عَلَى النَّبِيِّ ۚ يٰٓاَيُّهَا الَّذِيْنَ اٰمَنُوْا صَلُّوْا عَلَيْهِ وَسَلِّمُوْا تَسْلِيْمًا ۝ ثم يقول صلى الله عليك يا محمد، من يقولها سبعين مرة ناداه ملك صلى الله عليك يا فلان ولم تسقط له حاجة، كذا في الشفا قال القاري في شرحه : رواه البيهقي وابن أبي فديك ووثقه جماعة واحتج به أصحاب الكتب الستة ومعنى قوله أي في الحديث (فضائل حج ص ١٩٠)

quoted, the wording is 'Ya Muhammad', then this should be taken into consideration and it then does not remain prohibited.

Hazrat Shaikh Mouana Muhammad Zakariyya رَحْمَةُ اللّٰه mentioned:

I personally feel that a visitor to the grave of Rasulullah صَلَّى اللّٰهُ عَلَيْهِ وَسَلَّمَ should, at every visit, recite the following seventy times with complete humility:

اَلصَّلَاةُ وَالسَّلَامُ عَلَيْكَ يَا رَسُوْلَ الله

Sunnats and Aadaab of Madinah Munawarrah

1. After performing hajj or umrah, ensure that you proceed to Madinah Munawwarah and visit the Raudhah Mubaarak. Hazrat Rasulullah ﷺ mentioned in the Hadith, "The one who performs hajj and does not come to visit me has indeed shown ill-conduct and disrespect towards me." (Al Durarul Muntathirah #411 & Al Ikhtiyaar 1/175)

2. When visiting the Raudhah Mubaarak, keep in mind the Hadith, "Whoever visits my qabr (grave), my intercession becomes binding for him." (Al Maqaasidul Hasanah #1125)

3. Take ghusl, wear your best clothing and apply itr before going to make Salaam at the Raudhah Mubaarak. (Al Hindiyyah 1/265)

4. Our Ulamaa mention it is good for one to recite Surah Kausar 1000 times before entering Madinah Munawwarah. This is a means of Rasulullah ﷺ becoming pleased.

5. One should give sadaqah before going to the Raudhah Mubaarak.

6. After entering Musjid Nabawi, perform two rakaats Tahiyyatul Musjid, make istighfaar and dua, and thereafter proceed to confer Salaam upon our Master, Hazrat Rasulullah ﷺ. It is better to read a short Salaam that you understand rather

than reading a Salaam that you do not understand from a book or card etc. (Al Ikhtiyaar 1/175)

7. Recite once الصَّلَوةُ والسَّلَامُ عَلَيْكَ يَا رَسُوْلَ الله, then read إِنَّ اللهَ وَمَلَائِكَتَهُ يُصَلُّوْنَ عَلَى النَّبِي 70 times. Thereafter, seek intercession in these words:

يَا رَسُوْلَ اللهِ أَسْأَلُكَ الشَّفَاعَةَ وَأَتَوَسَّلُ بِكَ إِلَى اللهِ فِيْ أَنْ أَمُوْتَ مُسْلِمًا عَلَى مِلَّتِكَ وَسُنَّتِكَ

O Rasul of Allah ﷺ! I beg you to intercede for me (on the day of Qiyaamah), and I ask Allah تَبَارَكَوَتَعَالَى, in Your name, to bless me to pass away as a Muslim and upon your Deen and sunnah. (Majma' Al Anhur 1/313)

8. Thereafter, convey the Salaams of anyone who requested you to do so in these words: اَلسَّلَامُ عَلَيْكَ يَا رَسُوْلَ اللهِ مِنْ جَمِيْعِ مَنْ أَوْصَانِيْ بِالسَّلَامِ عَلَيْكَ *(Salaam upon you O Rasulullah ﷺ from all those who have requested me to convey Salaams)* (Al Ikhtiyaar 1/176)

9. Go to the Raudhah Mubaarak at least twice a day to convey Salaams. Thereafter, convey Salaams to Hazrat Rasulullah ﷺ after every salaah, from wherever you are in the Haram.

10. Try to recite Durood Shareef 1000 times or more daily. (Al Hindiyyah 1/266)

11. Do not engage in any conversations in Musjid Nabawi. (Al Hindiyyah 1/321)

12. Perform two rakaats of Shukr Salaah often, and thank Allah تَبَارَكَوَتَعَالَى for blessing you to come to this blessed place. (Maraaqil Falaah pg. 283)

13. Make the dua of Hazrat Umar رَضِىَ اللّٰهُ عَنْهُ:

"O Allah! Grant me martyrdom in Your path, and allow my death to take place in the city of Rasulullah صَلَّى اللّٰهُ عَلَيْهِ وَسَلَّم!" (Saheeh Bukhaari #1890)

14. In Madinah Munawwarah, make ta'leem of the kitaab Fazaail-e-Hajj (read the section on Madinah Munawwarah).

15. Visit Uhud on a Thursday as this is mustahab. Recite a portion of the Quraan Majeed and convey the rewards to the martyrs of Uhud. (Maraaqil Falaah pg. 285)

16. Visit Musjid Quba on a Saturday as this is mustahab. It is mustahab to walk and also to go by conveyance. (Saheeh Muslim #1399 & Maraqil falaah pg. 285)

17. Take sadaqah monies to distribute among the poor in Madinah Munawwarah.

18. Make at least one khatam of the Quraan Majeed in Makkah Mukarramah and one in Madinah Munawwarah.

19. Try to visit the cemetery of Jannatul Mu'alla in Makkah Mukarramah, and Jannatul Baqee in Madinah Munawwarah often (a good time is after the Ishraaq Salaah). Make dua for Allah تَبَارَكَوَتَعَالَى to reserve a place for you to be buried in Jannatul Baqee. (Al Ikhtiyaar 1/177 & Al Maslak Al Mutaqassit pg. 501)

CHAPTER THIRTEEN

Poems in Praise of our Beloved Nabi صَلَّى ٱللَّهُ عَلَيْهِ وَسَلَّمَ

NAAT OF HAZRAT QARI SIDDEEQ AHMAD BANDWI رَحِمَهُ ٱللَّهُ

تمنا ہے کہ گلزارِ مدینہ اب وطن ہوتا

وہاں کے گلشنوں میں کوئی اپنا بھی چمن ہوتا

How I wish Madinah was my home, and that I had my own little garden in the gardens of Madinah.

بسر ابِ زندگی اپنی دیارِ قدس میں ہوتی

وہیں جیتا وہیں مرتا وہیں گور و کفن ہوتا

I wish I could pass my life in the sacred land of Madinah, wherein I will live, die and be buried.

میسر بال و پر ہوتے تو میں اڑ کر پہنچ جاتا

زہے قسمت کہ اپنا آشیاں ان کا چمن ہوتا

I wish I had wings, then I would fly to Madinah, And I wish I had the good fortune of having my nest in that garden.

یہی ہے آرزو ثاقب یہی اپنی تمنا ہے

کہ پیوندِ بقیعِ پاک اپنا بھی بدن ہوتا

This is my desire, this is my wish that my body be attached to the blessed land of Baqee.

URDU QASEEDAH OF HAZRAT MOULANA QAASIM NANOTWI رَحمَهُ ٱللَّه

نہ ہوے نغمہ سرا اس طرح سے بلبل زار

کہ آئی ہے نئے سر سے چمن چمن میں بہار

The nightingale bursts forth in a song of happiness, the freshness of springtime in the garden now prevails.

ہر اک کو حسبِ لیاقت بہار دیتی ہے

کسی کو برگ کسی کو گل اور کسی کو بار

And in accordance with their capability, to some a leaf and to some a rose, to some a fruit.

خوشی سے مرغِ چمن ناچ ناچ گاتے ہیں

کفِ ورق سے بجاتے ہیں تالیاں اشجار

Birds of the garden in joyfulness do dance and sing, and the trees shaking their leaves, with clapping applaud.

بُجھائی ہے دلِ آتش کی بھی تپش یا رب

کرم میں آپ کو دشمن سے بھی نہیں انکار

O You Sustainer of all, who the fire to coolness did command, and not even to an enemy kindness does refuse.

یہ قدرِ خاک ہے، ہیں باغ باغ وہ عاشق

کبھی رہے تھا سدا، جن کے دل کے بیچ غبار

So great Your reward for the lowliest of Your lovers, now jubilant, even though with heavy hearts their days they have passed.

یہ سبزہ زار کا رتبہ ہے شجرۂ موسیٰ

بنا ہے خاص تجلی کا مطلعِ انوار

The green meadows the rank of Moosa's عَلَیْہِ السَّلَام tree have attained. And now the radiance of a special light of Allah تَبَارَكَ وَتَعَالیٰ reflect.

اسی لئے چمنستان میں رنگہ مہندی نے

کیا ظہور ورق ہائے سبزہ میں ناچار

And thus in the orchard a wealth of colour is seen, as every form of plant life in greenness is clouded.

پہنچ سکے شجر طور کو کہیں طوبیٰ

مقام یار کو کب پہنچے مسکن اغیار

As the tree of Mount Toor has no likeness to the tree of Tooba in Paradise. So the abode of the beloved has no likeness to the abode of an intruder.

زمین و چرخ میں خ میں ہو کیوں نہ فرق چرخ و زمیں

یہ سب کا بار اُٹھائے وہ سب کے سر پر بار

As the earth and sky are distant from each other and different, so the earth bears the burden of all, while the sky bears the burden hanging above.

کرے ہے ذرّۂ کوۓ محمدی سے خجل

فلک کے شمس و قمر کو زمین لیل و نہار

The earth belittles the sun and moon by night and day, because of the particles of soil surrounding Muhammad's ﷺ body.

فلک پہ عیسیٰ و ادریس ہیں تو خیر سہی

زمیں پہ جلوہ نما ہیں محمد مختار

In the heavens Isa عَلَيْهِ السَّلَامُ and Idrees عَلَيْهِ السَّلَامُ are found, it is true, but here on earth do shine the splendour of Muhammad ﷺ the great.

فلک پہ سب سہی پر ہے نہ ثانئ احمد

زمیں پہ کچھ نہ ہو پر ہے محمدی سرکار

And whether all the heavens are filled they still lack his presence, and even if the earth is empty and Muhammad ﷺ is there, it's filled indeed!

ثنا کر اس کی فقط قاسم اور سب کو چھوڑ

کہاں کا سبز ہ کہاں کا چمن کہاں کی بہار

O Qaasim, praise him alone and discard your praise for others, whose beauty has his ever freshness in a fragrant garden even in the midst of Spring.

الٰہی کس سے بیان ہو سکے ثنا اس کی

کہ جس پہ ایسا تری ذاتِ خاص کا ہو پیار

O Allah, who is there that can indeed with adequacy praise him? Him for whom Your being has expressed such infinite love?

جو تو اسے نہ بناتا تو سارے عالم کو

نصیب ہوتی نہ دولتِ وجود کی زنہار

Had you not created him then in truth, not this world nor anything in it would have enjoyed the joy of existence.

کہاں وہ رتبہ کہاں عقلِ نار سا اپنی

کہاں وہ نورِ خدا اور کہاں یہ دیدۂ زار

How can my intellect perceive his exalted rank? How can my limited eyes perceive the light of Allah تَبَارَكَ وَتَعَالٰى؟

چراغِ عقل ہے گل اس کے نور کے آگے

زباں کا مُنھ نہیں جو مدح میں کرے گفتار

Before the shine of his light the lamp of my reason died off, and my tongue has not the words to express his worthy praise.

جہاں کہ چلتے ہوں پر عقلِ کل کے بھی پھر کیا

لگی ہے جان جو پہنچیں وہاں مرے افکار

Where even the wings of wisdom lag far behind, and so even my imaginative powers, though soaring high.

مگر کرے مری روح القدس مدد گاری

تو اس کی مدح میں میں بھی کروں رقم اشعار

Yet Allah, if Your noble spirit do guide me, then in humbleness I too in his praise would pen down these lines.

جو جبریل مدد پر ہو فکر کی میرے

تو آگے بڑھ کے کہوں اے جہان کے سردار

And while Jibreel's عَلَيْهِ ٱلسَّلَامْ *helps to stir my thoughts, I shall say unto him, "O Muhammad* صَلَّى ٱللَّهُ عَلَيْهِ وَسَلَّمَ, *chosen from amongst all men."*

تو فخر کون و مکاں زبدۂ زمین و زماں

امیرِ لشکرِ پیغمبراں شہِ ابرار

You are the pride of space and time, the glory of this earth, and you are the leader of the host of Ambiyaa, those truly saintly beings.

تو بوئے گل ہے اگر مثل گل ہیں اور نبی

تو نورِ شمس گر اور انبیاء ہیں شمس و نہار

If we compare the Ambiyaa to a rose, you are the fragrance thereof, and if they are the shining sun of the day, you are the rays thereof.

حیاتِ جان ہے تو ہیں اگر وہ جانِ جہاں

تو نورِ دیدہ ہے گر ہیں وہ دیدۂ بیدار

If they are the life of the world, you are the essence of life, and where they are the sense of sight, you are the light of eyes.

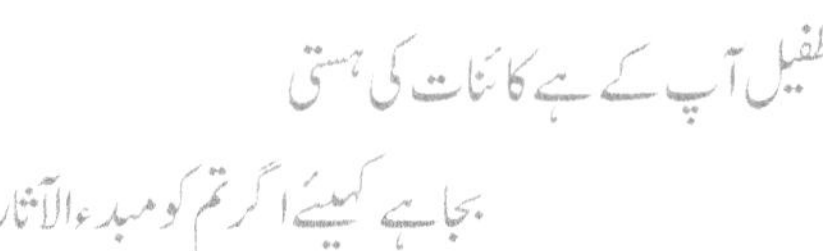

طفیل آپ کے ہے کائنات کی ہستی

بجا ہے کہیئے اگر تم کو مبدءالآثار

Through you has come into existence all that exists, and so be it for you
are the first of all creation.

جلوہ میں تیرے سب آئے عدم سے تابِ وجود

قیامت آپ کی تھی دیکھیئے تو اک رفتار

Through you has all been brought from non-existence into being, that
life-giving blessing from you did come.

جہاں کے سارے کمالات ایک تجھ میں ہیں

ترے کمال کسی میں نہیں مگر دو چار

All the excellence of this world in you is found, and except for one or two,
your merits are found in none.

پہنچ سکا ترے رتبہ تلک نہ کوئی نبی

ہوئے ہیں معجزہ والے بھی اس جگہ ناچار

Not one Nabi could ever reach to your noble rank, even though among
them workers of miracles are found.

جو انبیاء ہیں وہ آگے تری نبوت کے

کریں ہیں امتی ہونے کا یا نبی اقرار

And every Nabi shall express belief in your Nubuwwwat and a follower of
your mission shall he be.

لگاتا ہاتھ نہ پیٹے کو بوالبشر کے خدا

اگر ظہور نہ ہوتا تمہارا آخر کار

Never would Allah تَبَارَكَ وَتَعَالَىٰ have looked upon Aadam عَلَيْهِ ٱلسَّلَامُ had your appearance not been made at last.

خدا کے طالبِ دیدار حضرت موسیٰ

تمہارا لیجے، خدا آپ طالبِ دیدار

Moosa عَلَيْهِ ٱلسَّلَامُ was indeed desirous of seeing Allah تَبَارَكَ وَتَعَالَىٰ, and behold with you, Allah تَبَارَكَ وَتَعَالَىٰ Himself was desirous of meeting you.

کہاں بلندیِ طور اور کہاں تری معراج

کہیں ہوے ہیں زمین آسمان بھی ہموار

How can the heights of Mount Toor compare with the heights of your Mi'raaj (ascension), has the heavens and the earth ever been traversed as with you?

جمال کو ترے کب پہنچے حسنِ یوسف کا

وہ دل رُبائے زلیخا تو شاہد ستار

Never will the beauty of Yusuf عَلَيْهِ ٱلسَّلَامُ approach your shining countenance, even though Zulaikha had been bewitched thereby.

رہا جمال پہ تیرے حجابِ بشریت

نجانا کون ہے پکچھ بھی کسی نے جز ستار

Your glory had the veil of humanity over it, so none except Allah تَبَارَكَ وَتَعَالَىٰ could discern your total reality.

سما سکے تری خلوت میں کب نبی و ملک

خدا اغیور تو اُس کا حبیب اور اغیار

Neither Nabi nor angel could intrude into your seclusion with Allah

تَبَارَكَ وَتَعَالَ, and you are His beloved so all others are mere outsiders.

نہ بن پڑا وہ جمال آپ کا سا اک شب بھی

قمر نے گو کہ کروڑوں کیئے چڑھاؤ اتار

The moon could not attain to your beauty even for one night, although it

went into millions of revolutions.

خوش نصیب یہ نسبت کہاں نصیب مرے

تو جس قدر ہے بھلا میں برا اسی مقدار

To my good fortune I have a likeness with you, that in similar measure

as you are good, so am I weak.

نہ پہنچیں گنتی میں ہر گز ترے کمالوں کی

مرے بھی عیب شہِ دوسرا شہِ ابرار

Never can the sum of my defects be equal to the total of your virtues, O

leader of both worlds, and king of virtuous ones.

عجب نہیں تری خاطر سے تیری امت کے

گناہ ہو ویں قیامت کو طاعتوں میں ثمار

No wonder on the day of Judgement, the sins of your followers will be

counted as obedience for your sake.

بکھیں گے آپ کی امّت کے جُرم ایسے گراں

کہ لاکھوں مغفرتیں کم سے کم پہ ہوں گی نثار

So high will the sins of your Ummah be valued that tons of pardon be lavishly granted to a few of them.

تِرے بھروسہ پہ رکھتا ہے غُرّۂ طاعت

گناہِ قاسم بر گشتہ بخت بد اطوار

So ill-fated and sinful, this Qaasim hopefully relies on you, that through you his sins be changed to acts of obedience.

تمہارے حرفِ شفاعت پہ عفو ہے عاشق

اگر گناہ کو ہے خوفِ غصہ قہار

When sinners fear the wrath of Allah تَبَارَكَ وَتَعَالَى, Most Great, a mere word of intercession from you brings forgiveness and pardon.

یہ سُن کے آپ شفیعِ گناہ گاراں ہیں

کیئے ہیں میں نے اکٹھے گناہ کے انبار

Having heard that on behalf of sinners you will intercede, have I gathered piles of sins, to be forgiven.

تِرے لحاظ سے اتنی تو ہو گی تخفیف

بشر گناہ کریں اور ملائک استغفار

Out of consideration for you, this favour is granted, that while men do sins, angels pray for their forgiveness.

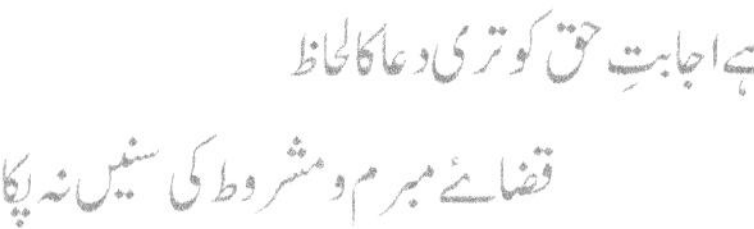

So well is Allah تَبَارَكَ وَتَعَالَى disposed to your prayers that even conditional
fates voice is stilled.

Sinful even though I am, yet I remain yours, so am I known, though
worthless I am.

It would be insulting to you that your dog should bear my name, but an
honour to me to be so connected with you.

While the best of creation you are, the worst am I, and while master of
both worlds you are, the lowest am I.

For years have I longed to open to you my heart, if ever I get a chance to
reach your Raudhah.

مگر جہاں ہو فلک آستاں سے بھی نیچا

وہاں ہو قاسمؔ بے بال و پر کا کیونکہ گزار

But where even the heaven is lower than your threshold, there is it most difficult for Qaasim to find a way.

دیا ہے حق نے تجھے سب سے مرتبہ عالی

کیا ہے سارے بڑے چھوٹوں کا تجھے سردار

The highest rank did Allah تَبَارَكَ وَتَعَالَى graciously grant unto you, and to be chief over all has He elevated you.

جو تو ہی ہم کو نہ پوچھے تو کون پوچھے گا

بنے گا کون ہمارا تیرے سوا غم خوار

If you do not care for us, then who shall? And who besides you, can truly console us all?

لیا ہے سگ نمط ابلیس نے مرا پیچھا

ہوا ہے نفس موا سانپ سا گلے کا بار

Indeed does Shaitaan constantly pursue me like a dog, and my nafs (carnal self) hangs around my neck like a snake.

رجا و خوف کی موجوں میں ہے، امید کی ناؤ

کہ ہو سگانِ مدینہ میں میر انام شمار

In huge waves of hope and fear the boat of my future lies, hoping that I may be counted among the obedient dogs of Madinah.

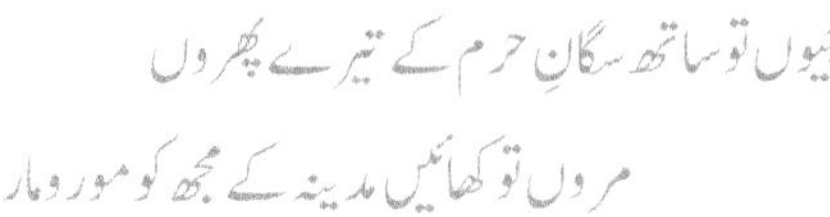

جیوں تو ساتھ سگانِ حرم کے تیرے پھروں

مروں تو کھائیں مدینہ کے مجھ کو مور و مار

I hope that among the dogs of your sacred Haram I shall roam, till the end of my days, and that I be eaten by the ants and snakes of Madinah.

اڑا کے باد مری مشتِ خاک کو پس مرگ

کرے حضور کے روضہ کے آس پاس نثار

And I hope that on having turned to dust at death, the wind shall spread my dust over the Raudhah Mubaarak.

و لے یہ رتبہ کہاں مُشتِ خاکِ قاسم کا

کہ جائے کوچہ اطہر میں تیرے بن کے غبار

Alas, the earthly remains of Qaasim can hardly reach that holy place even in the shape of dust.

غرض نہیں مجھے اس سے بھی کچھ رہی لیکن

خدا کی اور تری الفت سے میر اسینہ فگار

About other things I care not much, except that forever my heart be sore with love for Allah تَبَارَكَ وَتَعَالَیٰ and for you.

لگے وہ تیرِ غمِ عشق کا مرے دل میں

ہزار پارہ ہو دل خونِ دل میں ہو سر شار

And I wish that such an arrow pierces and breaks my heart into a thousand pieces, still delighted while shedding blood.

لگے وہ آتشِ عشق اپنی جان میں جس کی

جلا دے چرخِ ستم گر کو ایک ہی جھونکار

That my soul be filled with such burning love, which, in one blaze, burn
down the oppressive sky.

تمہارے عشق میں رو رو کے ہوں نحیف اتنا

کہ آنکھیں چشمۂ آبی سے ہوں دورنِ غبار

May it then be that through my love for you so much I weep, that weak
in my body I become, and my eyes be like fountains shedding tears.

رہے نہ منصبِ شیخ المشائخی کی طلب

نہ جی کو بھائے یہ دنیا کا کچھ بناؤ سنگار

Then no aspiration will remain in me to spiritual heights, and for me the
adornment of the world will have no charm.

ہوا اشارہ میں دو ٹکڑے جوں قمر کا جگر

کوئی اشارہ ہمارے بھی دل کے ہو جا پار

Through a sign from you the moon was split in two, and now we look for
a gesture to cleave our hearts.

تو تھام اپنے تئیں حد سے پا نہ دھر باہر

سنبھال اپنے تئیں اور سنبھل کے کر گفتار

And O Qaasim, now you compose yourself and step not beyond bounds,
and withhold yourself while talking in a cautious way.

ادب کی جا ہے یہ چپ ہو تو اور زبان بند کر

وہ جانے چھوڑ اسے پر نہ کر تو کچھ اصرار

For this is a spot that silence and respect demands, so silence do give.

بس اب دُرود پڑھ اُس پر اور اُس کی آل پہ تو

جو خوش ہو تجھ سے وہ، اور اس کی عترتِ اطہار

Send only Salaat on him (Durood) and his descendants, that he and his progeny will be pleased with you.

الٰہی اس پر اور اس کی تمام آل پہ بھیج

وہ رحمتیں کہ عدد کر سکے نہ ان کو شمار

O Allah! send upon Rasulullah ﷺ and all his family such blessings that cannot be counted.

MASNAWI OF MULLA JAAMI' رَحْمَةُٱللَّهُ

ز مجبوری برآمد جان عالم

ترحّم یا نبی اللہ ترحّم

O Rasul of Allah ﷺ, the seal of Prophethood, bestow your generous attention (upon us), for greatly bereaved is the world since your demise.

نہ آخر رحمۃ للعالمینی

ز محروماں چرا غافل نشینی

Are you not indeed the last of the messengers and their seal. Thus, it is not possible for you to then ignore us in this pitiable plight?

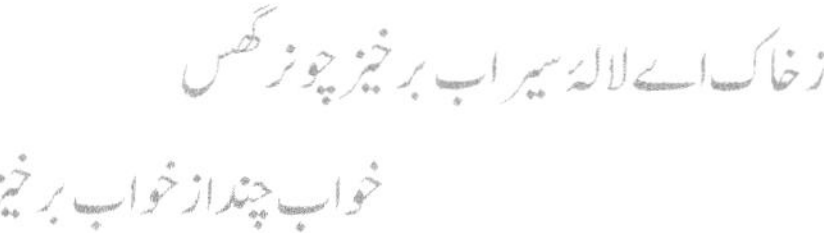

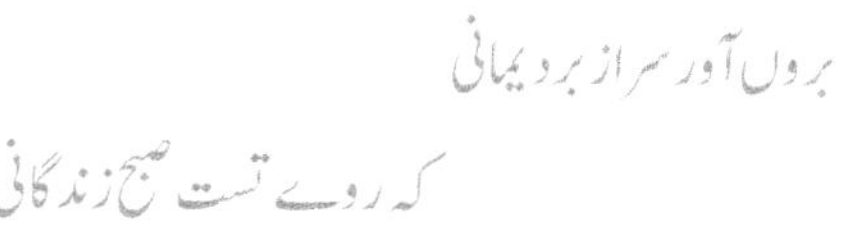

O dearest one, through your evergreen freshness, grace this world now and attend to us from the depths of your absorption (in the love of Allah تَبَارَكَ وَتَعَالَىٰ) filling us with guiding light.

بروں آور سر از برد یمانی

کہ روے تست صبح زندگانی

Lift your blessed countenance from within your Yemeni shroud, for your blessed face is the beginning of life and is the light of the day.

شب اندوه مارا روز گرداں

زرویت روز ما فیروز گرداں

Turn the darkness of our sorrowful night into the radiance of a bright day, and crown this day of ours with success.

بہ تن در پوش عنبر بوے جامہ

بسر بربند کافوری عمامہ

(O Rasul of Allah ﷺ) Don your fragrant garments, and place on your blessed head the white turban

فرود آویز از سر گیسواں را

فگن سایہ بپا سر درواں را

Allow your dark and precious locks of hair to hang down so that their shade may fall upon your blessed feet.

ادیم طائفی نعلین پا کن

شراک از رشتہ جانہائے ما کن

Wrap your feet in your shoes from the hills of Taa'if and make your straps bind our souls.

جہانے دیدہ کردہ فرش راہ اند

چو فرش اقبال پا بوس تو خواہند

This entire universe desires to be spread at your feet, and sincerely wishes for your honourable steps.

Come forth from your Raudhah Mubaarak into the Nabawi Musjid, so that we may kiss and lay our heads on the dust under your feet where you tread.

O Rasulullah ﷺ, grant refuge and help to the needy and console the hearts of those filled with love for you.

Indeed, we are sinners, drowned in the sea of our sins. Yet great is the thirst of our endeavour to follow your way.

You are the rain cloud of mercy and your generosity demands that help be granted to the thirsty seeker in search of you.

خوشا کز گرد رہ سویت رسیدیم

بدیدہ گرد از کویت کشیدیم

How wonderful would be that day when to your abode I shall come and blacken my eyes with the dust of Madinah. (May Allah تَبَارَكَ وَتَعَالَى hasten that day of my arrival in Madinah, to refresh my eyes with the dust of Madinah).

بمسجد سجدہ شکرانہ کردیم

چراغت راز جاں پروانہ کردیم

How wonderful would be that day, when after performing the salaah of thanks and the sajdah of thanks, my soul shall fly into the midst of the sacred Raudhah?

بگرد روضہ ات گشتیم گستاخ

دلم چوں پنجرہ سوراخ سوراخ

When in loving madness, overjoyed heart and overflowing yearning, I shall walk amidst your grave and the Green Dome.

زدیم از اشک ابر چشم بے خواب

دلم چوں پنجرہ سوراخ سوراخ

How glorious would be that day when from the clouds of my eyes, raindrops of tears shall sprinkle upon the threshold of your Haram and your grave.

گہے رفتیم زاں ساحت غبارے

گہے چیدیم زو خاشاک و خارے

When in joyful bliss I shall feel blessed to sweep away the dust of your Haram in ecstasy, to remove all the dust from around you.

ازاں نور سواد دیدہ دادیم

وزیں بر ریش دل مرہم نہادیم

Though dust be hurtful to the eyes, yet your dust is a light and cure for me, and though litter is of no benefit to wounds, to me the litter of Madinah shall be a perfect cure for the ills of my heart.

بسوۓ منبرت رہ بر گرفتیم

زچہرہ پایہ اش در زر گرفتیم

To your honoured mimbar shall I go and rubbing thereupon my face, which will go pale out of love for you, hoping that it shall become golden.

ز محرابت بسجدہ کام جستیم

قدم گاہت بخون دیدہ شستیم

Then (I shall go) to your musalla and your mimbar to stand in salaah fulfilling my hearts desires. Standing where you once stood, to wash your footsteps in the streams of my blood (of love).

بپاۓ ہر ستوں قد راست کردیم

مقام راستاں در خواست کردیم

Then to every pillar of your Musjid I will stand in utmost humbleness.
Begging of Allah تَبَارَكَوَتَعَالَى for faith and the ranks of the Siddeeq.

زداغ آرزویت بادل خوش

زدیم ازدل بهر قندیل آتش

Indeed, will the great hopes and desires of my heart in extreme pleasure,
cause every candle on earth to glow most brightly.

کنوں گرتن نہ خاک آں حریم است

بحمد اللہ کہ جاں آں جا مقیم است

Though my body does not appear in your presence as yet, grateful am I
to Allah تَبَارَكَوَتَعَالَى that my soul is there for me.

بخود درماندہ ام از نفس خود راے

ببیں درماندۂ چندیں ببخشاے

O Rasulullah صَلَّیاللهُعَلَیْهِوَسَلَّم, frustrated have I become, dejected of my
selfishness. Help this helpless soul and turn your gaze of favour towards
him.

اگر نبودے چو لطفت دست یارے

زدست ما نیاید ہیچ کارے

If your loving kindness is not showered upon us, paralysis would
overtake us and defeated shall we be.

قضا می افگند از راہ مارا

خدا را از خدا در خواہ مارا

Our ill-fate has turned us from Allah's ﷽ path of righteousness. You make dua to Him on our behalf for complete guidance.

کہ بخشد از یقین اوّل حیاتے

دہد آنگہ بکار دیں ثباتے

(This dua was then said), O Allah, firstly grant us true faith in a goodly, fruitful life. And guide us, O Allah, to be steadfast in following the Deen.

چو ہول روز رستاخیز خیزد

بآتش آبرو دے مانریزد

When we meet the terrors of Qiyaamah, the Rabb of the day of Qiyaamah shall save us from it with honour and dignity.

کند با ایں ہمہ گمراہئ ما

ترا اذن شفاعت خواہئ ما

In spite of our numerous heinous sins, Allah ﷽ shall grant Muhammad ﷺ, the power to intercede for us, without which we will be lost.

چو چوگاں سر فگندہ آدری روے

بمیدانِ شفاعت امّتی گوے

You shall arrive on the plains of reckoning, while we, encircled by our sins shall look on as you shall bend your head in dua, calling out, "Forgive my Ummah, O Allah! Forgive them."

بحسن اہتمامت کار جامی

طفیل دیگراں یا بد تمامی

And may through your glorious efforts and the blessings of the pious,

this Jaami' also be included amongst the accepted and pardoned ones.

Aameen.

SALAAM IN THE COURT OF THE BEST OF HUMANITY ﷺ

Prepared by Faqeehul Ummat, Hadhrat Mufti Mahmood Hasan Gangohi رحمه الله

بڑھاپا ہے چلا ہوں سوئے طیبہ

In my old age I am walking towards Yasrib

لرز لڑ کھڑ اتا سر جھکائے

Trembling, staggering with my head stooping low

گناہوں کا ہے سر پر بوجھ بھاری

My head is heavy with the burden of my sins

پریشاں ہوں اسے اب کون اٹھائے

I am worried, now who will carry this load of mine

کبھی آیا جو آنکھوں میں اندھیرا

Sometimes darkness veils my eyes all of a sudden

تو چکرا کر قدم بھی ڈگمگائے

Drowsiness renders my weak legs unstable

کبھی لاٹھی کبھی دیوار پکڑی

Sometimes a stick I hold and sometimes a wall

کبھی پھر بھی قدم جمنے نہ پائے

Then too my feet do not become steady at all

نہ بیٹا ہے نہ پوتا ہے نہ بھائ

کوئی گھر میں نہیں جو ساتھ جائے

I have no son, no grandson and no brother

There's no one at home to go with me yonder

نہیں کچھ آرزو اب واپسی کی

وہیں رکھے خدا واپس نہ لائے

I have no desire to return home

May Allah keep me there never to return

مگر چلتا رہوں گا دھیرے دھیرے

دیاوالا میری نیّا تَرائے

But I would carry on walking step by step

O Merciful One! Let my boat stay afloat

وہاں جا کر کہوں گا گڑ گڑا کر

سلام اس پر جو گرتوں کو اٹھائے

I would go there and cry profusely and say

Salaam upon Him who raises the fallen

سلام اُس پر جو سوتوں کو جگائے

سلام اس پر جو روتوں کو ہنسائے

Salaam upon Him who awakens the sleeping

Salaam upon Him who makes those who are crying laugh

سلام اس پر جو اجڑوں کو بسائے

Salaam upon Him who
shelters the homeless

سلام اس پر جو بھوکوں کو کھلائے

Salaam upon Him who feeds the
hungry

سلام اس پر جو پیاسوں کو پلائے

Salaam upon Him who
quenches the thirsty

سلام اس پر جو گریوں کو سجائے

Salaam upon Him who adorns the
times

CHAPTER FOURTEEN

Forty Durood upon Hazrat Rasulullah صَلَّى ٱللَّهُ عَلَيْهِ وَسَلَّمَ

سَلَامٌ عَلَى عِبَادِهِ الَّذِينَ اصْطَفَى

سَلَامٌ عَلَى الْمُرْسَلِينَ

١) اَللّٰهُمَّ صَلِّ عَلَى مُحَمَّدٍ وَعَلَى آلِ مُحَمَّدٍ وَأَنْزِلْهُ الْمَقْعَدَ الْمُقَرَّبَ عِنْدَكَ

O Allah تَبَارَكَ وَتَعَالَى, shower your choicest Durood (blessings) on Hazrat Muhammad صَلَّى ٱللَّهُ عَلَيْهِ وَسَلَّمَ and upon the family of Hazrat Muhammad صَلَّى ٱللَّهُ عَلَيْهِ وَسَلَّمَ, and grant him the lofty position of Maqaam-e-Mahmood on the day of Qiyaamah

٢) اَللّٰهُمَّ رَبَّ هَذِهِ الدَّعْوَةِ الْقَائِمَةِ وَالصَّلَوةِ النَّافِعَةِ صَلِّ عَلَى مُحَمَّدٍ وَارْضَ عَنِّى رِضًا لَا تَسْخَطُ بَعْدَهُ أَبَدًا

O Allah تَبَارَكَ وَتَعَالَى, Rabb of this lasting call and this beneficial dua, confer Your special blessings upon Hazrat Muhammad صَلَّى ٱللَّهُ عَلَيْهِ وَسَلَّمَ and bless

me with Your everlasting pleasure after which You would never be displeased with me.

٣) اَللّٰهُمَّ صَلِّ عَلٰى مُحَمَّدٍ عَبْدِكَ وَرَسُوْلِكَ وَصَلِّ عَلَى الْمُؤْمِنِيْنَ وَالْمُؤْمِنَاتِ وَالْمُسْلِمِيْنَ وَالْمُسْلِمَاتِ

O Allah ﵎, send your choicest blessings upon Hazrat Muhammad ﷺ your slave and messenger, and descend blessings upon the believing men and women.

٤) اَللّٰهُمَّ صَلِّ عَلٰى مُحَمَّدٍ وَّعَلٰى آلِ مُحَمَّدٍ وَبَارِكْ عَلٰى مُحَمَّدٍ وَّعَلٰى آلِ مُحَمَّدٍ وَّارْحَمْ مُحَمَّدًا وَآلَ مُحَمَّدٍ كَمَا صَلَّيْتَ وَبَارَكْتَ وَرَحِمْتَ عَلٰى إِبْرَاهِيْمَ وَعَلٰى آلِ إِبْرَاهِيْمَ إِنَّكَ حَمِيْدٌ مَجِيْدٌ

O Allah ﵎, bestow Your special mercy upon Hazrat Muhammad ﷺ and the family of Hazrat Muhammad ﷺ, and shower Your choicest blessings upon Hazrat Muhammad ﷺ and the family of Hazrat Muhammad ﷺ and shower Your special mercy upon Hazrat Muhammad ﷺ and the family of Hazrat Muhammad ﷺ, as You bestowed Your mercy, showered Your blessings, and showered Your special mercy upon Hazrat Ebrahim ﵇ and the family of Hazrat Ebrahim ﵇. Indeed, You are praiseworthy and most glorious.

٥) اَللّٰهُمَّ صَلِّ عَلٰى مُحَمَّدٍ وَّعَلٰى آلِ مُحَمَّدٍ كَمَا صَلَّيْتَ عَلٰى آلِ إِبْرَاهِيْمَ إِنَّكَ حَمِيْدٌ مَجِيْدٌ، اَللّٰهُمَّ بَارِكْ عَلٰى مُحَمَّدٍ وَّعَلٰى آلِ مُحَمَّدٍ كَمَا بَارَكْتَ عَلٰى آلِ إِبْرَاهِيْمَ إِنَّكَ حَمِيْدٌ مَجِيْدٌ

O Allah تَبَارَكَ وَتَعَالَى, shower Your mercy upon Hazrat Muhammad صَلَّى ٱللَّهُ عَلَيْهِ وَسَلَّمَ and the family of Hazrat Muhammad صَلَّى ٱللَّهُ عَلَيْهِ وَسَلَّمَ, as You showered Your mercy upon the family of Hazrat Ebrahim عَلَيْهِ ٱلسَّلَامُ. Indeed, You are praiseworthy and most glorious. O Allah تَبَارَكَ وَتَعَالَى, shower Your blessings upon Hazrat Muhammad صَلَّى ٱللَّهُ عَلَيْهِ وَسَلَّمَ and the family of Hazrat Muhammad صَلَّى ٱللَّهُ عَلَيْهِ وَسَلَّمَ, as You showered Your blessings upon the family of Hazrat Ebrahim عَلَيْهِ ٱلسَّلَامُ. Indeed, You are praiseworthy and most glorious.

٦) اَللّٰهُمَّ صَلِّ عَلَى مُحَمَّدٍ وَّعَلَى آلِ مُحَمَّدٍ كَمَا صَلَّيْتَ عَلَى آلِ إِبْرَاهِيْمَ إِنَّكَ حَمِيْدٌ مَّجِيْدٌ وَبَارِكْ عَلَى مُحَمَّدٍ وَّعَلَى آلِ مُحَمَّدٍ كَمَا بَارَكْتَ عَلَى آلِ إِبْرَاهِيْمَ إِنَّكَ حَمِيْدٌ مَّجِيْدٌ

O Allah تَبَارَكَ وَتَعَالَى, shower Your mercy upon Hazrat Muhammad صَلَّى ٱللَّهُ عَلَيْهِ وَسَلَّمَ and the family of Hazrat Muhammad صَلَّى ٱللَّهُ عَلَيْهِ وَسَلَّمَ, as You showered Your mercy upon the family of Hazrat Ebrahim عَلَيْهِ ٱلسَّلَامُ. Indeed, You are praiseworthy and most glorious. O Allah تَبَارَكَ وَتَعَالَى, shower Your blessings upon Hazrat Muhammad صَلَّى ٱللَّهُ عَلَيْهِ وَسَلَّمَ and the family of Hazrat Muhammad صَلَّى ٱللَّهُ عَلَيْهِ وَسَلَّمَ, as You showered Your blessings upon the family of Hazrat Ebrahim عَلَيْهِ ٱلسَّلَامُ. Indeed, You are praiseworthy and most glorious.

٧) اَللّٰهُمَّ صَلِّ عَلَى مُحَمَّدٍ وَّعَلَى آلِ مُحَمَّدٍ كَمَا صَلَّيْتَ عَلَى إِبْرَاهِيْمَ إِنَّكَ حَمِيْدٌ مَّجِيْدٌ، اَللّٰهُمَّ بَارِكْ عَلَى مُحَمَّدٍ وَّعَلَى آلِ مُحَمَّدٍ كَمَا بَارَكْتَ عَلَى إِبْرَاهِيْمَ إِنَّكَ حَمِيْدٌ مَّجِيْدٌ

O Allah تَبَارَكَ وَتَعَالَى, shower Your mercy upon Hazrat Muhammad صَلَّى ٱللَّهُ عَلَيْهِ وَسَلَّمَ and the family of Hazrat Muhammad صَلَّى ٱللَّهُ عَلَيْهِ وَسَلَّمَ, as You showered Your mercy upon Hazrat Ebrahim عَلَيْهِ ٱلسَّلَامُ. Indeed, You are praiseworthy and most glorious. O Allah تَبَارَكَ وَتَعَالَى, shower Your blessings upon Hazrat Muhammad صَلَّى ٱللَّهُ عَلَيْهِ وَسَلَّمَ and the family of Hazrat Muhammad صَلَّى ٱللَّهُ عَلَيْهِ وَسَلَّمَ, as You showered Your blessings upon Hazrat Ebrahim عَلَيْهِ ٱلسَّلَامُ. Indeed, You are praiseworthy and most glorious.

٨) اَللّٰهُمَّ صَلِّ عَلٰى مُحَمَّدٍ وَّعَلٰى آلِ مُحَمَّدٍ كَمَا صَلَّيْتَ عَلٰى إِبْرَاهِيْمَ وَعَلٰى آلِ إِبْرَاهِيْمَ إِنَّكَ حَمِيْدٌ مَّجِيْدٌ وَبَارِكْ عَلٰى مُحَمَّدٍ وَّعَلٰى آلِ مُحَمَّدٍ كَمَا بَارَكْتَ عَلٰى إِبْرَاهِيْمَ إِنَّكَ حَمِيْدٌ مَّجِيْدٌ

O Allah تَبَارَكَ وَتَعَالَى, shower Your mercy upon Hazrat Muhammad صَلَّى ٱللَّهُ عَلَيْهِ وَسَلَّمَ and the family of Hazrat Muhammad صَلَّى ٱللَّهُ عَلَيْهِ وَسَلَّمَ, as You showered Your mercy upon Hazrat Ebrahim عَلَيْهِ ٱلسَّلَامُ and the family of Hazrat Ebrahim عَلَيْهِ ٱلسَّلَامُ. Indeed, You are praiseworthy and most glorious. O Allah تَبَارَكَ وَتَعَالَى, shower Your blessings upon Hazrat Muhammad صَلَّى ٱللَّهُ عَلَيْهِ وَسَلَّمَ and the family of Hazrat Muhammad صَلَّى ٱللَّهُ عَلَيْهِ وَسَلَّمَ, as You showered Your blessings upon Hazrat Ebrahim عَلَيْهِ ٱلسَّلَامُ and the family of Hazrat Ebrahim عَلَيْهِ ٱلسَّلَامُ. Indeed, You are praiseworthy and most glorious.

٩) اَللّٰهُمَّ صَلِّ عَلٰى مُحَمَّدٍ وَّعَلٰى آلِ مُحَمَّدٍ كَمَا صَلَّيْتَ عَلٰى إِبْرَاهِيْمَ وَبَارِكْ عَلٰى مُحَمَّدٍ وَّعَلٰى آلِ مُحَمَّدٍ كَمَا بَارَكْتَ عَلٰى إِبْرَاهِيْمَ إِنَّكَ حَمِيْدٌ مَّجِيْدٌ

O Allah تَبَارَكَ وَتَعَالَى, shower Your mercy upon Hazrat Muhammad صَلَّى ٱللَّهُ عَلَيْهِ وَسَلَّمَ and the family of Hazrat Muhammad صَلَّى ٱللَّهُ عَلَيْهِ وَسَلَّمَ, as You showered Your mercy upon Hazrat Ebrahim عَلَيْهِ ٱلسَّلَامُ, and shower Your blessings upon Hazrat Muhammad صَلَّى ٱللَّهُ عَلَيْهِ وَسَلَّمَ and the family of Hazrat

Muhammad ﷺ, as You showered Your blessings upon Hazrat Ebrahim السلام. Indeed, You are praiseworthy and most glorious.

(١٠) اَللّٰهُمَّ صَلِّ عَلٰى مُحَمَّدٍ وَّعَلٰى آلِ مُحَمَّدٍ كَمَا صَلَّيْتَ عَلٰى إِبْرَاهِيمَ إِنَّكَ حَمِيْدٌ مَجِيْدٌ، اَللّٰهُمَّ بَارِكْ عَلٰى مُحَمَّدٍ وَّعَلٰى آلِ مُحَمَّدٍ كَمَا بَارَكْتَ عَلٰى آلِ إِبْرَاهِيمَ إِنَّكَ حَمِيْدٌ مَجِيْدٌ

O Allah تَبَارَكَوَتَعَالَى, shower Your mercy upon Hazrat Muhammad ﷺ and the family of Hazrat Muhammad ﷺ, as You showered Your mercy upon Hazrat Ebrahim السلام. Indeed, You are praiseworthy and most glorious. O Allah تَبَارَكَوَتَعَالَى, shower Your blessings upon Hazrat Muhammad ﷺ and the family of Hazrat Muhammad ﷺ, as You showered Your blessings upon the family of Hazrat Ebrahim السلام. Indeed, You are praiseworthy and most glorious.

(١١) اَللّٰهُمَّ صَلِّ عَلٰى مُحَمَّدٍ وَّعَلٰى آلِ مُحَمَّدٍ كَمَا صَلَّيْتَ عَلٰى آلِ إِبْرَاهِيمَ وَبَارِكْ عَلٰى مُحَمَّدٍ وَّعَلٰى آلِ مُحَمَّدٍ كَمَا بَارَكْتَ عَلٰى آلِ إِبْرَاهِيمَ فِي الْعَالَمِيْنَ إِنَّكَ حَمِيْدٌ مَجِيْدٌ

O Allah تَبَارَكَوَتَعَالَى, shower Your mercy upon Hazrat Muhammad ﷺ and the family of Hazrat Muhammad ﷺ, as You showered Your mercy upon the family of Hazrat Ebrahim السلام, and shower Your blessings upon Hazrat Muhammad ﷺ and the family of Hazrat Muhammad ﷺ, as You showered Your blessings upon the family of Hazrat Ebrahim السلام in both the worlds. Indeed, You are praiseworthy and most glorious.

(١٢) اَللّٰهُمَّ صَلِّ عَلٰى مُحَمَّدٍ وَّ أَزْوَاجِهِ وَذُرِّيَّتِهِ كَمَا صَلَّيْتَ عَلٰى آلِ إِبْرَاهِيمَ وَبَارِكْ عَلٰى مُحَمَّدٍ وَّأَزْوَاجِهِ وَذُرِّيَّتِهِ كَمَا بَارَكْتَ عَلٰى آلِ إِبْرَاهِيمَ إِنَّكَ حَمِيْدٌ مَجِيْدٌ

O Allah تَبَارَكَ وَتَعَالَى, *shower Your mercy upon Hazrat Muhammad* صَلَّى ٱللَّهُ عَلَيْهِ وَسَلَّمَ *and his wives and his offspring, as You showered Your mercy upon the family of Hazrat Ebrahim* عَلَيْهِ ٱلسَّلَامُ, *and shower Your blessings upon Hazrat Muhammad* صَلَّى ٱللَّهُ عَلَيْهِ وَسَلَّمَ *and his wives and his offspring, as You showered Your blessings upon the family of Hazrat Ebrahim* عَلَيْهِ ٱلسَّلَامُ. *Indeed, You are praiseworthy and most glorious.*

١٣) اَللّٰهُمَّ صَلِّ عَلَى مُحَمَّدٍ وَّعَلَى أَزْوَاجِهِ وَذُرِّيَّتِهِ كَمَا صَلَّيْتَ عَلَى آلِ إِبْرَاهِيْمَ وَبَارِكْ عَلَى مُحَمَّدٍ وَّعَلَى أَزْوَاجِهِ وَذُرِّيَّتِهِ كَمَا بَارَكْتَ عَلَى آلِ إِبْرَاهِيْمَ إِنَّكَ حَمِيْدٌ مَّجِيْدٌ

O Allah, shower Your mercy upon Hazrat Muhammad صَلَّى ٱللَّهُ عَلَيْهِ وَسَلَّمَ *and his wives and his offspring, as You showered Your mercy upon the family of Hazrat Ebrahim* عَلَيْهِ ٱلسَّلَامُ, *and shower Your blessings upon Hazrat Muhammad* صَلَّى ٱللَّهُ عَلَيْهِ وَسَلَّمَ *and his wives and his offspring, as You showered Your blessings upon the family of Hazrat Ebrahim* عَلَيْهِ ٱلسَّلَامُ. *Indeed, You are praiseworthy and most glorious.*

١٤) اَللّٰهُمَّ صَلِّ عَلَى مُحَمَّدٍ النَّبِيِّ وَأَزْوَاجِهِ أُمَّهَاتِ الْمُؤْمِنِيْنَ وَذُرِّيَّتِهِ وَأَهْلِ بَيْتِهِ كَمَا صَلَّيْتَ عَلَى إِبْرَاهِيْمَ إِنَّكَ حَمِيْدٌ مَّجِيْدٌ

O Allah تَبَارَكَ وَتَعَالَى, *shower Your mercy upon Hazrat Muhammad* صَلَّى ٱللَّهُ عَلَيْهِ وَسَلَّمَ *and his wives who are the mother's of the believers, his offspring, and his household as You showered Your mercy upon Hazrat Ebrahim* عَلَيْهِ ٱلسَّلَامُ. *Indeed, You are praiseworthy and most glorious.*

١٥) اَللّٰهُمَّ صَلِّ عَلَى مُحَمَّدٍ وَّعَلَى آلِ مُحَمَّدٍ كَمَا صَلَّيْتَ عَلَى إِبْرَاهِيْمَ وَعَلَى آلِ إِبْرَاهِيْمَ
وَبَارِكْ عَلَى مُحَمَّدٍ وَّعَلَى آلِ مُحَمَّدٍ كَمَا بَارَكْتَ عَلَى إِبْرَاهِيْمَ وَتَرَحَّمْ عَلَى مُحَمَّدٍ وَّعَلَى
آلِ مُحَمَّدٍ كَمَا تَرَحَّمْتَ عَلَى إِبْرَاهِيْمَ وَعَلَى آلِ إِبْرَاهِيْمَ

O Allah تَبَارَكَوَتَعَالَى, *shower Your mercy upon Hazrat Muhammad*
and the family of Hazrat Muhammad ﷺ, *as You*
showered Your mercy upon Hazrat Ebrahim عَلَيْهِٱلسَّلَامُ *and the family of*
Hazrat Ebrahim عَلَيْهِٱلسَّلَامُ, *and shower Your blessings upon Hazrat*
Muhammad ﷺ *and the family of Hazrat Muhammad*
ﷺ, *as You showered Your blessings upon Hazrat Ebrahim*
عَلَيْهِٱلسَّلَامُ, *and shower Your compassion upon Hazrat Muhammad*
and the family of Hazrat Muhammad ﷺ, *as You*
showered Your compassion upon Hazrat Ebrahim عَلَيْهِٱلسَّلَامُ *and the family*
of Hazrat Ebrahim عَلَيْهِٱلسَّلَامُ.

١٦) اَللّٰهُمَّ صَلِّ عَلَى مُحَمَّدٍ وَّعَلَى آلِ مُحَمَّدٍ كَمَا صَلَّيْتَ عَلَى إِبْرَاهِيْمَ وَعَلَى آلِ إِبْرَاهِيْمَ
إِنَّكَ حَمِيْدٌ مَّجِيْدٌ، اَللّٰهُمَّ بَارِكْ عَلَى مُحَمَّدٍ وَّعَلَى آلِ مُحَمَّدٍ كَمَا بَارَكْتَ عَلَى إِبْرَاهِيْمَ
وَعَلَى آلِ إِبْرَاهِيْمَ إِنَّكَ حَمِيْدٌ مَّجِيْدٌ، اَللّٰهُمَّ تَرَحَّمْ عَلَى مُحَمَّدٍ وَّعَلَى آلِ مُحَمَّدٍ كَمَا
تَرَحَّمْتَ عَلَى إِبْرَاهِيْمَ وَعَلَى آلِ إِبْرَاهِيْمَ إِنَّكَ حَمِيْدٌ مَّجِيْدٌ، اَللّٰهُمَّ تَحَنَّنْ عَلَى مُحَمَّدٍ
وَّعَلَى آلِ مُحَمَّدٍ كَمَا تَحَنَّنْتَ عَلَى إِبْرَاهِيْمَ وَعَلَى آلِ إِبْرَاهِيْمَ إِنَّكَ حَمِيْدٌ مَّجِيْدٌ، اَللّٰهُمَّ
سَلِّمْ عَلَى مُحَمَّدٍ وَّعَلَى آلِ مُحَمَّدٍ كَمَا سَلَّمْتَ عَلَى إِبْرَاهِيْمَ وَعَلَى آلِ إِبْرَاهِيْمَ إِنَّكَ
حَمِيْدٌ مَّجِيْدٌ

O Allah تَبَارَكَوَتَعَالَى, *shower Your mercy upon Hazrat Muhammad*
and the family of Hazrat Muhammad ﷺ, *as You*
showered Your mercy upon Hazrat Ebrahim عَلَيْهِٱلسَّلَامُ *and the family of*

Hazrat Ebrahim عَلَيْهِ ٱلسَّلَامُ. Indeed, You are praiseworthy and most glorious. O Allah تَبَارَكَ وَتَعَالَى, shower Your blessings upon Hazrat Muhammad صَلَّى ٱللَّهُ عَلَيْهِ وَسَلَّمَ and the family of Hazrat Muhammad صَلَّى ٱللَّهُ عَلَيْهِ وَسَلَّمَ, as You showered Your blessings upon Hazrat Ebrahim عَلَيْهِ ٱلسَّلَامُ and the family of Hazrat Ebrahim عَلَيْهِ ٱلسَّلَامُ. Indeed, You are praiseworthy and most glorious. O Allah تَبَارَكَ وَتَعَالَى, shower Your compassion upon Hazrat Muhammad صَلَّى ٱللَّهُ عَلَيْهِ وَسَلَّمَ and the family of Hazrat Muhammad صَلَّى ٱللَّهُ عَلَيْهِ وَسَلَّمَ, as You showered Your compassion upon Hazrat Ebrahim عَلَيْهِ ٱلسَّلَامُ and the family of Hazrat Ebrahim عَلَيْهِ ٱلسَّلَامُ. Indeed, You are praiseworthy and most glorious. O Allah تَبَارَكَ وَتَعَالَى, shower Your special mercy upon Hazrat Muhammad صَلَّى ٱللَّهُ عَلَيْهِ وَسَلَّمَ and the family of Hazrat Muhammad صَلَّى ٱللَّهُ عَلَيْهِ وَسَلَّمَ, as You showered Your special mercy upon Hazrat Ebrahim عَلَيْهِ ٱلسَّلَامُ and the family of Hazrat Ebrahim عَلَيْهِ ٱلسَّلَامُ. Indeed, You are praiseworthy and most glorious. O Allah تَبَارَكَ وَتَعَالَى, shower Your peace upon Hazrat Muhammad صَلَّى ٱللَّهُ عَلَيْهِ وَسَلَّمَ and the family of Hazrat Muhammad صَلَّى ٱللَّهُ عَلَيْهِ وَسَلَّمَ, as You showered Your peace upon Hazrat Ebrahim عَلَيْهِ ٱلسَّلَامُ and the family of Hazrat Ebrahim عَلَيْهِ ٱلسَّلَامُ. Indeed, You are praiseworthy and most glorious.

١٧) اَللَّهُمَّ صَلِّ عَلَى مُحَمَّدٍ وَعَلَى آلِ مُحَمَّدٍ وَّبَارِكْ وَسَلِّمْ عَلَى مُحَمَّدٍ وَّ عَلَى آلِ مُحَمَّدٍ وَّارْحَمْ مُحَمَّدًا وَّآلَ مُحَمَّدٍ كَمَا صَلَّيْتَ وَبَارَكْتَ وَتَرَحَّمْتَ عَلَى إِبْرَاهِيمَ وَعَلَى آلِ إِبْرَاهِيمَ فِي الْعَالَمِيْنَ إِنَّكَ حَمِيْدٌ مَّجِيْدٌ

O Allah تَبَارَكَ وَتَعَالَى, shower Your mercy upon Hazrat Muhammad صَلَّى ٱللَّهُ عَلَيْهِ وَسَلَّمَ and the family of Hazrat Muhammad صَلَّى ٱللَّهُ عَلَيْهِ وَسَلَّمَ, and shower Your blessings and peace upon Hazrat Muhammad صَلَّى ٱللَّهُ عَلَيْهِ وَسَلَّمَ

and the family of Hazrat Muhammad ﷺ, and shower Your compassion upon Hazrat Muhammad ﷺ and the family of Hazrat Muhammad ﷺ, as You showered Your mercy, blessings, and compassion upon Hazrat Ebrahim عَلَيْهِ السَّلَامُ and the family of Hazrat Ebrahim عَلَيْهِ السَّلَامُ in all the worlds. Indeed, You are praiseworthy and most glorious.

١٨) اَللّٰهُمَّ صَلِّ عَلٰى مُحَمَّدٍ وَّعَلٰى آلِ مُحَمَّدٍ كَمَا صَلَّيْتَ عَلٰى إِبْرَاهِيْمَ وَعَلٰى آلِ إِبْرَاهِيْمَ إِنَّكَ حَمِيْدٌ مَجِيْدٌ ، اَللّٰهُمَّ بَارِكْ عَلٰى مُحَمَّدٍ وَّعَلٰى آلِ مُحَمَّدٍ كَمَا بَارَكْتَ عَلٰى إِبْرَاهِيْمَ وَعَلٰى آلِ إِبْرَاهِيْمَ إِنَّكَ حَمِيْدٌ مَجِيْدٌ

O Allah تَبَارَكَ وَتَعَالٰى, shower Your mercy upon Hazrat Muhammad ﷺ and the family of Hazrat Muhammad ﷺ, as You showered Your mercy upon Hazrat Ebrahim عَلَيْهِ السَّلَامُ and the family of Hazrat Ebrahim عَلَيْهِ السَّلَامُ. Indeed, You are praiseworthy and most glorious. O Allah تَبَارَكَ وَتَعَالٰى, shower Your blessings upon Hazrat Muhammad ﷺ and the family of Hazrat Muhammad ﷺ, as You showered Your blessings upon Hazrat Ebrahim عَلَيْهِ السَّلَامُ and the family of Hazrat Ebrahim عَلَيْهِ السَّلَامُ. Indeed, You are praiseworthy and most glorious.

١٩) اَللّٰهُمَّ صَلِّ عَلٰى مُحَمَّدٍ عَبْدِكَ وَرَسُوْلِكَ كَمَا صَلَّيْتَ عَلٰى آلِ إِبْرَاهِيْمَ وَبَارِكْ عَلٰى مُحَمَّدٍ وَّعَلٰى آلِ مُحَمَّدٍ كَمَا بَارَكْتَ عَلٰى آلِ إِبْرَاهِيْمَ إِنَّكَ حَمِيْدٌ مَجِيْدٌ

O Allah تَبَارَكَ وَتَعَالٰى, shower Your mercy upon Hazrat Muhammad ﷺ, Your servant and Messenger, as You showered Your mercy upon Hazrat Ebrahim عَلَيْهِ السَّلَامُ, and shower Your blessings upon Hazrat

Muhammad ﷺ and the family of Hazrat Muhammad ﷺ, as You showered Your blessings upon the family of Hazrat Ebrahim عليه السلام. Indeed, You are praiseworthy and most glorious.

٢٠)   اَللّٰهُمَّ صَلِّ عَلٰى مُحَمَّدٍ النَّبِيِّ الْأُمِّيِّ وَعَلٰى آلِ مُحَمَّدٍ كَمَا صَلَّيْتَ عَلٰى إِبْرَاهِيمَ وَبَارِكْ عَلٰى مُحَمَّدٍ النَّبِيِّ الْأُمِّيِّ كَمَا بَارَكْتَ عَلٰى إِبْرَاهِيمَ إِنَّكَ حَمِيْدٌ مَجِيْدٌ

O Allah تبارك وتعالى, shower Your mercy upon Hazrat Muhammad ﷺ, the unlettered Nabi,and upon the family of Hazrat Muhammad ﷺ, as You showered Your mercy upon Hazrat Ebrahim عليه السلام, and shower Your blessings upon Hazrat Muhammad ﷺ, the unlettered Nabi, as You showered Your blessings upon Hazrat Ebrahim عليه السلام. Indeed, You are praiseworthy and most glorious.

٢١)   اَللّٰهُمَّ صَلِّ عَلٰى مُحَمَّدٍ عَبْدِكَ وَرَسُوْلِكَ النَّبِيِّ الْأُمِّيِّ وَعَلٰى آلِ مُحَمَّدٍ اَللّٰهُمَّ صَلِّ عَلٰى مُحَمَّدٍ وَّعَلٰى آلِ مُحَمَّدٍ صَلٰوةً تَكُوْنُ لَكَ رِضًى وَّلَهُ جَزَآءً وَّلِحَقِّهِ أَدَآءً وَّ اَعْطِهِ الْوَسِيْلَةَ وَالْفَضِيْلَةَ وَالْمَقَامَ الْمَحْمُوْدَ الَّذِيْ وَعَدْتَّهُ وَاجْزِهِ عَنَّا مَا هُوَ أَهْلُهُ وَاجْزِهِ أَفْضَلَ مَا جَازَيْتَ نَبِيًّا عَنْ قَوْمِهِ وَرَسُوْلًا عَنْ أُمَّتِهِ، وَصَلِّ عَلٰى جَمِيْعِ إِخْوَانِهِ مِنَ النَّبِيِّيْنَ وَالصَّالِحِيْنَ يَا أَرْحَمَ الرَّاحِمِيْنَ

O Allah تبارك وتعالى, shower your special mercy upon Hazrat Muhammad ﷺ, Your slave and Your messenger, the unlettered messenger, and upon the family of Hazrat Muhammad ﷺ. O Allah تبارك وتعالى, shower your special mercy upon Hazrat Muhammad ﷺ and upon the family of Hazrat Muhammad ﷺ, such mercy which would please You and which is a reward for him, and which truly fulfils his rights. And grant him Al-Waseelah and Al-Fadeelah (Your special Grace) and Al-Maqaam al-Mahmood (the honour of interceding to Allah تَبَارَكَ وَتَعَالَى to commence the reckoning on the day of Qiyaamah) which You have promised him. Reward him on our behalf with a reward he is deserving of and reward him with the best You have ever rewarded a Nabi on behalf of his people and a messenger on behalf of his followers. And shower Your mercy upon all his brothers from amongst the Ambiyaa and the righteous servants, O Most Merciful of those who show mercy.

٢٢) اَللّٰهُمَّ صَلِّ عَلٰى مُحَمَّدٍ النَّبِيِّ الْأُمِّيِّ وَعَلٰى آلِ مُحَمَّدٍ كَمَا صَلَّيْتَ عَلٰى إِبْرَاهِيْمَ وَعَلٰى آلِ إِبْرَاهِيْمَ وَبَارِكْ عَلٰى مُحَمَّدٍ النَّبِيِّ الْأُمِّيِّ وَعَلٰى آلِ مُحَمَّدٍ كَمَا بَارَكْتَ عَلٰى إِبْرَاهِيْمَ وَعَلٰى آلِ إِبْرَاهِيْمَ إِنَّكَ حَمِيْدٌ مَجِيْدٌ

O Allah تَبَارَكَ وَتَعَالَى, shower Your mercy upon Hazrat Muhammad ﷺ, the unlettered Nabi, and upon the family of Hazrat Muhammad ﷺ, as You showered Your mercy upon Hazrat Ebrahim عَلَيْهِ السَّلَام, and the family of Hazrat Ebrahim عَلَيْهِ السَّلَام, and shower Your blessings upon Hazrat Muhammad ﷺ, the unlettered Nabi, and upon the family of Hazrat Muhammad ﷺ, as You showered Your blessings upon Hazrat Ebrahim عَلَيْهِ السَّلَام and the family of Hazrat Ebrahim عَلَيْهِ السَّلَام. Indeed, You are praiseworthy and most glorious.

٢٣) اَللّٰهُمَّ صَلِّ عَلٰى مُحَمَّدٍ وَّعَلٰى أَهْلِ بَيْتِهِ كَمَا صَلَّيْتَ عَلٰى إِبْرَاهِيْمَ إِنَّكَ حَمِيْدٌ مَجِيْدٌ اَللّٰهُمَّ صَلِّ عَلَيْنَا مَعَهُمْ اَللّٰهُمَّ بَارِكْ عَلٰى مُحَمَّدٍ وَّعَلٰى أَهْلِ بَيْتِهِ كَمَا بَارَكْتَ عَلٰى

إِبْرَاهِيْمَ إِنَّكَ حَمِيْدٌ مَجِيْدٌ، اَللّٰهُمَّ بَارِكْ عَلَيْنَا مَعَهُمْ، صَلَوَاتُ اللهِ وَصَلَوَاتُ الْمُؤْمِنِيْنَ عَلٰى مُحَمَّدٍ النَّبِيِّ الْأُمِّيِّ

O Allah تَبَارَكَ وَتَعَالٰى, shower your special mercy upon Hazrat Muhammad صَلَّى ٱللَّهُ عَلَيْهِ وَسَلَّمَ and upon the people of his household as You showered mercy upon Hazrat Ebrahim عَلَيْهِ ٱلسَّلَامُ. Indeed, You are praiseworthy and most glorious. O Allah تَبَارَكَ وَتَعَالٰى, shower Your mercy upon us together with them. O Allah تَبَارَكَ وَتَعَالٰى, shower Your blessings upon Hazrat Muhammad صَلَّى ٱللَّهُ عَلَيْهِ وَسَلَّمَ and the people of his household in the manner You showered Your blessings upon Hazrat Ebrahim عَلَيْهِ ٱلسَّلَامُ. Indeed, You are praiseworthy and most glorious. O Allah تَبَارَكَ وَتَعَالٰى, shower Your blessings upon us together with them.

٢٤) اَللّٰهُمَّ اجْعَلْ صَلَوَاتِكَ وَرَحْمَتَكَ وَبَرَكَاتِكَ عَلٰى مُحَمَّدٍ وَّآلِ مُحَمَّدٍ كَمَا جَعَلْتَهَا عَلٰى آلِ إِبْرَاهِيْمَ إِنَّكَ حَمِيْدٌ مَجِيْدٌ وَبَارِكْ عَلٰى مُحَمَّدٍ وَعَلٰى آلِ مُحَمَّدٍ كَمَا بَارَكْتَ عَلٰى إِبْرَاهِيْمَ وَعَلٰى آلِ إِبْرَاهِيْمَ إِنَّكَ حَمِيْدٌ مَجِيْدٌ

O Allah تَبَارَكَ وَتَعَالٰى, shower Your special mercy, compassion and blessings upon Hazrat Muhammad صَلَّى ٱللَّهُ عَلَيْهِ وَسَلَّمَ and the family of Hazrat Muhammad صَلَّى ٱللَّهُ عَلَيْهِ وَسَلَّمَ as You showered upon the family of Hazrat Ebrahim عَلَيْهِ ٱلسَّلَامُ. Indeed, You are Praiseworthy and most glorious. And shower Your blessings upon Hazrat Muhammad صَلَّى ٱللَّهُ عَلَيْهِ وَسَلَّمَ and the family of Hazrat Muhammad صَلَّى ٱللَّهُ عَلَيْهِ وَسَلَّمَ as You showered Your blessings upon Hazrat Ebrahim عَلَيْهِ ٱلسَّلَامُ and the family of Hazrat Ebrahim عَلَيْهِ ٱلسَّلَامُ. Indeed, You are Praiseworthy and most glorious.

٢٥) وَصَلَّى اللهُ عَلَى النَّبِيِّ الْأُمِّيِّ

May Allah تَبَارَكَ وَتَعَالَى shower His special mercy upon Hazrat Muhammad ﷺ, the unlettered Nabi.

(صيغ السلام)

٢٦) اَلتَّحِيَّاتُ لِلّٰهِ وَ الصَّلَوَاتُ وَالطَّيِّبَاتُ، اَلسَّلَامُ عَلَيْكَ أَيُّهَا النَّبِيُّ وَرَحْمَةُ اللهِ وَبَرَكَاتُهُ، اَلسَّلَامُ عَلَيْنَا وَعَلَى عِبَادِ اللهِ الصَّالِحِينَ ، أَشْهَدُ أَنْ لَّا إِلٰهَ إِلَّا اللهُ وَأَشْهَدُ أَنَّ مُحَمَّدًا عَبْدُهُ وَرَسُوْلُهُ

All verbal praises, physical praises and monetary praises be for Allah تَبَارَكَ وَتَعَالَى. May the special peace of Allah تَبَارَكَ وَتَعَالَى descend upon you, O Nabi ﷺ, and Allah's choicest mercies and blessings. May peace descend upon us and upon all the pious servants of Allah تَبَارَكَ وَتَعَالَى. I bear witness that there is no deity except Allah تَبَارَكَ وَتَعَالَى and I bear witness that Hazrat Muhammad ﷺ is His servant and messenger.

٢٧) اَلتَّحِيَّاتُ الطَّيِّبَاتُ الصَّلَوَاتُ لِلّٰهِ اَلسَّلَامُ عَلَيْكَ أَيُّهَا النَّبِيُّ وَرَحْمَةُ اللهِ وَبَرَكَاتُهُ اَلسَّلَامُ عَلَيْنَا وَعَلَى عِبَادِ اللهِ الصَّالِحِينَ أَشْهَدُ أَنْ لَّا إِلٰهَ إِلَّا اللهُ وَأَشْهَدُ أَنَّ مُحَمَّدًا عَبْدُهُ وَ رَسُوْلُهُ

All verbal praises, monetary praises and physical praises are for Allah تَبَارَكَ وَتَعَالَى. May the special peace of Allah تَبَارَكَ وَتَعَالَى descend upon you, O Nabi ﷺ, and Allah's choicest mercies and blessings. May peace descend upon us and upon all the pious servants of Allah تَبَارَكَ وَتَعَالَى. I bear witness that there is no deity except Allah تَبَارَكَ وَتَعَالَى and I bear witness that Hazrat Muhammad ﷺ is His servant and messenger.

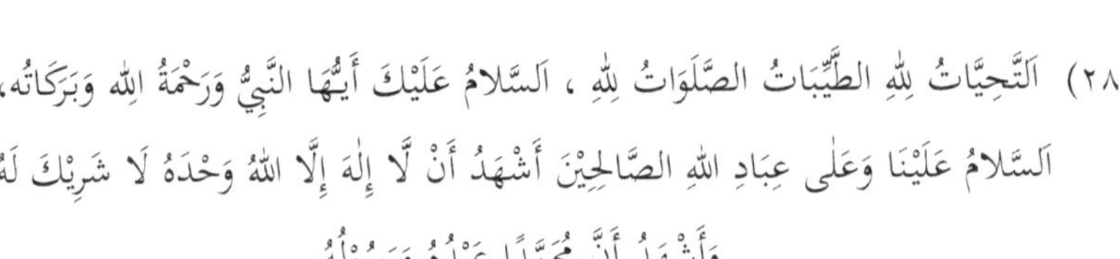

٢٨) اَلتَّحِيَّاتُ لِلّٰهِ الطَّيِّبَاتُ الصَّلَوَاتُ لِلّٰهِ ، اَلسَّلَامُ عَلَيْكَ أَيُّهَا النَّبِيُّ وَرَحْمَةُ اللهِ وَبَرَكَاتُهُ، اَلسَّلَامُ عَلَيْنَا وَعَلَى عِبَادِ اللهِ الصَّالِحِيْنَ أَشْهَدُ أَنْ لَّا إِلٰهَ إِلَّا اللهُ وَحْدَهُ لَا شَرِيْكَ لَهُ وَأَشْهَدُ أَنَّ مُحَمَّدًا عَبْدُهُ وَرَسُوْلُهُ

All verbal praises are for Allah تَبَارَكَوَتَعَالَى, and all monetary praises and physical praises are for Allah تَبَارَكَوَتَعَالَى. May the special peace of Allah تَبَارَكَوَتَعَالَى descend upon you, O Nabi صَلَّىَاللَّهُعَلَيْهِوَسَلَّمَ, and Allah's choicest mercies and blessings. May peace descend upon us and upon all the pious servants of Allah تَبَارَكَوَتَعَالَى. I bear witness that there is no deity except Allah تَبَارَكَوَتَعَالَى who is alone and has no partner, and I bear witness that Hazrat Muhammad صَلَّىَاللَّهُعَلَيْهِوَسَلَّمَ is His servant and messenger.

٢٩) اَلتَّحِيَّاتُ الْمُبَارَكَاتُ الصَّلَوَاتُ الطَّيِّبَاتُ لِلّٰهِ سَلَامٌ عَلَيْكَ أَيُّهَا النَّبِيُّ وَرَحْمَةُ اللهِ وَبَرَكَاتُهُ، سَلَامٌ عَلَيْنَا وَعَلَى عِبَادِ اللهِ الصَّالِحِيْنَ ، أَشْهَدُ أَنْ لَّا إِلٰهَ إِلَّا اللهُ وَأَشْهَدُ أَنَّ مُحَمَّدًا عَبْدُهُ وَرَسُوْلُهُ

All verbal praises which are full of blessings, all physical praises and all monetary praises are for Allah تَبَارَكَوَتَعَالَى. May the special peace of Allah تَبَارَكَوَتَعَالَى descend upon you, O Nabi صَلَّىَاللَّهُعَلَيْهِوَسَلَّمَ, and Allah's choicest mercies and blessings. May peace descend upon us and upon all the pious servants of Allah تَبَارَكَوَتَعَالَى. I bear witness that there is no deity except Allah تَبَارَكَوَتَعَالَى, and I bear witness that Hazrat Muhammad صَلَّىَاللَّهُعَلَيْهِوَسَلَّمَ is His servant and messenger.

٣٠) بِسْمِ اللهِ وَبِاللهِ ، اَلتَّحِيَّاتُ لِلّٰهِ وَالصَّلَوَاتُ وَالطَّيِّبَاتُ اَلسَّلَامُ عَلَيْكَ أَيُّهَا النَّبِيُّ وَرَحْمَةُ اللهِ وَبَرَكَاتُهُ اَلسَّلَامُ عَلَيْنَا وَعَلَى عِبَادِ اللهِ الصَّالِحِيْنَ أَشْهَدُ أَنْ لَّا إِلٰهَ إِلَّا اللهُ وَأَشْهَدُ أَنَّ مُحَمَّدًا عَبْدُهُ وَرَسُوْلُهُ أَسْأَلُ اللهَ الْجَنَّةَ وَأَعُوْذُ بِاللهِ مِنَ النَّارِ

I begin with the name of Allah تَبَارَكَ وَتَعَالَى and with the assistance of Allah تَبَارَكَ وَتَعَالَى. All verbal praises, physical praises and monetary praises be for Allah تَبَارَكَ وَتَعَالَى. May the special peace of Allah تَبَارَكَ وَتَعَالَى descend upon you, O Nabi صَلَّى ٱللَّهُ عَلَيْهِ وَسَلَّمَ, and Allah's choicest mercies and blessings. May peace descend upon us and upon all the pious servants of Allah تَبَارَكَ وَتَعَالَى. I bear witness that there is no deity except Allah تَبَارَكَ وَتَعَالَى and I bear witness that Hazrat Muhammad صَلَّى ٱللَّهُ عَلَيْهِ وَسَلَّمَ is His servant and messenger. I ask Allah تَبَارَكَ وَتَعَالَى for Paradise and I seek His refuge from Jahannum.

(٣١) اَلتَّحِيَّاتُ الزَّاكِيَاتُ لِلّهِ الطَّيِّبَاتُ الصَّلَوَاتُ لِلّهِ ، اَلسَّلَامُ عَلَيْكَ أَيُّهَا النَّبِيُّ وَرَحْمَةُ اللهِ وَبَرَكَاتُهُ، اَلسَّلَامُ عَلَيْنَا وَعَلَى عِبَادِ اللهِ الصَّالِحِينَ ، أَشْهَدُ أَنْ لَّا إِلَهَ إِلَّا اللهُ وَأَشْهَدُ أَنَّ مُحَمَّدًا عَبْدُهُ وَرَسُولُهُ

All verbal praises and all pure actions are for Allah تَبَارَكَ وَتَعَالَى, and all monetary praises and all physical praises are for Allah تَبَارَكَ وَتَعَالَى. May the special peace of Allah صَلَّى ٱللَّهُ عَلَيْهِ وَسَلَّمَ descend upon you, O Nabi تَبَارَكَ وَتَعَالَى, and Allah's choicest mercies and blessings. May peace descend upon us and upon all the pious servants of Allah تَبَارَكَ وَتَعَالَى. I bear witness that there is no deity except Allah تَبَارَكَ وَتَعَالَى, and I bear witness that Hazrat Muhammad صَلَّى ٱللَّهُ عَلَيْهِ وَسَلَّمَ is His servant and messenger.

(٣٢) بِسْمِ اللهِ وَبِاللهِ خَيْرِ الْأَسْمَاءِ، اَلتَّحِيَّاتُ الطَّيِّبَاتُ الصَّلَوَاتُ لِلّهِ ، أَشْهَدُ أَنْ لَّا إِلَهَ إِلَّا اللهُ وَحْدَهُ لَا شَرِيْكَ لَهُ وَأَشْهَدُ أَنَّ مُحَمَّدًا عَبْدُهُ وَرَسُولُهُ ، أَرْسَلَهُ بِالْحَقِّ بَشِيْرًا وَّنَذِيْرًا، وَأَنَّ السَّاعَةَ آتِيَةٌ لَّا رَيْبَ فِيهَا ، اَلسَّلَامُ عَلَيْكَ أَيُّهَا النَّبِيُّ وَرَحْمَةُ اللهِ وَبَرَكَاتُهُ، اَلسَّلَامُ عَلَيْنَا وَعَلَى عِبَادِ اللهِ الصَّالِحِينَ ، اَللّهُمَّ اغْفِرْلِيْ واهْدِنِي

I begin with the name of Allah and with the assistance of Allah تَبَارَكَ وَتَعَالَى, *whose name is the best of all names. All verbal praises, all monetary devotions and all physical praises are for Allah* تَبَارَكَ وَتَعَالَى. *I bear witness that there is no deity except Allah* تَبَارَكَ وَتَعَالَى, *who is alone and has no partner, and I bear witness that Hazrat Muhammad* صَلَّى اللَّهُ عَلَيْهِ وَسَلَّمَ *is His servant and His messenger. He sent him with the truth as a bearer of glad-tidings and as a warner. (And I bear witness) that the Final Hour is coming without any doubt. May the special peace of Allah* تَبَارَكَ وَتَعَالَى *descend upon you, O Nabi* صَلَّى اللَّهُ عَلَيْهِ وَسَلَّمَ, *and Allah's choicest mercies and blessings. May peace descend upon us and upon all the pious servants of Allah* تَبَارَكَ وَتَعَالَى. *O Allah, forgive me and guide me.*

(٣٣) اَلتَّحِيَّاتُ الطَّيِّبَاتُ وَالصَّلَوَاتُ وَالْمُلْكُ لِلهِ ، اَلسَّلاَمُ عَلَيْكَ أَيُّهَا النَّبِيُّ وَرَحْمَةُ اللهِ وَبَرَكَاتُهُ

All verbal praises, all monetary devotions, all physical praises, and the entire kingdom belongs to Allah تَبَارَكَ وَتَعَالَى. *May the special peace of Allah* تَبَارَكَ وَتَعَالَى *descend upon you, O Nabi* صَلَّى اللَّهُ عَلَيْهِ وَسَلَّمَ, *and Allah's choicest mercies and blessings.*

(٣٤) بِسْمِ اللهِ، اَلتَّحِيَّاتُ لِلهِ الصَّلَوَاتُ لِلهِ الزَّاكِيَاتُ لِلهِ ، اَلسَّلاَمُ عَلَى النَّبِيِّ وَرَحْمَةُ اللهِ وَبَرَكَاتُه، اَلسَّلاَمُ عَلَيْنَا وَعَلَى عِبَادِ اللهِ الصَّالِحِينَ ، شَهِدْتُ أَنْ لَّا إِلَهَ إِلَّا اللهُ شَهِدْتُ أَنَّ مُحَمَّدًا رَّسُوْلُ اللهِ

I begin in the name of Allah تَبَارَكَ وَتَعَالَى. *All verbal praises, all physical praises and all pure actions are for Allah* تَبَارَكَ وَتَعَالَى. *May the special peace of Allah* تَبَارَكَ وَتَعَالَى *descend upon you, O Nabi* صَلَّى اللَّهُ عَلَيْهِ وَسَلَّمَ, *and Allah's choicest mercies and blessings. May peace descend upon us and upon all the pious servants of Allah* تَبَارَكَ وَتَعَالَى. *I bear witness that there is no deity except Allah* تَبَارَكَ وَتَعَالَى, *and I bear witness that Hazrat Muhammad* ﷺ *is His servant and messenger.*

(٣٥) اَلتَّحِيَّاتُ الطَّيِّبَاتُ الصَّلَوَاتُ الزَّاكِيَاتُ لِلّٰهِ، أَشْهَدُ أَنْ لَّا إِلٰهَ إِلَّا اللهُ وَحْدَهُ لَا شَرِيكَ لَهُ وَأَنَّ مُحَمَّدًا عَبْدُهُ وَرَسُوْلُهُ، اَلسَّلَامُ عَلَيْكَ أَيُّهَا النَّبِيُّ وَرَحْمَةُ اللهِ وَبَرَكَاتُهُ، اَلسَّلَامُ عَلَيْنَا وَعَلَى عِبَادِ اللهِ الصَّالِحِيْنَ

All verbal praises, monetary devotions, physical praises and pure actions are for Allah تَبَارَكَ وَتَعَالَى. *I bear witness that there is no deity except Allah* تَبَارَكَ وَتَعَالَى, *who is alone and has no partner, and I bear witness that Hazrat Muhammad* ﷺ *is His servant and messenger. May the special peace of Allah* تَبَارَكَ وَتَعَالَى *descend upon you, O Nabi* ﷺ, *and Allah's choicest mercies and blessings. May peace descend upon us and upon all the pious servants of Allah* تَبَارَكَ وَتَعَالَى.

(٣٦) اَلتَّحِيَّاتُ الطَّيِّبَاتُ الصَّلَوَاتُ الزَّاكِيَاتُ لِلّٰهِ، أَشْهَدُ أَنْ لَّا إِلٰهَ إِلَّا اللهُ وَأَشْهَدُ أَنَّ مُحَمَّدًا عَبْدُ اللهِ وَرَسُوْلُهُ، اَلسَّلَامُ عَلَيْكَ أَيُّهَا النَّبِيُّ وَرَحْمَةُ اللهِ وَبَرَكَاتُهُ، اَلسَّلَامُ عَلَيْنَا وَعَلَى عِبَادِ اللهِ الصَّالِحِيْنَ

All verbal praises, monetary devotions, physical praises and pure actions are for Allah تَبَارَكَ وَتَعَالَى. *I bear witness that there is no deity except Allah* تَبَارَكَ وَتَعَالَى, *and I bear witness that Hazrat Muhammad* ﷺ *is His servant and messenger. May the special peace of Allah* تَبَارَكَ وَتَعَالَى *descend upon you, O Nabi* ﷺ, *and Allah's* تَبَارَكَ وَتَعَالَى *choicest mercies and blessings. May peace descend upon us and upon all the pious servants of Allah* تَبَارَكَ وَتَعَالَىٰ.

٣٧) اَلتَّحِيَّاتُ الصَّلَوَاتُ لِلهِ ، اَلسَّلَامُ عَلَيْكَ أَيُّهَا النَّبِيُّ وَرَحْمَةُ اللهِ وَبَرَكَاتُه ، اَلسَّلَامُ عَلَيْنَا وَعَلَى عِبَادِ اللهِ الصَّالِحِيْنَ

All verbal praises and physical forms of worship are for Allah تَبَارَكَ وَتَعَالَىٰ. *May the special peace of Allah* تَبَارَكَ وَتَعَالَىٰ *descend upon you, O Nabi* صَلَّى اللّٰهُ عَلَيْهِ وَسَلَّمَ, *and Allah's* تَبَارَكَ وَتَعَالَىٰ *choicest mercies and blessings. May peace descend upon us and upon all the pious servants of Allah* تَبَارَكَ وَتَعَالَىٰ.

٣٨) اَلتَّحِيَّاتُ لِلهِ الصَّلَوَاتُ الطَّيِّبَاتُ، اَلسَّلَامُ عَلَيْكَ أَيُّهَا النَّبِيُّ وَرَحْمَةُ اللهِ، اَلسَّلَامُ عَلَيْنَا وَعَلَى عِبَادِ اللهِ الصَّالِحِيْنَ ، أَشْهَدُ أَنْ لَّا إِلٰهَ إِلَّا اللهُ وَأَشْهَدُ أَنَّ مُحَمَّدًا عَبْدُهُ وَرَسُوْلُهُ

All verbal praises, physical praises and monetary devotions are for Allah تَبَارَكَ وَتَعَالَىٰ. *May the special peace of Allah* تَبَارَكَ وَتَعَالَىٰ *descend upon you, O Nabi* صَلَّى اللّٰهُ عَلَيْهِ وَسَلَّمَ, *and Allah's* تَبَارَكَ وَتَعَالَىٰ *choicest mercies. May peace descend upon us and upon all the pious servants of Allah* تَبَارَكَ وَتَعَالَىٰ. *I bear witness that there is no deity except Allah* تَبَارَكَ وَتَعَالَىٰ, *and I bear witness that Hazrat Muhammad* صَلَّى اللّٰهُ عَلَيْهِ وَسَلَّمَ *is His servant and messenger.*

٣٩) اَلتَّحِيَّاتُ الْمُبَارَكَاتُ الصَّلَوَاتُ الطَّيِّبَاتُ لِلهِ ، اَلسَّلَامُ عَلَيْكَ أَيُّهَا النَّبِيُّ وَرَحْمَةُ اللهِ وَبَرَكَاتُهُ، اَلسَّلَامُ عَلَيْنَا وَعَلَى عِبَادِ اللهِ الصَّالِحِيْنَ ، أَشْهَدُ أَنْ لَّا إِلٰهَ إِلَّا اللهُ وَأَشْهَدُ أَنَّ مُحَمَّدًا رَّسُوْلُ اللهِ

All verbal praises that are full of blessings, physical praises and monetary devotions are for Allah تَبَارَكَ وَتَعَالَىٰ. *May the special peace of Allah* تَبَارَكَ وَتَعَالَىٰ *descend upon you, O Nabi* صَلَّى اللّٰهُ عَلَيْهِ وَسَلَّمَ, *and Allah's* تَبَارَكَ وَتَعَالَىٰ

choicest mercies and blessings. May peace descend upon us and upon all the pious servants of Allah تَبَارَكَ وَتَعَالَى. I bear witness that there is no deity except Allah تَبَارَكَ وَتَعَالَى, and I bear witness that Hazrat Muhammad ﷺ is His servant and messenger.

٤٠) بِسْمِ اللهِ وَالسَّلَامُ عَلٰى رَسُوْلِ اللهِ

I begin in the name of Allah تَبَارَكَ وَتَعَالَى, and may peace descend upon the Messenger of Allah تَبَارَكَ وَتَعَالَى.

يا رب صل وسلم دائما أبدا على حبيبك خير الخلق كلهم

Undoubtedly, Hazrat Rasulullah ﷺ is the greatest human being and the pinnacle of Allah's ﷻ creation. It is the ultimate honour for every ummati of Hazrat Rasulullah ﷺ to be linked to Hazrat Rasulullah ﷺ, the Imaam of all the Ambiyaa of Allah ﷻ.

Hazrat Rasulullah ﷺ is the source of hidaayat (guidance) for humanity at large, for it was none other than Hazrat Rasulullah ﷺ who was chosen to show us the path of guidance through which we can earn eternal bliss and salvation. The ability to worship and recognize Allah ﷻ correctly, and simultaneously fulfil the rights of fellow humans, also depends entirely upon emulating the teachings of Hazrat Rasulullah ﷺ.

Thus, when Hazrat Rasulullah ﷺ is essentially the source of all good in this world and our guide to Paradise, and we are blessed to be his followers, then we can well imagine what rights he has over us and how indebted we are to him.

Among the rights that Hazrat Rasulullah ﷺ has over us is that we obey him in all that he has commanded, we lead a life in conformity to his mubaarak lifestyle, and we continuously recite Durood and Salaam upon him.

Lamentably, on account of our busy schedules and preoccupation with commitments and mundane activities, we have drifted far away from Hazrat Rasulullah ﷺ and lost track of our main objectives and priorities in life. In view of the present situation, the need was felt to once again rekindle the love of Hazrat Rasulullah ﷺ within our hearts, thereby enabling us to understand and follow the way of his mubaarak sunnah and reach Allah ﷻ. Hence, this book titled "The Gift of Durood and Salaam" has been prepared which contains the virtues of durood and incidents regarding love for Rasulullah ﷺ.